STIRLING DISTRICT LIBRARIES

3 8048 00149 2532

CANCELLED

D0311906

PORTRAIT OF THE ISLE OF MAN

Portrait of
THE ISLE OF MAN

by
E. H. STENNING

Fully revised and with new photographs by
JOHN GRIMSON

ROBERT HALE · LONDON

B
2

© *E. H. Stenning 1958, 1965, 1975 and 1978*
First edition 1958
Reprinted 1961
Reprinted 1962
Second edition 1965
Reprinted 1968
Reprinted 1972
Third edition 1975
Fourth edition 1978

Robert Hale Limited
Clerkenwell House
Clerkenwell Green
London EC1R 0HT

ISBN 0 7091 7027 0

914·289
STE

Printed in Great Britain by
Lowe & Brydone Printers Limited, Thetford, Norfolk

CONTENTS

ILLUSTRATIONS

Picture Credits

The new photographs in the fourth edition were supplied by: John Grimson, 3, 4, 5, 6, 7, 12, 13, 15, 17, 18, 19, 20, 21, 22, 23, 24; Manx Press Pictures, 9.

7

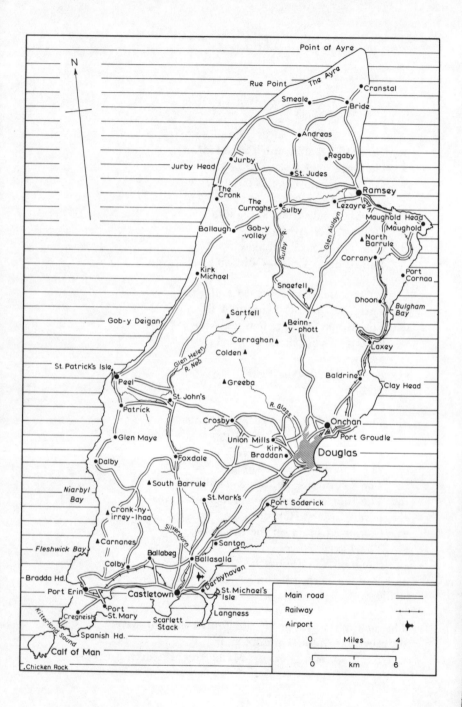

PREFACE TO THE FOURTH EDITION

I T is unusual for a portrait, once completed, to be revised at a later date (and by a different artist) to show the changes which have come over the subject since its first painting. Consequently, it is with some trepidation, and with the lightest possible strokes of the brush, that I have undertaken this revision of the late E. H. Stenning's masterly and ever-popular *Portrait of the Isle of Man*. And yet, revision had become necessary if the book was to depict the Island scene as it is today, rather than that of the 1950s, when the book was first written.

The past two decades have seen great changes in the Isle of Man and in the way of life of its people. The drift from the land and the growth of the towns have continued, and the structure and strength of the Manx economy have been transformed by a rise in immigration and by the growth of light industry and the financial sector. These changes have necessitated some revision of the text, particularly of the chapters on Legislation and on Trade, Industry and Commerce. Nevertheless, much of what Stenning wrote of the Island, its history and its people remains pertinent today, and I have left as much as possible of his original text intact, consistent with the requirement for the book to present an up-to-date picture of the Island.

Finally, the opportunity has been taken of incorporating a new series of photographs, thereby increasing the total number of illustrations whilst retaining the best of Stenning's originals.

Kirk Michael   JOHN GRIMSON
1977

PREFACE

THE GREAT and steady demand for *The Isle of Man* (County Books) has given ample proof that there are many (and an increasing number of) people who have found the Island an ideal place for a holiday, and a place of absorbing interest. For many years the Isle of Man meant just Douglas to thousands of north-countrymen and midlanders. They spent their holidays there (and found them very good) as they might have done at Blackpool, or Margate or a hundred other seaside summer resorts. But by degrees many of them found out that Douglas was not the whole of the Isle of Man, but beyond the glamour and glitter of that very pleasant and prosperous town, the Isle of Man had infinite interests for educated and intelligent people. Modern education ably assisted by radio and television has brought about a state of mind in a great number of people to show their interest in the history (ancient and natural), archaeology, social conditions, folklore, and manners and customs of the places in which they spend their holidays. The Isle of Man affords an ideal place to which to come, for it lies in the very centre of the British Isles, has a unique position, is far enough removed across the sea to make the journey thither sufficiently romantic, has a history quite different from any of its surrounding islands, has its own system of government, its own laws, its own marked nationality . . . a thousand points of difference from other British countries. Moreover, condensed into an ideal-sized area for a holiday all its interests lie displayed, so that within a few weeks everything of interest can be examined and understood under ideal conditions, with a book at hand to guide, and suggest. That is what this book hopes to be, a book of suggestions for those who wish to see and understand the real Isle of Man. But there is a wider public even than the holiday-maker to whom such a book appeals, the many students who come to the Island to undertake specific studies in various phases of Manx national life; the senior children of our schools; official folk who have to come to the Island on their "lawful occasions" and who like to know the general background of the folk they are visiting; and, just as important to the Manx overseas in all parts of the world, a multitude of whom have never had a

11

chance of visiting their fatherland, yet are so proud of it. All these good folk like to have, condensed into one volume, a summary of such information as this book hopes to give. To them and many others it is offered, written by one who came here, a young school-master, to stay for five years, and who has stayed for fifty to enjoy a life made delightful by the interests he has found here, as well as the affection he has both for the Island and all its charming people. He imagined that in "retirement" there would be plenty of leisure in which to acquire more information, verify facts, and look at things in less strenuous circumstances; but alas! life isn't like that, and retirement has brought more preoccupation than he found in working life! This must be the excuse for any errors of fact, which it is hoped are few.

Between the publication of *The Isle of Man* and now, the writer has had the joy of reading Mr. David Craine's wonderful book *Manannan's Isle*, which has thrown a flood of light on mediaeval Manx history. *Per contra*, the *Manx Museum Journal* has not been published*, and worst of all the departure of the curator of the Museum, Mr. B. R. S. Megaw, to another Celtic centre, to wit Edinburgh University, has removed a mentor whose judgment and opinion were always reliable, and always at my disposal.

I have to thank my former colleague, the present Vice Principal of King William College, Mr. S. Boulter, T.D., M.C., for checking over the information about the birds of the Island, and as before, my wife for her hard work in aranging, correcting, criticizing, and worst of all, proof-reading, without which help the work would not have been possible.

---

* *The Journal of the Manx Museum* is now published at irregular intervals.

CHAPTER ONE

INTRODUCTORY

DREADFUL TO relate, there are very many people even in these enlightened days who have very vague ideas about the Isle of Man, vague ideas not only of its uniqueness and interest, but even of its position. In the north country and the midlands it is known to multitudes as a competitor with Blackpool, a seaside resort of gaiety and glitter, mistaking Douglas for the Isle of Man. Further afield there are some who have heard that it has Home Rule, that it has a delightfully low Income Tax, that its bishop has an amusing title as " Bishop of Sodor and Man ", that Manx cats have no tails, and that twice a year there are motor-cycle races run there, races of hair-raising speed and skill.

First then, let it be realized that the Isle of Man is a unique part of the British Commonwealth. It is one of the British Isles, but forms no part of Great Britain, nor of the United Kingdom. It is a separate kingdom, and by lucky historical chance the monarch of Britain happens to be also the Lord of Mann. Further than that, it provides sidelights on the history of Britain from the Glacial periods right up to the present day.

Its position is really the " centrum " of the British Isles, approximately equidistant from the other countries of the group. Indeed it is a claim of its people that from its highest point, Snaefell, on a clear day one may see six kingdoms, England, Scotland, Wales, Ireland, Mann, and the kingdom of Heaven.

The ancient names of the Island are interesting. Julius Caesar (*Comm.*, Bk. V), 54 B.C., writes, "*In hoc medio cursu est insula quae apellatur Mona*" (" In the midway of the channel [i.e. the Irish Sea] is an island which is called Mona "). It has been claimed that this " Mona " is Anglesey, but Caesar would scarcely describe Anglesey as "*in hoc media cursu*". Pliny the Elder (A.D. 74) gives a list of the islands between Britain and Ireland, and quotes Mona, probably in this case Anglesey, and Monapia (probably the Isle of Man). Paulus Orosius (*circa* A.D. 400) in his *History*, Bk. I, writes, "*Hic etiam Menavia insula proxima est, et ipsa spatio non parva solo commoda aequae a Scotorum gentibus habitatur*" (" Here too in the sea [between Britain and Ireland] is Menavia, of no mean size, with fertile soil, inhabited by a tribe of Scots "). Claudius Ptolemy, the geographer of Hadrian's time, A.D. 125, calls it " Monaoida ", while Nennius, an Irish monk, A.D. 858, calls it " Eubonia ". After that the Irish and Welsh forms " Mannan " and " Mannaw " respectively are frequent, while an Icelandic saga of about the same period calls it " Mon ". In the Island itself, its first written name-form occurring on a runic cross in Kirk Michael is " Maun ". It is known to its children of today as " Mannin ", " Vannin ", or " Ellan Vannin ", Isle of Man. The base of all these early names would seem to be " Mon " (Highland Gaelic " monadh ", Welsh " mynydd ", Latin " mons ", a mountain), suggesting that it was named on account of the view from the surrounding isles as a mountain-mass rising from the sea. But this of course is very prosaic, and the suggestion of Professor Rhys is far more attractive and pleasing and is the derivation accepted by the romantics. This refers the name to the Celtic sea-god Manannan, the equivalent of Roman Neptune and Greek Poseidon. In Cormac's Glossary (about A.D. 900) it is recorded that " Mannin McLir was a celebrated merchant who lived in the Isle of Man. He was the most famous pilot in western Europe. He used to know, by studying the heavens, the period of fine and bad weather, and of their change one to the other." It goes on to state that " Hence the Scots and Britons have called him ' God of the Sea ' and they assert that McLir is literally ' Son of the Seas ', and the Isle of Man, it is said, is the Isle of Manannan McLir." A later addition to the legend is found in the *Book of Fermoy* (about A.D. 1400) which describes Manannan as a " pagan necromancer who possessed the ability to envelop himself and his island in a mist, to make them invisible to strangers and enemies ". And thereby hangs the tale of Royal visits to the Island, of which more anon.

The pre-history of the Island may be summarized in brief: Together with the rest of the British Isles it formed a part of the continental shelf of Europe, which many thousand years ago fell under the influence of the glacial periods. The sea-water evaporated over the equatorial regions, was turned to snow which fell upon the polar caps and did not return to the sea, so that the sea-level fell a matter of some 600 feet, thereby uncovering a large land tract which ran out beyond Ireland forming a great " Atlantis " area, and making the island a part of the Great Britain land mass. After the last of these glacial periods, when the snows had melted, the sea-level slowly rose, leaving at first a land bridge to Britain, thawing out the island, which meanwhile had been sheared by glacial action not only of its vegetation, but of its superficial rock strata as well. Across this land bridge the plants slowly invaded the island, followed quickly by certain animals, reptiles, insects, and of course birds. By this time the early Stone Age people of the north (Palaeolithic) had disappeared, and in course of time the Mesolithic man arrived, followed by Neolithic man, presumably 4,000-2,000 years B.C. What happened to Neolithic man still remains a mystery. It was never a numerous race, but it left its marks all over the Island, more especially in the coastal areas. It was succeeded by the people of the Bronze Age, who may have been the evolutionary successors of the same race, or another invasion from the Asia-European continent. The Bronze Age culture lasted on to the Celtic incursion which ultimately spread across the British Isles, possibly 500 years B.C. There are countless monumental remains, graves, barrows, house, and "village" sites, beautifully made weapons and pottery found in the Island. The coming of the Celts so well marked over all the British Isles has left a multitude of relics in the Island; their small round houses whose sites may be found everywhere in the lowland belt, their promontory fortresses, inland fortified farms, and early iron implements, and later their very large circular farm "manor" houses, and still later their Ogham stones, Christian symbols, keeills, and most interesting of all in this Island the incised stone slab known as the "Calf crucifixion". This Celtic civilization, which still to this day is the basis of Manx culture, carries the Island Story up to the ninth century A.D. Meanwhile, in Britain the Roman invasion and occupation of Britain, which left such a stamp on British life, failed to reach this Island. However, another invasion which left a comparatively minor mark on Britain left a very great impression here, from about the ninth century A.D.: the arrival of the Scandinavian Vikings. These fierce marauders came at first to plunder and destroy, then to settle down, and attach the Island to the Scandinavian empire, and finally to separate themselves from Scandinavia, and constitute a separate Scandinavian petty kingdom. They left a tremendous mark on Mann, Scandinavian names and words, a Scandinavian form of government (which has survived the centuries), stronger and more efficient forts on the coasts, and inland, such strongholds as Cronk Sumark, and Castleward, increasing their strength by a system of vitrification by fire; ship burials, and a set of magnificently carved stones with beautifully designed scroll work, and a depiction of their mythology. They stayed independent till they were defeated by the Scots in the thirteenth century.

All these things are writ large over the Island, and may be seen and examined by anybody who wishes to see them; and they form a fascinating study for anybody interested in our Island Story.

CHAPTER TWO

GEOLOGY AND GEOGRAPHY

THE GLACIAL period, we have seen, was a major factor in the physical evolution of the Island. The glaciers covered it over, as indeed they covered the whole of the British Isles except a small portion of southern England and Ireland. They left the Island geologically much as we find it today. They had traversed the sea beds, and pushed up, " bull-dozer " fashion, though infinitely slower, the sea deposits from the northern seas, and left them, as the ice melted, lying as soil on the basic rocks. They carried large boulders from Scotland and the north and left them lying as " erratics " all over the Island. They even planed off the slate, in places, e.g., Foxdale, Santan, and the Dhoon, right down to the level of the igneous granite; and they left grooves or striae where hard stones carried beneath the glaciers ploughed into the slate; those striae may be seen in almost every part of the exposed rock in the Island.

The actual geological strata visible in the Island now are:

Recent.	*Blown Sand* at the Ayre, Jurby, Andreas, Poylvaish and Langness.
	Peat in beds over the mountains and hills.
	Alluvium and river drift over most of the Southern plain.
	Marine raised beach at Derbyhaven and Cass-ny-hawin.
Glacial.	*Sand and gravel mounds.* The Bride hills and isolated patches and mounds in many parts.
	Boulder clay and rubble drift. Blue Point, and S. of Port Cranstal.

Carboniferous.	Limestone series round Castletown.
	Basement sandstone of Peel.
	Basement conglomerate of Langness, Ballasalla and Peel.
Upper Cambrian.	*Manx slates.*	Barrule Slates.
		Crush conglomerates.
		Agneash Grits.
		Lonan and Niarbyl flags.
Igneous Rocks.	*Granite.*	Santan, Foxdale and Dhoon.

The Manx slates are a series of their own. Their nearest relatives in Britain are the Skiddaw slates. They are singularly deficient in fossils. There are worm tracks, castings and burrows, mainly of Palaeochorda major (or allied species); Chondrites, and a few Trilobites have been found in the Cronk Sumark quarry, Sulby. The general thickness of the slate over the Island area is about 2,000 feet. The Manx shales do not make good building stone. They gave rise to a "local" technique in the sixteenth century. The stone was removed from the quarry in slabs lengthwise, and these slabs were broken down into suitably sized "bricks" for the construction of walls etc. A specially good quarry in a most inconvenient position at the foot of Spanish Head yielded magnificent tough beams, 15 feet and more in length, many of which may be seen in use as gate-posts and foot-bridges. These beams have remarkable elasticity. A beam 15 feet long, and about 2 inches thick, will bend 2 inches in the centre without breaking. From the Gob-y-volley quarry beams of 24 feet length have been obtained. A great deal of flooring of Rushen Castle was made of such slabs in the eighteenth-century alterations. The crush conglomerate, well shown in Sulby Glen and in the cliffs at Gob-y-deigan, consists of a slaty matrix into which other and harder rock fragments have been forced by crushing. The intrusive fragments are sometimes small pebbles, and sometimes blocks of many feet in length. The Chasms between Port St. Mary and the Calf, below Cregneish, are another interesting feature of the Manx series. All visitors should go and see these gigantic rifts, caused presumably by severe earth movements. They are vertical rifts of varying widths from a few inches to several feet, descending the whole height of the 200-feet cliffs, and into the depths of the sea below. But care must be taken, for the clefts are overgrown with heather and undergrowth. Incidentally, at the top of the Chasms cliff at a slightly lower level, and cut off in great part by the clefts is a Neolithic burial circle, Cronk Karran, affording an intriguing

B

problem to determine which was the earlier, the chasms or the circle. The famous Sugar-loaf Rock immediately below the Chasms is a mass of slate which has faulted downwards. The bedding of the slates is approximately horizontal, so that the chasms cut the bedding plane at right angles.

Manx slates are of an early series, and include a great many intrusions from the igneous rocks below. Quartz veins form a network through the lower layers, visible almost everywhere. There are classic examples of greenstone dykes in Castletown Bay where at Dreswick Point on Langness their partial erosion (since they are softer than the slate) by the sea has left a succession of "cuts" through the contours of the reef; while another equally remarkable dyke cuts right through the limestone at Scarlett. On the slates was laid down, in early Carboniferous times, the basement conglomerate (pudding stone) seen at its best on Langness where the beds lie horizontal and unconformable on the slates, which in several places have faulted downwards, leaving the conglomerate as a series of arches, well worth seeing even by non-geological visitors.

Nearer Castletown and Derbyhaven the conglomerate has been entirely sheared off, presumably by glacial action, and over the slate has been blown a mass of sand forming an ideal golf course.

The eastern edge of Castletown Bay and the northern end of Derbyhaven Bay show the Carboniferous limestone which underlies a shallow alluvial-drift soil over a square running from Langness to Kentraugh, inland to Grenaby, thence to the mouth of the Santan River, about three miles square. The formation is best seen at Scarlett (where much erosion of the upper soil has laid the rock bare); in the Scarlett, Ballahot, and Ballasalla quarries; and on the shore at Derbyhaven. The formation shows very graceful folds approximating to horizontal, sometimes only a few inches below soil level, while at other places the soil is deep and contains bands of clay in the sand and forms water basins from which the wells of old Castletown obtained their water. The whole area was preserved by an extensive downward fault of the whole mass before the glacial period, so that it was spared the fate of being "planed off" by glacier action, and thus was preserved to form the building stone from which Castle Rushen, the old houses of Castletown, King William's College, and incidentally all the harbour works of the Island, were constructed, and which gave to distant views of Castletown that lovely blue "atmosphere" so striking to the visitor when he approaches the ancient capital. The value of the stone is attested by the wonderful state of preservation of Rushen Castle, whose stones are as clean-cut and free from weathering as when they were built in, 800 years ago. The limestone has very abundant fossils easily obtainable by the geologist and of which there is a fine collection in the Manx Museum. At Poylvaish and towards the west, the stone was much modified by volcanic action, and formed almost black beds of Poylvaish "marble" which was quarried extensively because it took a polish like marble, providing mantelpieces for all the more pretentious houses in Castletown. It also made handsome gravestones. But alas it weathered very badly, and within a few years the surface flaked away and the inscriptions are now very difficult to read, as may be seen in the churchyards of Malew, Arbory and Santan, and ever further afield in the Island. The steps of Wren's new St. Paul's Cathedral brought great fame to these quarries, from which they were hewn, but sad to say, these steps, too, weathered so severely that within a few years they had to be replaced by more durable material, a sequel not commented on in insular circles!

The Scarlett area is made the more interesting by the presence of much volcanic activity. There are masses of basalt, volcanic ash and debris, forming probably the most interesting feature of Manx geology.

The great basalt sill, known locally as Cromwell's Walk, together with the Stack Rock are the filling out of a great chasm by molten material from below, probably during the time of formation of the limestone. During this time a great amount of volcanic material was ejected, and the lava filled in depressions in the limestone rock, forming a mass of coarse agglomerate, while all around fell pumaceous material.

The Stack Rock itself consists of semi-crystalline basalt of nearly vertical columns. The sides of the Stack are almost vertical, except on the shore side, which is reasonably easy of access at low water. It is perfectly safe to visit, but visitors should remember to watch the tide.

The red sandstone of Peel forms a small patch in the form of a semi-circle of radius about a mile round Peel, upon which patch Peel and St. Patrick's Island are based. All round, the edges have faulted, in a manner somewhat similar to the limestone area at Castletown. The sandstone of this area provides the only freestone in the Island. Of this stone are built the castle and cathedral, and most of the ancient houses of Peel, forming a picture, seen from the distance in all directions as "a rose-red city, half as old as Time". The sandstone includes very few fossils, and those mainly corals. There are many quartz inclusions but no slate. Much has been written as to the place of this sandstone in the geological series. The general opinion seems to be in favour of connecting it with the Carboniferous conglomerate of Langness on which later the limestone was laid down.

Manx granite, of which the greatest exposure occurs at Granite mountain, Foxdale, is yellowish grey, well mottled, and pleasing to the eye. It has not been quarried for building purposes, though when the Lancashire and Yorkshire roads were " setted ", there was a great export of granite setts from the Island to provide this want. In the days succeeding the glacial period when the Santan and Silverburn rivers were swift flowing torrents, blocks of granite were washed down and may still be seen in their beds. These blocks were removed in great numbers to be used for building stone for many cottages and barns, where they are very apparent as one walks round the countryside. The granite bosses at Dhoon and Santan have been vigorously worked to provide road metal for the Manx roads.

The northern plain has great geological interests, first of all because of the structure of the Bride hills, which mark the deposits dropped at the foot of some great glacier, of a mass of drift and detritus, which have fine exposures at the two coastal ends, Knock-y-dooney to the west, and Shellag Point to the east, among the grandest drift cliffs in the British Isles.

Immediately north of the slate buttress from Sulby to Lezayre is the wide expanse of curragh (marsh) land, the bed possibly of some vast lake, or wide river bed. This curragh-land has been in a small part drained, to form good farm land, and further draining schemes are in hand, but the area is covered with marsh vegetation, and is a natural sanctuary for multitudes of aquatic and other birds, and provides an entomologist's paradise.

There is a salt deposit under the blown sand of the Ayre. Many borings have been made in the Ayre region, mainly in the hope of finding coal seams, but though the same strata series were found as in the Cumberland field, there was no sign of coal.

GEOGRAPHY OF THE ISLAND

The geography of a place is obviously the outcome of its geology. The main factor of the geography of the British Isles was obviously the return of the sea after the glacial era to form the Channel, the Irish and North Seas, and, in the case of this

Island, leaving it "insulated". Another great factor was the formation as the ice melted of gigantic rivers which scoured out deep valleys and glens, later to become covered with soil and vegetation to make the Island the wonderful place it is. For sheer natural beauty it forms an attraction to visitors. During the past hundred years an ever increasing tourist "trade" has kept the Island in the public eye as a place that "exports kippers, and imports trippers". Today the Island somewhat anomalously owes its prosperity rather to its imports than its exports!

For those who come over be it said that even the approach to the Island is a revelation if that approach be by sea or air, in fine, or wild and misty weather. There are days when the Island is continuously in view right from the Mersey bar, when minute by minute it seems to be rising Venus-like from the sea. Again there are those days when nothing can be seen until the full glory bursts out when the boat gets within a few miles' distance, then on those stormy days when the mountains look so grand and defiant of the breakers lashing against their base. And one has the same impression in coming by air, though in much swifter sequence.

With relation to Greenwich, Douglas has a longitude of approximately $4\frac{1}{2}°$ W., so that local time is 18 minutes late on Greenwich's time, hence the local comment that any event starting within a quarter of an hour of schedule time, is "over-punctual".

The length of the Island along its main axis, which runs from S.W. to N.E., is 30 miles, and its width at right-angles to this axis is 9-10 miles. Its area is 145.325 acres or 227 square miles. The area of the Isle of Wight, with which the most frequent comparison is made, is only 147 square miles.

We have seen that geologically the Island consists of a central mountain mass. This mass is cut across from east to west by a deep, central valley, a valley interesting in that, though its highest point is only 150 feet above sea level, yet it is in reality a double river valley formed by what must have been two mighty rivers now represented by the Rhenass which flows west, and the Dhoo flowing east, both now shrunk to mere trickles. Laxey Glen is a typical glacial valley. The mountain mass composed of Manx slates rises abruptly from the northern plain, but sinks gradually and easily to the south. The central valley is known locally as the "Plains of Heaven".

The northern massif is roughly shaped like a hand with four fingers pointing north, each finger being a ridge of mountain country separated from its neighbour by a deep glen and each comprising a considerable peak. The peaks from east to west being North Barrule (1,854 feet), Slieu Meanagh (1,257 feet), Mount Karrin (1,084 feet) and Slieu Curn (1,153 feet) (Scacafell, or Skyhill, the scene of King Orry's victory over the Manx which brought the Scandinavian domination of the island A.D. 1079, is a buttress of Slieu Meanagh). The three river glens between the four "fingers" are Glen Auldyn to the east, a deep, well-wooded glen at its northern end, wonderfully sheltered, with many sub-tropical shrubs round its comfortable sizeable houses, ending up more barely, right at the base of Snaefell. In the middle is Sulby glen, the most magnificent and splendid of the Manx glens, very deep and surrounded by overpowering mountains where may be seen ravens and falcons among the rocky crags, and traversed by the largest of the Manx rivers. Sulby glen, too, runs up to the very base of Snaefell, and affords the finest of all Manx scenery. Moreover, an excellent road runs right the way down from the Mountain road at the Bungalow,[1] to the exit in Sulby guarded by Cronk Sumark with its vitrified Viking summit fort. The western glen is Glen Dhoo, opening into Ballaugh glen, which is another glacier-formed valley. It too is traversed along the northern side by another wonderful mountain road, narrow, but fit for motor traffic, and running up to the mountain road at Brandywell, through wild scenery of great beauty.

The east side of the mountain massif is really a hog's back starting from North Barrule, and running to Clagh Ouyr (1,808 feet), the whole ridge running above 1,750 feet. Between Clagh Ouyr and Snaefell is the col that carries the mountain road (of motor-cycle race fame) at about 1,400 feet. Snaefell is the highest peak in the Island (2,036 feet). From Snaefell and indeed from the whole of this ridge are to be seen on a clear day the finest of views, the whole of the coast of Southern Scotland from the Mull of Galloway to Solway Firth, the coast of England from the Solway to the Mersey. From North Barrule the whole north of the Island from Ramsey nestling at the foot, to the Point of Ayre, every field and building pin-pointed except for the village of Bride, hidden behind the Bride hills, and away to the west (as also from Snaefell) the Mourne Mountains of Ulster, the opening of Belfast Lough, and the shipping through the North Channel. Snaefell is now, sad to say, rather smothered by various masts and buildings which are concerned with radio, television, and communication with and location of trans-Atlantic aircraft.

From a point just to the north of the Bungalow the descent of

[1] The Bungalow (now demolished was formerly a refreshment bar for passengers on the Manx Electric Railway (see p. 135).

Laxey glen may be carried out on its northern face (the electric cars descend on the southern face) along the old Snaefell mine track, through the charming little hamlet of Agneash. Alternatively the pedestrian may cross the col and climb up Beinn-y-Phott (1,790 feet), known familiarly as "Penny Pot", and thence to Slieu Carn (1,460 feet) and the mystic witch-ridden Garraghan (1,640 feet).

The western flank of this mass is scarcely less interesting, beginning at Slieu Curn (1,153 feet), followed by a stiff climb to the top of Slieu Freoghane (1,601 feet), which has a very steep fall to Kirk Michael down a grass-covered "roof side", very difficult to descend and more difficult to ascend, either of which processes will afford a considerable amount of amusement if one cares for a couple of hours' good exercise.

The third peak is Sartfell (1,490 feet), followed by Colden (1,599 feet), quite close to Garraghan but separated from it by a very deep valley.

Manx 'pedestrians like during their career to undertake the walk along the backbone of the Isle of Man from Ramsey to Port Erin. Probably many a visitor would like to emulate this feat, which must be done in one day. For this purpose North Barrule is usually climbed in the early morning summer hours, and the hog's back taken as described to Garraghan. There comes the crux. The very hardy descend the deep valley and climb Colden, but the less ambitious, from the top of Garraghan, turn back and essay the rim of the glen round to Injebreck Hill, and so to Colden, not descending below the 1,300-foot contour. From Colden the going is direct by Slieu Ruy (1,570 feet) to Greeba (1,383 feet) and so down into the central valley. The valley is crossed and from Ballacraine the southern massif is attacked by climbing Slieu Whallian, the Witches' Hill, or alternatively by Archallagan and Foxdale up South Barrule (1,586 feet), then Cronk-ny-arrey-lhaa (The Hill of the morning watch) (1,433 feet), the Carnanes, followed by a heart-breaking (at this stage of the journey) descent to Fleshwick Bay, and up the other side on to Bradda Head. There are tracks the whole way, and the whole course is through heather and ling and gorse, in summer and autumn a glorious carpet of beauty, and gorgeous views everywhere.

The Island itself is a "child of the south-west wind". This is the prevailing wind, that brings the fiercest gales and heaviest seas. The seas sweep right up the length of the Island on both sides, driving the tide along both flanks with relentless force, heaping up against every jutting rock, hurling themselves on Langness, and the Stack, and Spanish Head and the Calf with enormous fury. Aeons of years with such gales have scoured the bases of the cliffs and left them completely denuded. There is still enough force left in the seas, after they have passed the Niarbyl reef and Maughold Head, to eat away the sandy "broughs" of Michael and Ballaugh and Jurby, and the soft cliffs north of Ramsey. Inland the trees bow down to the force of the gales, and grow "away from the wind" in eerie shapes, so that a casual glance anywhere will show one the direction of S.W.

Much of the mountain mass is uncultivated, although an increasing area has been afforested in recent years. From time to time one encounters high stone walls made without mortar, very difficult to negotiate. These walls usually have long cross-beam stones which may be used as steps. But pedestrians must remember that a heavy wall falling upon one is a dangerous proposition.

The mountain roads of some of the northern areas have been mentioned. The main trunk is the mountain road from Ramsey to Douglas, a road of perfect surface. From it, roads join the other mountain roads mentioned, and there is a cross road from a junction south of the Bungalow over to Kirk Michael. This is joined at Brandywell cottage by probably the most beautiful of them all, the West Baldwin road from Braddan Bridge up the West Baldwin Valley past the Douglas Reservoir, with a very steep climb up Injebreck, starting from a stiff hair-pin bend, but equally lovely in either direction. Brandywell Cottage, usually now for some unknown reason better known as Brandywine Cottage, is a reminder that in the last century when the Manx mountains were covered with vast flocks of sheep, after lambing time, they were all driven hither for assortment and branding, and the well was the "Branding" well.

From the Bungalow the grandest road of all starts to run down Sulby glen. The descent, at first gradual, runs past a circular sheep-fold, often mistaken for a "Stone-circle", and then the descent becomes more severe and enters the trees around Tholt-y-Will, round two sharp hair-pin bends and then descends deeper and deeper between the towering mountains, and above, and later beside, the Sulby River, and so, down to Gob-y-volley with Cronk Sumark blocking the mouth of the glen, a mere pimple against the massive mountains behind.

There are equally lovely walks and drives in the southern mountain areas. A perfect mountain road starts near Rushen Church and passes over the col between South Barrule and the

Cronk-ny-irrey-lhaa. From the highest point the road to the left leads to the path which descends to the lovely little keeill on the Lag-ny-killey (q.v.), while the right-hand road leads to a second junction at the 1,000-foot mark, where it is joined by a similar road coming up from the south. From this point there are two alternative routes, one straight ahead along what is known as the "Shoulder Road", which after four miles of glorious heather-land brings one to the Castletown-Peel road above Foxdale; while the other, running north, traverses the little table-land known as "the Round Table" and through even lovelier country drops down to Dalby. From Dalby the Niarbyl should be visited. This is a reef of flagstone jutting out into the sea. Viewed from the Niarbyl the coast scenery is magnificent. From the "Shoulder Road", as it passes the disused mines, another narrow lane glorious to walk, and just possible for a car, known by the curious name of "Snuff the Wind", leads down to St. John's.

In nearly all these mountain roads there are gates, but, in order to help the motorist, beside each gate is a sheep-stop made of a grating over which the car can pass but not sheep.

It must not be imagined that all the best scenery is in the mountain regions. Nothing could be more delightful than to wander undisturbed across the Ayre in the north, to be lost in the curraghs of Ballaugh and Jurby, to explore the east side glens, or in the south to walk down the Santan gorge, a wonderful cleft with steep cliffs on either hand where the Santan river has found its way along the great "fault", with the limestone to the south and the shale to the north. The gorge bursts into the sea at the Cass-ny-hawin. From Port St. Mary another lovely excursion is to climb up the cliff path to the Chasms and go on round the National Trust property above Spanish Head and Blackhead, and watch the sea-birds and feast one's eyes on the Calf.

For those interested in lighthouses, there are six on the Island, controlled, not as in Britain by Trinity House, but by the Northern Lights Board of Scotland. They are:

Langness. One white flash every 10 seconds. In fog a siren 5 seconds every 45 seconds. (Known locally as "The Buggane".)

The Chicken Rock. Badly damaged by fire in 1960, the tower is unmanned and exhibits a low-powered automatic light and fog signal.

The Calf. Completed in 1968 to replace the Chicken Rock light. One white flash every 15 seconds. In fog one siren blast every 45 seconds.

The Point of Ayre. A red and a white flash every half-minute. In fog three siren blasts every 90 seconds.

Maughold Head. Three white flashes every 30 seconds. One siren blast every 90 seconds.

Douglas Head. Six white flashes every 30 seconds. One siren blast every 20 seconds. (Known locally as "Wailing Wilfred".)

In its climate too the Island is unique. Its weather is almost unpredictable even by its own fisher-folk. It seems to be a sort of no-man's land in the eyes of the weather gods, and one is thrown back more and more on Manannan McLir. Conditions vary as to rainfall, fog, snow, and hours of sunshine in the Island itself. The east side has, as may be realized from the position of the mountain mass, a higher rainfall than the west, and the uplands naturally receive more rain than the lowlands.

The annual statistics show that the climate is exceedingly equable, with an average winter isotherm approximating to that of Falmouth. The lowlands receive an average rainfall of 36 inches, an average daily sunshine period of 4.28 hours, an average maximum temperature of 53.2°F and minimum of 44.3°F.

From these data it will be seen that the Island shares with the south and west coasts an equable climate, a high winter temperature with a cool summer temperature. In fact no statistics can give an adequate idea of Manx weather. They do not tell of the brilliant cloudless summer and autumn days, the magnificent sunrises and sunsets (which soulless scientists attribute largely to the dust of Lancashire and Belfast on either distant horizon). They tell nothing of the comparative freedom from thunderstorms, of the wonderful displays of the Aurora, or of the long evenings which almost meet the early sunrises. Nor *per contra* do they give any idea of Manannan's fogs which play the strangest of tricks, encircling the coasts and keeping the land clear, smothering the south and blotting out Ronaldsway Airport but leaving Jurby clear. Again they tell nothing of the subtropical plants that flourish all over the Island, fuchsias which are the glory of every cottage, of dracaenias (so-called palms) in full bloom, of veronicas, olearias, escallonias, making delightful hedges, and of camellias, clianthus and magnolias. Nor do they tell of the rarity of snowstorms, or sharp frost. It is true that winter brings chilly winds from the east and north-east that almost convince one that the thermometer is lying. But the purity of the air, its freedom from dust, make it the healthy invigorating place it is. "Vigorous" is perhaps the adjective that best describes it, a climate that braces one and inspires the wish to be up and doing.

CHAPTER THREE

PRE-HISTORY

THE FIRST of the inhabitants of the Island who left their records here were the Mesolithic folk whose culture is known as Tardenoisian, from its similarity to the relics found around Tardenois in northern France. They were a fishing, hunting, nomadic people who seemed to have reached Mann by way of Ireland, where their weapons and implements are found in considerable supply. They are found very sparsely in Great Britain. But in Ireland they are classified as the Bann type. They are singularly dainty. They are found in large numbers around Castletown, in fields and gardens, all across Ronaldsway Airport, on the raised beach just south of the Cass-ny-hawin round Port St. Mary, Peel, Michael and Ramsey, always near the shore of low-lying coasts. Their houses were of the most primitive type. Examples were found near Glen Wyllin, Michael, small sunk circular structures.

The Mesolithic culture was succeeded by a race, known as Neolithic, which seems to have worked its way north from the Mediterranean, by way of south-western France, Brittany, and Great Britain. They were a race of farmers and hunters, who settled down in small "farms" in which they grew cereals, ground their own corn in typical querns, and bred animals for food and milk. Their tools and weapons were more massive and of far greater variety and utility. They made useful pottery, at first crude, but later well designed and decorated in "false relief". They are known best by their burial places, megalithic in structure, large communal graves or "barrows" in which their cremated remains were buried in "galleries" paved with quartz pebbles, the whole (often vast) grave roofed over with wooden beams, wattles, turf, and often large stone cairns.

In the graves they placed stores of food and drink in pottery urns, shell-fish, and grain, and often arrows, spears and hunting implements, food and sustenance for the "long journey". Besides using flint for their tools they used as well quartz, bone and basalt. They must, too, have been traders, for in their houses are found articles and materials which must have been brought from far-distant places. The culture is thought to have reached the British Isles 4000-2000 B.C. The best known Neolithic monuments in the Island are:

1. The Meayll or Mull circular grave at Cregneish, Rushen.
2. Gorry Castle or Cashtal-yn-Ard, Maughold.
3. King Orry's Grave, Gretch Veg, Laxey.
4. The Cloven Stones at Baldrine, Lonan.
5. The Stone Circle, Ballakelly, Santan.
6. The Giant's Grave, Liaght-ny-Foawr, Kew, German.

The burial tumuli of the earliest Neolithic type were circular in form, made by erecting a ring of stones about three or four feet high, mounting around this a bank of earth, and covering it over with a substantial roof of wood, wattles and earth. Many such circles exist more or less despoiled in many localities on the Island, the least damaged being that at the Chasms, Cronk Karran. In course of time such tumuli collapsed and their stones formed a miniature quarry of portable material, used by the farmers to repair walls, or provide gate posts, so that today only a few stones mark the spot where the tumulus was.

The Meayll (or Mull) Circle is unique in the British Isles. It is a megalithic stone circle just below the summit of Mull Hill, Cregneish. Its ancient Manx name was Rhullick-y-lag-sliggagh (The graveyard of broken slates). The circle consists of six chambers termed by their investigators "tritaphs" or "three-armed" graves. These tritaphs are in two groups of three on the circumference of the circle. Two arms of each tritaph are cir-cumferential, the third radial and outside the circle. The two sets are separated by a broad passage pointing almost exactly N. and S. The units are made of huge slabs of local slate, the largest 8 feet long, 3 feet wide and 6 inches thick. These are all sunk into the earth, making chambers about 2 feet deep below the surface level. The complete structure is difficult to estimate, since the monument has been terribly mutilated through the ages. Pos-sibly the whole area was roofed-in to form a huge "barrow", alternatively each tritaph may have been separately roofed over, so as to form a six-tumuli cemetery. The N. and S. alignment of the "passage-way" tempts one to think it was a definite passage having reference to the sun, and not roofed over. The radial

passage of each tritaph suggests that entrance was made by this
means, and that the urns were deposited by a near relative crawl-
ing in to leave the ashes in them.   Each unit had a flagged floor.
Almost certainly each tritaph was roofed over with slate slabs, but
these, being of portable size, and readily uncovered, have mostly
been removed.   In 1897 when the first investigation was made

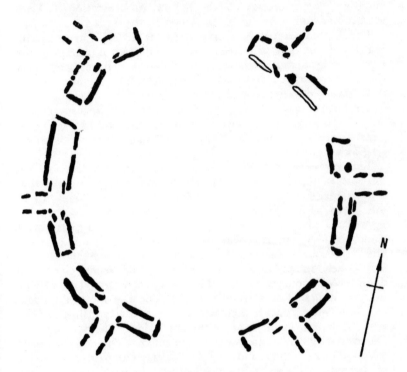

THE MEAYLL CIRCLE

there were the remains of twenty-six urns, but a host of others
must have been removed and smashed.   They were found, as
would be expected, in the tangential cists, and in the inside ends
of the "crawls".   At the same time, five knives were found and a
scraper.   A marked feature was the large number of white quartz
pebbles found in and on the "flooring".   The urns were all about
9 inches to a foot in height, of diverse shape and pattern.   Some
showed a simple type of decoration of short lines scratched on the
lip, and long diagonal lines on the body and small hollows all

probably made by a pointed "style". The urns were fashioned
from local clay. One or two had a recurved lip. The pyre may
have been in the N.-S. passage way, though no trace of burning was
found. Quite close to the circle but lower down the hill to the
south-east are to be seen the remains of the ancient village of
which presumably the circle was the "cemetery". Its traditional
name is "Lag-ny-boirray", "the hollow of botheration". Here
were found four urns similar to those in the graves.

The Cashtal-yn-Ard or Gorry Castle is in Ballachrink Farm,
Maughold. It, too, is a megalithic burial place standing on the
top of the headland north-west of Port Cornaa. It has been many
times despoiled in times past. Recent careful excavation shows
it to have been a remarkably fine example of a "gallery grave".
When built it was at least 40 yards long, 15 wide, and covered an
area of about 500 square yards. It was in the form of a long-oval
barrow with a pyre area, an "approach", and a horned forecourt.
The axis lies roughly E. and W.

The approach was from the east end, but this portion has
in past centuries been very much despoiled, and all that
can be made out now is a series of four or five steps up to
the grave area. Near the top of these steps is located the
"pyre", of blackened earth surrounding a built-up platform of
stone about 6 feet by 3 feet. At the west end is an unusually
fine "forecourt" marked by a semicircle of eight tall standing stones, in plan, like two horns. The semicircle has a
diameter of about 12 yards. The forecourt was paved. Of the
upright stones of this semicircle, those on the south side were
mostly missing, though their sockets were clearly visible. They
were "balanced" with those on the north side. The most westerly
pair were large and "dog-toothed" in shape. The next two pairs
were not quite so high and were flat slabs. The pair on each side
of the entrance were by far the largest. Between them was the
"crawl" or entrance to the grave gallery, between two massive
stones, leaning inward towards each other, and leaving between
them a triangular opening about 3 feet high and about the same
width. Between this entrance and the pyre area was constructed
the grave gallery, consisting of a series of five compartments,
separated by upright slabs, each compartment having an oblong
plan, about 8 feet in length and 5 feet in width. These compartments were roofed over with timber, wattles, and earth, with grass
covering, and enclosed as one long barrow. The side boundaries
on each side were marked by lateral walls converging towards the
east. It is presumed from the existence of the pyre area that bodies

were burned, and the ashes placed in earthenware urns, and
deposited by the relatives in the gallery. During early excava-
tions many pottery fragments were found, neolithic in character,
of the "windmill" or "Avebury" type, several stone implements,
and some fragments of human bone, one considerable fragment
of the skull of a young woman. There are tumuli in the area
which have been completely despoiled, all thought to have been
of the "long barrow" type, suggesting a civilization somewhat
different from that of the Meayll circle. The size of the structure
makes it one of the largest in the British Isles.

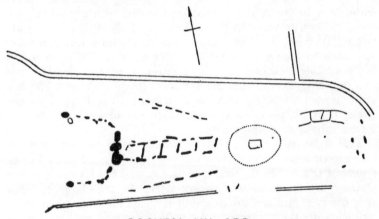

CASHTAL-YN-ARD

King Orry's Grave, Gretch Veg, Laxey, is another huge long-
barrow of complex design. It has been very much mutilated, and
the old Lonan-Ramsey road appears to have been cut right
through it, so that it now appears to be made up of two separate
halves, of which the east end has been carefully excavated, but not
the west. The earliest description is that of Feltham, 1798, which
suggests that there was a forecourt at each end. Today the
"main" entrance and crawl appear to be at the west end, while
the largest megalith is at the east. Possibly when the east portion
has been carefully excavated it will be found that there were two
separate barrows. If the two halves were part of the same barrow,
it was indeed immense. The western half showed a collapsed
barrow, possibly built up on the style of the Cashtal-yn-Ard.
Only one small piece of pottery was found, a fragment of earthenware somewhat like that found at the Meayll circle. The lack of

such finds is not surprising since the two halves have formed for centuries parts of two cottage gardens.

The Cloven Stones or Giant's Grave, Baldrine, Lonan, have always been a puzzle. The site is now surrounded by houses and bungalows, so all that can be written about it must be taken from past records. In the Swarbreck MS. (1815) in the Manx Museum it is recorded " Mr. Millburne informed us that about seven years since, he with two or three miners opened the mound to the depth of five feet, and discovered a human skull and some thigh bones, which from their uncommon size must have belonged to a person of gigantic stature ". When surveyed in 1865 a plan was drawn, showing it to be an almost circular barrow, with a two-compart-ment gallery grave. On the N.E. edge of the barrow there are two pillars 6 to 7 feet high, which presumably formed the entrance approach to the chambers. The taller stone is split from top to bottom along a cleavage line of the stone apparently while it was in situ. But the split has given rise to many traditions, the one most often told being that on this stone King Orry tried the strength of his sword, and presumably the strength of his arm, for he split it at a single blow.

The Ballakelly Circle, Santan, stands near the old Douglas-Castletown road. The earliest account of it is found in Maining's *Guide* of 1822: " In the parish of Santan and not far distant from Oatland are the remains of a cairn altar. It is not large, but it is very distinct, and the stones are of considerable size. The stone sepulchre in the centre is exposed to view and is composed of very large stones placed at regular intervals, and though there are some on the west the circle does not seem to have been completed."

Some of the stones have interesting " cup " markings, the date and origin of which are indeterminate. The monument was pre-sumably a very large round barrow which has been very ruthlessly destroyed down the ages. It was almost certainly very much larger, but many of its stones, which are of just the useful shape, have been taken away and used as gate-posts, and for a long dis-tance around there are such posts in a multitude of fields.

The Giant's Grave, Liaght-ny-Foawr, Kew, German, is another barrow which has been greatly despoiled. It too appears today as an avenue of stones, probably of the same general plan of a line of chambered graves.

The Neolithic Age was succeeded by the Bronze Age, but it is an open question whether this age and culture were due to a further incursion of another race from Europe, or whether it was the result of a natural evolutionary process in the history of the

Neolithic folk. The graves at least were quite different from the long-barrows. They were indeed small stone-lined, stone-covered graves, very shallow constructed constantly being uncovered in process of ploughing, or showing as low tumuli on the face of fields. They contain usually only one burial, the body crouched up with knees against chin. A graveyard of such burials occurs on the summit of Chapel Hill, at Balladoole, Arbory, where the graves lie within the ramparts of a later Iron-Age occupation. Other Bronze-Age burial mounds form more distinctive features in the countryside, as, for example, in the two stone circles at Arragon Mooar, Santon. The prominent summit cairn on Cronk-ny-irree-lhaa, Rushen, marks a large burial mound which may be from the late Neolithic or early Bronze Age. A striking example of the internal structure of a Bronze-Age burial mound is afforded by the 'Giant's Grave' (not the same one as previously identified by that colloquialism, although it lies in the same parish) at St. John's, where the road passing the west side of Tynwald Hill has been cut through the mound, exposing a cist of large stone slabs in the roadside banking.

The pottery, ornaments, implements and weapons of the Bronze Age show considerable advance in utility, and marked development in ornamentation and design. In the Museum may be seen a fine earthenware beaker of the period, the Baroose beaker from Lonan, beautifully decorated with fine point markings, and the Cronk Aust urn from Lezayre, a sample of " false relief " pottery of a type rarely found in England, but more common in Ireland and Scotland. There may also be seen bronze swords, palstaves, daggers, and spearheads. There are upwards of fifty Bronze Age sites in the Island, more in the north than elsewhere. A very interesting stone of the Bronze Age was found at Cronk-yn-How while excavating the keeill there, in Lezayre. It is a slab of slate about 2 feet 5 inches wide and 2 inches thick engraved lightly with several primitive drawings. The engravings are, one of a strongly antlered deer, well drawn, and several attempts to draw a doe with fawn at heel. The Abbé Breuil thought it bore a general likeness to many Scandinavian stones of the Bronze Age. Mr. Petersen of the Trondheim Museum thought it was earlier than the Bronze Age, unique in the British Isles, and the earliest representation of human art therein. The stone was built into the wall of a keeill which had been built on a Neolithic site. The stone has been broken off, and it is conjectured that the broken-off part may have had drawings offensive to the Christian taste.

As in Britain and Ireland, there are to be seen many monoliths, large standing stones or menhirs, in many parts of the Island, more especially in the south and central parts (few in the northern plain).   There is no certain knowledge of the origin of these stones, though much folk-lore is centred round them.   There is a particularly fine example between Ballaqueen and Port St. Mary station, about 9 feet above ground and very deeply set, weighing several tons.   Another stands beside the cross roads (round-about) not many yards away, less massive but quite impressive.   Another above the main Douglas-Castletown road near Ballalona Bridge, Santan, is a massive top-heavy stone which in order to maintain its balance must be very deep-set.

At Berk in Michael, again quite close to a tumulus, stands another menhir.   None of these stones have any markings, but near the base of that at Berk carved in the native rock is a rectangular " nest " of cup-markings reminiscent of the ancient game of " nine-holes ".

CHAPTER FOUR

THE CELTIC PERIOD

T HE ISLE OF MAN is above all things Celtic even to this day.   All kinds of invasions and incursions have happened since the time the Celtic invasion of the British Isles reached Mann, but through it all it remains staunchly Celtic . . . as Celtic as wild Wales, or Brittany, or the highlands of Scotland.   The term " Kelt " is derived from the Greek " keltoi ", the name given to the tall, fair inhabitants of northern Europe, in contradistinction to the short, dark Mediterranean type.   It is doubtful whether the Greeks had any knowledge of the " black Celt " of western Europe during the first millennium B.C.

The fate of the pre-Celtic (presumably Bronze Age or Neolithic race) is not known.   It never was a large population.   It may have received the Celtic invader on equal terms, intermarried and formed part of the succeeding generation.   It may have been annihilated by war, or isolated in ever-decreasing areas till it died out.   Nothing definite is known.   The Celts certainly arrived in Britain during the Bronze Age.   Having arrived in all parts of Britain, they were later driven westward by further invasions from the Continent and eventually by the Anglo-Saxons in England, till they were only to be found in the highlands and islands of Scotland, in Wales, Mann and Ireland. In these areas the Celtic language remains. In the Island it survived invasions of Scandinavians and English and remained the vernacular right down to this century, but although there remain students of the Manx language who seek to preserve this aspect of the Island's heritage, it is. spoken fluently only by very few and by nobody normally. The first record of the language, showing its similarity to Irish, occurs in the *Glossary of Cormac*, A.D. 650, telling of the visit of the Irish poet Senchan to Mann, accompanied by about fifty pupils and fellow-poets. They landed in the Island and immediately met an old woman gathering sea-weed, who asked who they were. On being told they were poets, she gave them a couplet in her own language and challenged them to give another to complete it, which one of them immediately did to her satisfaction. Manx is also closely related to Highland-Gaelic. But it must be remembered that there never has been a Manx literature. The first written Manx was that of the Prayer Book of Bishop Phillips, 1610, and in that, as in all Manx, the spelling is purely phonetic, and further, it was only manuscript. We have already noted that in spite of building at least three castra in Lancashire, Manchester, Ribchester, and Lancaster, in spite of main roads ending at Fleetwood, and Holyhead, the Romans seem entirely to have neglected the Island. They drove the Welsh into their mountains, the Scots to their highlands, but, so far as can be seen, they made no organized attempt to colonize Mann. In Britain there were further invasions by the Scandinavians, the Anglo-Saxons, and the Danes, all of whom left their marks on the main island before William the Norman and his line consolidated it as a single nation. But of these invaders the Scandinavians only left their mark on the Isle of Man. In spite of the Scandinavians the Celtic language remained, and survived; place names and family names survived in great preponderance, the Celtic spirit and way of life survived, and the language survived, and to this very day the real Manx are Celtic in every way.

To the Celtic period the Island owes its Church in very great degree, as will be shown in the chapter on the Manx Church. Little is known of the Celtic political system, and in any case the Manx political system is Scandinavian, of which a great deal is known. The land tenure system has been well worked out. Like the Scandinavian system in its early days, the Celtic system was for all purposes a "udal". Land was held in small areas by a conquering chieftain, and was owned by him alone, and passed on to his children. So too, in the Celtic system, land was owned in small areas by families. To this very day holdings have the family name Ballakelly, Ballamaddrell, Ballanorris. The prefix "balla" means a homestead. The feudal system in which land was given out to supporters of the king, on condition of the provision of a "feu" of fighting men, was never introduced into the Island in spite of many unsuccessful efforts by the Lords to force it on them. The successful struggle to retain the "udal" has been one of the more interesting features of Manx history. Further, the Island still retains a great degree of Celtic land organization. The Celtic custom was to amalgamate into one unit known as a "treen" four "quarterlands" or "kerroos" (farmsteads), and to make each treen responsible for the upkeep of a small church or "keeill". There are in the Island today at least 200 known sites of keeills, a good number of which are still marked by their foundations. The treen names remain to this day. The treens occupied all the arable land. Rough land outside the treen was known as "intack". It could be used for grazing land by the owners of the quarterlands.

During the Celtic period, too, Christianity was introduced into the Island by way of Ireland, and the disciples of St. Patrick. This is dealt with in the chapter on "The Church".

Writing, too, was introduced in this same period, in the form of oghams, and for the first time names and facts could be recorded. Of such ogham inscriptions there are about 300 known in the British Isles, and of these there are six fine examples in Mann. Of these, two were found at Ballaqueen, Port St. Mary, and two at Bemaken Friary, Arbory, and one each in Andreas and Maughold. Those at Ballaqueen were inscribed:

(a) "OF BAIVAIDU SON OF CONVALI"
(b) "OF DAVAIDU THE DRUID'S SON"

The Arbory stones are inscribed:

(a) OF CUNAMALGUS SON OF . . .
(b) OF MAQLEOG . . .

Of these, the claim to be the "Druid's Son" is of interest, for there are no signs of any Druidic influence in the Island. Caesar in his commentaries is almost the sole contemporary authority on British Druidism, while Cicero added some further information of the cult in Brittany. But in the Island there are no Druidic names

(Druidale farm under Snaefell is a modern name for "Eary Kelly"). The sacred oak tree is rare today in the Island, though it is true that it was more common in bygone days, as is shown by the supplies of bog-oak; mistletoe, important at the mid-winter festival, is very rare.

Of the Arbory stones that "OF MAQLEOG" is interesting as the earliest example in "writing" of the use of MAQ as "Son of . . ." Maqleog is therefore the modern "Clague" of son of Leog, and the very widespread family of Clague in the Island may claim to be, if not the oldest family, the earliest recorded Manx family in the Island. There were two other stones. The Andreas stone has a bi-lingual inscription in Ogham-Latin inscribed:

(In Ogham): AMBECATOS MAQI AOCATUS.

(In Latin):   AMMECAT FILIUS ROCAT.

Thus verifying that Maqi and Filius are equivalent.

The Maughold stone also is bi-lingual, in this case Ogham-Runic.

It is well known that Manx names commonly begin with hard C or K or Q, all equivalent to Maq, e.g. Clucas (McLucas), Corrin (McOrry), Kelly (M'Helli, or son of war), Kissack (MacIsaac), Quilliam (MacWilliam), Quiggin (McVige = Son of Knowledge), Quirk (M'Ceorc, son of (my) heart), Quayle (M'Phail = Paul).

Early in this period the discovery of iron-smelting reached western Europe and spread to the Isle of Man, and in monuments of this and succeeding periods it is common to find iron implements, weapons, ornaments and utensils.

The Isle of Man has a multitude of Celtic monuments, and more and more come to light with each succeeding year. The primitive Celt lived in a small round house of "rath" of the same type but much larger than his Neolithic forbears. Remains of such houses are to be found in every part of the Island as round mounds or tumuli about 9-12 feet in diameter. They were very typical. They had a central fireplace; the lower portion of the walls was a sunk stone circle. The roof was usually conical and made of wooden beams covered with wattles or brushwood and then turfed. Just outside the house was a "midden" in which bones and mollusc shells may still be found. As age succeeded age, some of the houses became larger and larger, but still remained circular in plan, necessitating the erection of posts to assist in supporting the roof. The spaces were partitioned off, the outside was occupied by a ring of "stables" and sheds, and stores. Several members of the same family "set up house" in compartments round the inside and the house became one of which the "round house" near Castletown (of which there is a lovely little model in the Museum) is a typical example. This house shows a civilization living prosperously at peace. It stands beside the Dumb stream on the outskirts of Castletown. It was approached by a causeway, through what was probably a considerable marsh. In form it consisted of two concentric circles about 180 feet across. The outer ring of posts was the stockade, into which the animals of the farm could be driven. The inner circle, about 90 feet in diameter, was a large "manor" or farmhouse. Between the supporting posts were fitted brushwood and wattle walls. The centre was occupied by a great fire-hearth, floored with the local marble slabs. The house was the centre of the owner's "allodium", owned and farmed by himself, his family and his servants. The house, because of its turf roof and flat structure, would be scarcely visible from a little distance, for its total height above ground would be barely twelve feet. The various floors showed clearly that the house had been held by many succeeding generations.

This house would be of date probably in the first or second century A.D., and represents a house and allodium of a rapidly developing Celtic family. Between it, and the earlier Celtic houses above-mentioned, are to be found others of varying degrees of progress, making a series in which can be read the evolution of a race. The small houses increased in size, in the better wall-formation, in the appearance of roof-posts needed for the increasing expanse of roof area, in the construction of entrance passages, and now with increased space, of ledges round the walls which would afford permanent seating, and possibly sleeping space. Just before the second World War, when the Island antiquarians realized that the building of the airport at Ronaldsway would blot out an area very full of antiquarian interest, containing so much of the Island's history, made what alas! was an all-too-brief investigation of the area. But a large Celtic village was found, in which the round houses were grouped together, and the groups surrounded by walls, considered to have been built during the first four centuries of the Christian era, since the site showed signs of Viking occupation at a later date. Many relics of the period are to be seen in the Museum, such things as spindle-whorls, combs, needles and pins of bone, many bronze ornaments, finely decorated, a finger ring, and a very fine example of a graduated balance-arm.

The Celts, too, inaugurated a system of promontory fortresses, mostly on the headlands at river-mouths, and on some of the bluffs beside the banks of the rivers. These were round houses fortified by ramparts on the landward side. They were later modified by the Vikings (q.v.). And on South Barrule, the hill of Watch and Ward, they built a huge fortification containing many "raths", revealed by aerial photography. This mountain became the chief site in the south of Watch and Ward (q.v.).

CHAPTER FIVE

THE SCANDINAVIAN PERIOD

THE CELTIC period seems to have been an age of peace and prosperity, of farming, fishing, and trading. There was constant communication with Ireland, and presumably Scotland. But round about A.D. 780 the Scandinavian Vikings (or creek men) began to build seaworthy boats and venture far abroad. Indeed they reached Iceland about A.D. 860 and later Greenland, and presumably the continent of North America. They would certainly have reached Shetland and Orkney fairly early and presumably made more and more frequent visits to the rest of the British Isles. They came first to sack, and plunder, and harry, but it was not many centuries before they decided to conquer and remain. By the time they came to settle, the Island was well Christianized, as we may judge from the famous " Crucifixion stone " already mentioned, as well as the multitude of Celtic grave crosses in the Island. They left their names on our shores, and indeed inland, Garwick, Soderick, Grenwick, Stacka, Scholaby, Colby, Ronaldsway (Ronald's path or ford), Sartfell (dark mountain), Snaefell, and countless others. They even left some personal names, Kinvig (the creek man), Corkell (MacThorkell, Thor's Kettle), Corjeag (Macuart-ayg, He of the dark eyes), Cottier (Mac otter, a sacred animal of the Norse), and Crennell (MacRegnal, Ruler of the gods).

The first recorded raid on Ireland occurred in 798, if we may believe the *Annals of Ulster*. But from internal evidence we know that before Christianity was established in Norway, the Scandidinavian pagan religion was well established in Mann. This evidence is afforded by the wonderful Scandinavian tombstones and monuments found in the Island. Christianity was made compulsory in Norway by Olaf I (Tryggvesson), King from 969-1000. It is by no means certain when Norwegian Christianity reached the Vikings in Mann. But it is certain that the Viking pagan religion came into the Island, and if it did not destroy the early Celtic Christianity, it at least suppressed it, and became the main religion.

Three wonderful stones remain as pagan religious records, and show the Sigurd story from the Saga of the Norse Gods. These stones were found respectively in the parishes of Jurby, Maughold and Malew, while a fourth and later stone from Andreas shows a transition from paganism back to Christianity. All four stones are from the hands of different sculptors.

The story of Sigurd, which has been immortalized by Wagner in the " Ring " series of operas, begins with the mischief-maker of the gods, Loki. Loki comes upon Otter (who is really a prince under a curse) devouring a salmon. As a matter of fact, Otter has magical powers, and not only Loki, but even Odin, are afraid of him. Odin agrees with Loki to pay tribute to Otter, to ensure his help, and in order to accomplish this, Loki undertakes to steal the Ring of the Nibelungs which carries disaster wherever it goes. Sigurd, a mortal and a very fine character beloved of Odin, essays to kill Fafnir the dragon that harasses the land. Fafnir has wound her body round a vast treasure which Sigurd has sworn to obtain, as a present for his wife Brunhilde. But Sigurd has a dwarf, Regin, who has traitorous designs, and has agreed to kill Sigurd, when he has obtained the treasure, and give the treasure to Otter. Odin, to aid Sigurd, suggests to him that the best way to kill Fafnir is to tunnel under her, and thrust her through with a spear from below. This he does, cuts out her heart, and roasts it in slices, cooking them by roasting them on his sword. The dragon's blood runs down the sword and scalds him, and to ease the pain he puts his hand in his mouth. But tasting the dragon's blood gives him power to understand the meanings of the songs of the birds, and they tell him of the treachery of Regin. Such is the story told on these three crosses.

The two stones from Malew and Jurby tell the same part of the story but in differing figures. The Jurby stone shows Fafnir writhing in death agony, not knowing whence came the wound delivered by a tiny Sigurd below, in his tunnel. In a panel beneath may be seen Sigurd with three rings from Fafnir's heart toasting them over a ring of flames. Grani, Sigurd's horse, stands by, and overhead the birds are twittering their message to Sigurd.

In the Malew stone Sigurd is holding his burnt hand in his mouth, and a far more dignified Grani appears ready to start on a long journey.

The Maughold stone is somewhat later and finer designed. It is the shaft of a cross, and is broken, but shows enough of the story to suggest that it originally had the whole story. It was found forming the lintel of a window of a Ramsey outhouse! The beginning of the story is at the base, and shows Loki, and Otter and the salmon. At the top of the column is the end of the story, Sigurd with Grani loaded with treasure, Fafnir slain, and the nasty little dwarf Rani slain also. Doubtless all the rest of the story was told on the mutilated sides.

Two other pagan carved stones are of great interest, the Heimdall slab at Jurby, and the Thor stone of Bride. The former shows Heimdall, the janitor of Valhalla (the abode of the gods) blowing his great horn to summon the gods to their last great meeting before the end of all things.

The Thor stone from Bride is probably the finest stone in the world of its kind. It depicts a Christian cross together with Norse mythology. It shows the passage of religion from pagan to Christianity. At the head of the shaft, two dwarfs uphold the firmament. Below the Christian cross stands Odin, the father of the gods. On the other side stands Thor, bearded, and wearing his Strength Belt and below him his gigantic opponent Ragnir with Main, Thor's son, who in the contest saved his father's life.

On another panel is the incident of Thor's fishing, with Thor using an ox-head for bait.

A somewhat similar cross, but probably still later, is in the Andreas collection. This shows a naked Odin, with raven on shoulder, in the twilight of the gods, while on the reverse side is the cross of Christ, and below it kneels a figure in prayer, carrying "the Book". Serpents writhe away below him and the Christian symbol of the fish, *ICHTHUS: Iesus CHristus THeou Uios Soter*, signified that Christ has "bruised the serpent's head".

So in the Isle of Man, covering these two and a half centuries, we have wonderfully carved stones which are redolent of history, stones of very great archaeological value and absorbing public interest, a collection nowhere equalled in Europe in such a small space. We see the abrupt close of the early Celtic Christianity, the appearance of a new pagan religion in its place, in a culture far in advance artistically, and then the gradual recovery of Christianity, the final return preceded by a stage in which the people "had a foot in both worlds", pagan and Christian.

There are good casts of all these crosses in the Museum.

It should be known by all those who are interested that when portions of crosses are found, they remain in the possession of the church authorities and are to be seen at the churches, sometimes in the porches, sometimes, as at Maughold and Michael, in specially built shelters, sometimes fixed outside on the walls.

Of the later Christian Scandinavian period, there are many carved stones with Bible studies, among which ought to be mentioned a " David in the Lions' Den " from Braddan, "Adam and Eve " from Bride, and a "Virgin and Child " from Maughold. It is just possible that this last stone may be eighth-century Celtic.

The main Viking invasion seems to have come in the ninth century. About the year 880 Harald Harfager, a harsh king of Scandinavia, tried to bring to heel his warring chiefs, and claimed the land tenure of the whole kingdom as his, in fact adopting the feudal system in opposition to the Norse. Many of the chieftains thereupon took their wives, families, and servants, and such goods as they could carry off, and settled down in lands overseas. In turn they settled in the Shetlands and Orkneys, which they named "Nordreys", or Northern Islands, and the Islands to the West of Scotland, the "Sudreys", or Southern Islands. These they formed into separate kingdoms. The chieftain who thus entered into the traditional history of the Isle of Man was known as Gorree, or in later versions Orry. He belongs largely to the sagas, unreliable in detail, but his name has been deeply woven into Manx history. The sagas give him a date of about 950. But unfortunately there is another and much more historically attested claimant for the title of King Orry, namely Godred Crovan King of Mann 1079-95. To him may be attributed three bulwarks of the state, a legislative body, a code of laws, and a standing army.

According to Skene, *Celtic Scotland*, he came to Mann and was ejected by Malcolm King of Scotland, and exiled. He returned and was refused by the Manx; he returned with his brother to fight against Harold of England at Stamford Bridge, then once again via Norway, bringing an army to re-conquer Mann. The tale is then taken up by the Cottonian MS. (British Museum), *Chronicon Manniae*, the record of the monks of Rushen Abbey. According to this, he landed at Ramsey Bay. He commanded 600 men, 300 of them he put in ambush, and with 300 he pushed forward. Tradition here inserts that on landing on a very clear night, he pointed to the Milky Way, shining brilliantly. "There," he said, " is my road, running straight from Norway to this place." Ever since then the Manx have called the Milky Way "Rad Mooar

Ree Goree" (The great road of King Orry). The Manx were encamped on Scacafell (now called Sky Hill) and they attacked from their camp with great ferocity. Godred fell back skilfully towards Ramsey till the enemy had passed his ambush, whereupon the Vikings attacking on two sides drove the Manx back towards the Sulby river, which was in flood, and, seeing no chance of escape, they surrendered. Godred spared them. *Chronicon* goes on to relate that Godred offered his Vikings the option of staying in the Island and dividing the lands among themselves, or of taking back what of value they could find, and leaving him with a faithful few to rule. In true Viking fashion they chose to plunder and return, and Godred was left, to make friends with his newly conquered people, which he appears to have done with very great success, for history and tradition agree that he was a highly respected and even much-loved king. For nearly 200 years the Island was ruled by Godred's descendants (1079-1266).

Interesting sidelights on this period are afforded in the ship-burials of the Island, of which three have been excavated, and possibly more will be found. The first was that at Knock-y-dooney, Andreas, the second at Balladoole, Arbory, and the third at Balla-mooar, Jurby. They point to a transition stage. The earlier Vikings came to plunder, and then withdrew in their boats. In the transition stage a certain number of chiefs came to settle down and become farmers and land-owners, but retained their war boats transformed to times of peace and used for fishing. Indeed for centuries the farmer-fisherman formed the backbone of the Manx nation.

The excavation of the Knock-y-dooney site was carried out by the famous Manx archaeologist Mr. P. M. C. Kermode in 1927. The other two were investigated by Dr. G. Bersu in 1945, and the approximate date of the burials was stated to have been about A.D. 850. Knock-y-dooney is a sandy hill just south of Rue Point. It is about 100 feet above sea-level on the top of the drift-gravel cliff overlooking the sea. Through the centuries it was a hill of "Watch and Ward". The tumulus excavated had a diameter of 51 feet and a height of about 7 feet above the surrounding level. Buried in this had been a boat filled with stones, and covered with sand. The timbers of the boat had decomposed, and disappeared, but the outline was clearly demonstrated by the iron marks in the soil, of bolts and nails. The boat was about 30 feet long, 6 feet wide and 3 feet deep. In the centre of the boat had lain the chief's body; in the prow the man's horse and harness. The custom was to equip the boat for the "journey to Odin". The chief's sword was by his side, enough fragments were found to show its size and shape. Of the spear, the head remained. There were also the leaden weights of his fishing gear, a smith's hammer and tongs (no doubt he had been a skilled smith as well), two knives, and an earthen bowl. Remains of leather showed he had worn leather foot-gear. The whole boat seems to have been covered with a timber and brush-wood cover, over which had been raised a cairn, and the whole structure covered with earth and turf. When the wood of the roof had perished the whole structure collapsed on the boat.

In the boat at Balladoole were relics showing that the owner was a wealthy and much-travelled man, for there were found in this case a cloak-pin, gilt buckles and ornaments all of Scandinavian origin, an enamel button with debased triquetra, a massive silver buckle, a silver-gilt strap-end of continental design, stirrups, spurs and harness of Irish design. The sword and spear had rusted away, but the shield-grip remained. There were burnt bones of horse and ox, pointing to a funeral sacrifice; and there were flints for fire-lighting. The excavation of the Jurby site had to be put off, because it was included during the War in the area of the Jurby aerodrome. But it had been earmarked for excavation, and the constructors of the aerodrome were careful not to damage it. There are other very obvious relics of Viking occupation in the Island. There are for instance about twenty tumuli around the coast of the Island (especially the south coast), and a few well inland, marked on the Ordnance maps as "Forts". The first of these to be carefully investigated was the Vowlan Fort on Ramsey Bay. This was found to be made up of several rectangular buildings built on what is known as the "three-aisle" plan of Viking structure. In the years 1950-52 the fort known as Cronk-ny-Merrieu at Port Grenaugh, Santan, was excavated by Mr. P. S. Gelling. It proved to be a rectangular Viking pattern fortified farm, on the edge of the cliff, protected on the landward side by a rampart, with a fosse. The building was definitely Scandinavian, probably of late eleventh century, but there were obvious signs that the rampart and fosse were earlier, and there were traces of earlier buildings on the same site as the Viking rectangular house. A building of the same dimensions has been set up in the field beside the fort, and it is hoped that at some future date a replica of the building will be completed.

In 1954 an even more interesting excavation was made at Close-ny-Chollagh, Arbory, overlooking Poylvaish Bay. Here again was the same scheme of fosse, rampart and fortified Viking house, almost identical in plan with that of Grenaugh. But deeper excavation under the Viking building revealed three circular Celtic houses or raths. In the Celtic houses one very significant "find" was made, viz. a brooch of very distinctive pattern of a type known in Britain to have been of the first century B.C. This discovery made it fairly certain that these coastal forts were Celtic in origin. The ramparts and fossae were of Celtic origin, and the fortified posts were taken over in the later period, and used by the Scandinavian folk who occupied the Island.

Again in 1956, the fort to the south of the Cass-ny-hawin in Malew, on the northern outskirt of the aerodrome, was investigated, and the same general result obtained, of a Celtic fort with in this case a rampart only, and inside, the Celtic site, over-built with a Viking house. In this case a "find" of a spear, or fish spearhead, and a two-edged knife of dagger-like form showed the Viking occupation. A somewhat similar result at the inland river fort at Ballanicholas in Santan showed the same general practice, for here the inland site is on a low cliff above the Santanburn, protected by a rampart on the opposite side.

Then further there are, very visible and accessible, two other Viking forts of a different kind, one at Cronk Sumark, Sulby in Lezayre, the other at Castleward in Braddan. These are the so-called "vitrified" forts. Cronk Sumark or Primrose Hill stands at the mouth of Sulby Glen, and is a rocky outcrop very steep to the N. and W., but having an easy slope to the E. and S. These easy slopes, again in the same manner as the coastal forts, are the defended sides. The hill has been quarried and the road to the quarry has cut through part of the outer defence rampart. Inside there is a newer, steeper bank which shows evident signs of vitrification. Within these two banks, and at the edge of the cliff, is a rectangular enclosure, which has not yet been excavated, but which would seem to have been another Viking fort. A "vitrified" fort is a fort whose ramparts have been modified by great heat. Wood placed on and in cavities of the rampart has been fired, and possibly covered in to maintain a great heat for a long time, so that the stones have to a large extent fused, to form a solid mass. Such forts are well known across northern Europe.

The Braddan fort of Castleward stands on a steep bluff above the River Glass for about half a mile east of the Mental Hospital. It is a solidly constructed fort surrounded by three terraces. Its terraces again show marked signs of vitrification. It has never been carefully investigated but in general form is an obvious Viking fort, and had, probably in the fortified area, Viking type houses as in the case of the other examples considered. It is not known if there was a previous Celtic settlement there.

One more Viking fortification often seen and easily accessible is the mound known as Cronk How Mooar about half a mile west of Kirk Christ, Rushen, and beside the Port Erin road to Ballachurry. It is a natural mound about 35 feet high, surrounded by a well-marked ditch. The ditch is man-made but the mound is a deposit of glacial drift, probably artificially shaped. In the top is a depression, which contained a rectangular " house " whose walls were sunk 3 or 4 feet below the surface, and consisted of large stone slabs about three feet apart and built up between with stone "cobbles". The area was about 18 feet by 10 feet and there was an entrance through the west wall. The only relic found on excavation was an iron-and-wood object identified in Scandinavia as an arrow of Viking age. The structure has been variously interpreted as a "motte-and-bailey" fort, a Viking fort precursor of the type usually found in Britain, and as a defended farm or storehouse.

The Braaid Circle, Marown, consists of a large circular Celtic-type house of approximately 40 feet diameter, and, adjacent to it, a rectangular Viking-like " house " and a peculiar boat-shaped building, each about 50 feet long. This is the only boat-shaped building known in the Island, but others are known in Britain, and a greater number in Scandinavia.

But, returning to recorded history, the line of Godred ruled until 1265, and they all more or less paid allegiance to the kings of Norway, who also elected bishops of the Island.

In 1134 Olaf I (of Mann) granted to the Savignian Abbey of Furness a tract of land at "Balisali" in Malew, for an abbey for the Island. This abbey was built and soon became the dominant factor in its life. In 1229 Simon of Argyll was reluctantly accepted as bishop of the Island, consecrated at Nidaros, came to the Island, built a fortress at Kirk Michael, which afterwards became Bishopscourt, and also reconstructed and enlarged on Peel Island the small church of St. German, which a century or so later became St. German's Cathedral.

The last Scandinavian King of Mann was Magnus, 1252-1265. He agreed to accept the overlordship of Alexander III of Scotland and to retain his title on furnishing the King of Scotland, when called upon, with five twenty-four-oared and five twelve-oared war galleys. The Sudreys were attached directly to the

Scottish kingdom. So the Manx-Scandinavian rule came to an end.

But Scandinavia had left its mark upon the Island, a mark which has lasted down the centùries. First and foremost it left a Scandinavian form of legislature. (See Legislature.) It also left a Manx Church organized upon western lines. (See Church.) It left a distinct influence on place and family names, though it left very little influence upon the language, which remained Celtic. It left two other interesting features which lasted through the following centuries, the guardian system of Watch and Ward, and the national alarm system of the "Crosh Vusta" or summoning cross. The Custom of Watch and Ward was placed first, presumably because of its importance, on the list of laws binding on the people of Mann, when in 1405 Sir John Stanley came to the Island to study the laws of his new kingdom. In the first record of that date, it is written: "Firste . . . that watche and ward be kepte throughe your lande as it ought to be, upon lyfe and lime for whoso faileth one nighte of ye watche forfeiteth bodye and goodes . . . whoso faileth any nighte in warde forfeiteth a wether to ye witnesses and ye warde, ye second nighte, a cow, and ye thrid nighte lyfe and lime to yr Lorde." It was obvious that in an island open to attack by sea, some sentry system must be maintained. In the Manx system nobody was exempt from the duty except the Coroners, Lockmen and Moars, the chief smith and miller of the parish. Four men from each parish were on duty at one time by day and four by night, making a total of fifty-six in the week. The times were from sunrise to sunset, for the day watch, and relief by the night watch at sunset. Each parish with the exception of Marown, which alone has no sea-border, had watch hills. Only the day watch went to the watch hill. The night watch used shore look-outs. Blundell, who saw the system working during the Civil War, said that "since the winds here are so boysterous on the summets of the hills so that widdows of the Island have to gather fuel to furnish to the warming of the men of the Watch: as well as for the beacons that are set there".

A list from the Castle Rushen papers of 1627 gives a list of persons on ward for day and night from each parish. In that year the two Deemsters, both by name Christian, were "on duty", one at Hangman's Hill in Lezayre, by day, the other in Malew, at the Port of Ronaldsway, for the night. The watch was under what was practically military discipline, and had to be properly armed and accoutred. In the early days they used their own arms, but after 1550 there are records of arms supplied by the legislative body. A map marked with the " beacon hills " shows a complete system all round the Island, and specially round the Island headlands. The night watches were at all the bays and inlets. The watch for each parish was under the control of the Captain of the Parish.

The token for summons of fighting men in case of emergency was the " Wooden Cross ", the " Crosh Vusta " or " mustering cross ". Captains of Parishes seemed to have had always ready in their homes these crosses, which were in case of alarm given to the lockman and probably other messengers, who took them round the villages and countryside as direct summonses to muster in the villages under the captains. Kelly's dictionary defines the " crosh " as " a wooden sword in the form of a cross ". A description from the eighteenth century says that the " crosh " was about two feet long, burnt at one end. In later times the use of the " crosh " was maintained as a general summons to a parish meeting. The last time it was used was at Patrick in 1843.

CHAPTER SIX

THE RULE OF THE STANLEYS

THE ATTACHMENT of the Isle of Man to Scotland by no means brought about an era of peace. Edward I of England, called to adjudicate between the claims of John Balliol and Robert Bruce, decided in favour of the former, but almost immediately dethroned him and claimed the crown for himself. He claimed the Isle of Man as well, and appointed Balliol as its governor. But Bruce defeated Edward II, and himself came to the Island, and in 1313 reduced and captured the Scandinavian stronghold where Castle Rushen now stands, and for twenty years Mann was again attached to Scotland. Edward III finally took back the Island in 1333, and appointed as " King of Mann " William de Montacute, and his heirs in perpetuity. He was succeeded by his son in 1344. During the lordship of these two barons, Castle Rushen was reconstructed on the site of the Scandinavian fortress and included much of the old fort in the keep of the new castle (see Castle Rushen). The second Montacute, now Earl of Salisbury, sold the kingship to William le Scrope,

Kitterland Sound and Calf of Man

The Sugar-loaf Rock

The coast below the Marine Drive

Lower Sulby
Glen

North Barrule
from Maughold

Cottage at
Niarbyl

King Orry's
Grave, Laxey

The Andreas Cross–Odin and his Raven

who with papal authority built the Castle and red-curtain wall at Peel (see Peel Castle) and repaired and enlarged the cathedral there. Scrope supported Richard II against Henry IV, who executed Scrope and gave the Island to Henry Percy, Duke of Northumberland. But the Percys rebelled against Henry and after their defeat at Shrewsbury in 1403 the Island was given to John Stanley, "Chivaler", for life, and in the next year the grant was confirmed in perpetuity, "with its castles, and royalties and the patronage of the bishopric, on paying homage and rendering two falcons to him and every future king of England on their coronation day". So the uneasy days came to an end, and the Stanley family ruled as Kings of Mann for 350 years. John Stanley was the grandson of the first Stanley to achieve fame, Adam, Royal Forester of the Wirral to King Stephen. He built a fortified house at Liverpool, became a Garter Knight, married the heiress of the family of Lathom House at Knowsley, a house that has been the family home ever since. His grandson Thomas, third Stanley to be King of Mann, was the first Earl, and he took his title as Earl of Derby, not from the famous midland town, but from his estate of Derby in Lancashire. He was a "catskin earl" with the privilege of wearing, like the dukes, four rows of ermine ("quatre-skin").

Sir John Stanley, first King, never visited the Island, but he sent his son John to interview the leading Islanders, receive their homage, and consult them as to the future of his realm. He appointed a Lancashire man as Governor, one Michael Blundell, and it is interesting to see down the centuries how the Derby family appointed a multitude of Lancashire men as officers in the Island. Their names stand out prominently, Walton, Blundell, Dutton, Preston, Fazakerley, Radcliffe, Bolton, Kirkham, Greenhalge. At the meeting with young John Stanley, which was virtually a Tynwald Court, the Islanders explained their ancient system of Government (see Legislature) and swore fealty under penalty of "drawing, quartering, and hanging" (horrible sequence!). Besides Blundell he left two commissioners, Tyldesley and Haysnap, to settle affairs generally. His father died in 1414, and young John became the second Lord of Mann. But the Manx were by no means settled, and tried to murder Walton, the new Governor, while he was holding a court of justice at Michael. This brought the Lord again to the Island. He summoned the "tennants and commons of Mann" to meet him at Raneurling Hill near Michael, and heard there in public from this "Tynwald" hill the case against the would-be murderers. They were

D

condemned to death. The bishop (Payl) swore fealty and the established laws of the land were confirmed by "Ye same Sir John Stanley by ye grace of Godde King of Mann and the Isles" and by the "best of ye commons of Mann".

On the eve of Lady Day 1423 the "King" summoned a Tynwald Court "his deemsters and twenty-four faithful Keys" at Castle Rushen. This Tynwald Court became the model on which the Stanleys based their rule. There is a record of some of the proceedings of a similar Tynwald Court held in 1429, virtually the Manx Magna Carta, with four main clauses:

i. Trial by battle was abolished and made illegal; in future all matters of contention to be settled by a jury.
ii. No man's goods may be confiscated except by lawful authority.
iii. Every man to be held responsible for debts incurred by his wife.
iv. Fixed standards of weights and measures to be enforced.

Until that time there had been no written law. The law as administered had always been "breast law" . . . decisions as determined by a succession of deemsters. Indeed the deemsters were the "repositories" of the law. There is still a considerable amount of breast law in the Manx courts, clearly accepted and equally binding with *lex scripta*, to this day. John II was succeeded by his son Thomas in 1432, who had been appointed Governor of Ireland, and later was made the "Comptroller of the Royal household", so had no time to devote to the Island's affairs. But his son Thomas (II) (first baron) had to follow a difficult path through the Wars of the Roses. His adroitness was phenomenal. He was a favourite esquire of Henry VI, for whom he fought at Northampton, he was appointed Chief Justice of Chester by Edward IV, and later Lord Steward of England. Richard Crookback made him Lord Constable, and when at Bosworth he watched from a distance his royal master being defeated, he picked up his crown from the thornbush, and placed it on the head of Henry Tudor, surely a record in baronial adroitness. He had married Margaret Beaufort, widow of Edward Tudor, so he was in fact step-father to King Henry VII. He was succeeded by his grandson Thomas III (first earl) in 1504. He it was who preferred to be "a powerful lord, rather than a petty king" and "Lord of Mann" became a title that has lasted to the present day.

Thomas III was succeeded by his son Edward, but as he was so young Cardinal Wolsey was appointed Commissioner till he came of age. He remained a strong Roman Catholic, but survived

Henry VIII's anger because he had joined the petition of several barons to urge the Pope to recognize the divorce of Catherine. He was ordered by the protestant supporters of Edward VI to give up the Island, which he declined to obey, was commended and rewarded by Mary, and equally appreciated by Elizabeth. He was a rich and outstandingly able and generous man. There is no record of his having visited the Island, but he took a very great interest in its affairs, and appointed an "Enquest" to investigate the great waste taking place in the economy of Castle Rushen and Peel Castle. This same Enquest was charged to make out a tariff of fees for certain officers, and fines for misdemeanours. His son Henry, Lord from 1572 to 1598, came to the Island in 1577, and presided at a Court of common law, and at a Tynwald Court, at which regulations were made for salmon and trout fishing, and the deemsters were asked to make a statement on "treasure trove". He was one of the commissioners who condemned to death Mary, Queen of Scots. His son named Ferdinando seems to have been one of the Elizabethan poet-courtier type and the Queen, when he died within seven months of succeeding, realizing he had only daughters, felt that Spain or France would look upon the Island as a useful base against her England, so assumed the lordship herself. She held this lordship all through her life, and tradition says she presented a clock to Castle Rushen (q.v.). The lordship was passed on to her successor James I, who passed it over successively to the Earl of Northumberland and then to the Earl of Salisbury.

In 1610 James restored the lordship to William Stanley (sixth earl), who took no interest in the Island; but his wife lived there, and so did his son James, Lord Strange, who when he succeeded in 1627 on the death of his mother became the "Great Stanley". He married the famous and much-respected Charlotte de la Tremoille.

During the lordship of the Great Stanley two famous Manxmen, both named Christian, left their mark on the Island history. One was Edward Christian (1603-61), son of the Vicar of Maughold, the other William Christian (1608-63), known to his fellow-countrymen as "Illiam Dhone" (Swarthy William), was the younger son of Deemster Ewan Christian of Milntown, Lezayre. Edward Christian went to sea early, became captain and owner of a ship, and amassed a considerable fortune in the East India Company. He left the sea and attached himself to the Duke of Buckingham, under whose aegis he was accepted at the Royal Court. He joined the Royal Navy and became captain of a frigate *Bonaventura* (37 guns). In 1627 he retired to his native Isle, and came to the notice of the Earl, who offered him the post of Captain of the Troops. The Earl wrote to his son, ". . . he is content to hold the office for as much or as little as it pleases me to pay him; he is excellent company, as rude as a sea-captain should be, but refined as one that hath been half a year at court". It is therefore amusing to find him being dismissed in 1639 for the reason that "the more I gave, the more he demanded". In the meanwhile he had been instructed to build a fort in the Lhen where the Manx militia might be trained. In 1634 the Lord Deputy of Ireland was complaining bitterly that Christian was in league with pirates and freebooters, and was harassing the shipping in the Irish sea. The Lord was trying to alter the land tenure in the Island to the English (feudal) system, and Christian was fomenting rebellion among his fellow-countrymen, and raised strong protest against fresh tithes. A revolt broke out during the Lord's absence in England. He returned hurriedly to the Island, and found that Christian had mustered a considerable body of militia, by means of the "Crosh". The Lord prevailed, and Christian was arrested and imprisoned in Peel Castle. There was a heavy indictment against him on ten main charges, including a charge of declaring for Parliament against the King. The sentence of the court was a fine of a thousand marks, and his "boddye to perpetual imprisonment, or till released by the Lord". As a matter of fact he was released when Commonwealth forces occupied the Island in 1651. In 1659 he entered into a plot against the Commonwealth governor, Challenor, and was again committed to Peel Castle, where he died in 1661. He was buried in his home church at Maughold.

William Christian appears first in Island affairs as Steward of the (dissolved) abbey lands in 1643, when he was also a member of the Keys. In that year his father the Deemster presented him with the farm of Ronaldsway, now completely covered by the airport. Strangely enough in view of his after-behaviour, he agreed to accept the property, not on the Manx system of the "straw" tenure, but on the Lord's new lease, a tenure for three lives. He was appointed "Receiver", virtually the Lord's land agent. In 1651 the Earl left the Island with a strong and well-equipped force of Manxmen, four from each parish, and with his own retainers provided a useful company for the Royalist cause. The Earl had fortified the Island considerably. In addition to the Lhen fort which Edward Christian had built, he made another similar one at Ballachurry in Andreas, which still stands. He built a strong stone fort guarding Douglas Bay, of which the name "Fort Street" alone remains a relic, and he further strengthened the armament of the fort on Fort Island (Derbyhaven). He built a very strong fort on St. Patrick's Island, Peel, whose ruins remain today, and another at Port Cranstal near the Point of Ayre.

For defence by sea the Earl provided the King's frigate *Elizabeth* and a number of 16-oared galleys each with two guns. Twice this "fleet" repulsed the Parliamentary fleet of five ships. The Earl joined Prince Rupert and with him was defeated at Marston Moor, at which battle many of his Manxmen died. He returned to the Island and remained there till the execution of the King (1649). During this period the Island was the refuge of many Royalists, but for the time Parliament made no demands for its surrender. The Earl spent his time training and equipping more troops.

In 1649 Parliament sent a formal demand for the surrender of the Island, to which demand the Lord replied "that with any more message of this sort, he would burn the paper and hang the bearer". Further, he declared he would "hold the Island for his Majesty".

In January 1651, Charles II in exile appointed him commandant of the King's forces in Lancashire and Cheshire. He thereupon took with him "300 Mancks Souldiers" and landed at Rossall, leaving his intrepid Countess, Charlotte, with John Greenhalge to control the Island, and William Christian as Receiver. The Earl was defeated at Wigan, but escaped to join Charles before the battle of Worcester, where he was captured and sent to Chester Castle. His Countess made every effort to save his life, and offered to surrender the Island on his behalf. But Cromwell was determined that he should die. "Darbie," he wrote, "will be tried at Chester and die at Bolton"; and so it was.

The Manx landowners were much incensed at what they considered was the Countess' offer to save herself and her husband at their expense. That too seems to have been the first idea of William Christian, for he seized all the Island strongholds other than the two castles. He then proceeded to open negotiations with the parliamentary forces. He sent word that the landing from their fleet would not be opposed. Colonel Duckinfield, their commander, after a very stormy crossing, landed in Ramsey Bay, and received a deputation of leading landowners with Christian as their spokesman, who agreed to surrender the Island if they might retain their ancient laws and liberties. He addressed the Countess as "widow of the Earl of Derby", which was the first intimation the poor soul had of her husband's fate. At first she was defiant, but soon realized that her garrison was disaffected, and indeed they had already surrendered the gatehouse of Rushen Castle, and the curtain wall. So she surrendered on condition that she and her children should be allowed to go free. To her belongs the honour of being the last opponent to surrender to Parliament.

Almost immediately William Christian and his brother Deemster John were summoned to London for consultation about the ancient laws and liberties. Both were confirmed in their offices, and in 1656 William was appointed Governor but in 1658 his arrest was ordered for misappropriation of public revenue. Little is known of his doings during the following years until the Restoration, but he certainly spent these years in England, probably in London, but when the Act of Indemnity was passed, believing himself to be included in the pardon, he returned to the Island. He had failed to realize that the Act of Indemnity did not cover the domain of the Lord of Mann. Charles, son of the Great Stanley, had been immediately restored to the lordship, and had returned to the Island, all too anxious to avenge the injury and insult to his family. He ordered the arrest of Illiam Dhone on a charge of rebellion. A jury of six unlettered labouring men was empanelled, men who were entirely ignorant of the purpose for which they were called, unable even to speak English, in which the case was heard, and three of them in direct employment of the Lord. Tradition says that twice they returned a verdict of "Not Guilty", but a third time they were told what they were expected to do. On their verdict Christian was committed to the General Gaol Delivery. But he refused to plead before this Court. This was an error of judgment on his part, for by the law of the time a refusal to plead was equivalent to a plea of "Guilty", so the case was taken to the Deemster and Keys. The Keys returned a majority verdict of "Guilty". Christian was condemned to be "hanged, drawn, and quartered", but in deference to the disconsolate state of his wife, the verdict was commuted to being "shotte to death". The sentence was carried out on January 2nd, 1663, at Hangohill in Malew, and his body was interred the same day in the nave of Malew Church, where his tombstone may be seen today. A petition for pardon was sent to Charles II, but the execution was hurried on, and Charles' stay of execution arrived much too late. The King commanded that all the properties and land should be returned to the widow and children and ordered the arrest of the Deemsters who had passed sentence, to be held for " condign punishment ".

During the lordship of Earl Charles, Bishop Barrow, acting as his governor or " sword-bishop ", seized Hangohill farm, Malew, belonging to John Lace, in order to finance " Bishop Barrow's Trust ", a fund intended for the training of young Manx men as clergy. This seizure the Earl supported in an attempt to insist that the Manx folk held their land on a " feudal " system, and not as freeholders. Lace appealed to the Keys, and twice they returned a decision " The land is John Lace's ". But the Earl threatened the Keys with severe penalties if they insisted, and they gave way.

The " murder " of Illiam Dhone, and this attempt to feudalize the ownership of land, made the Stanley rule very unpopular, and tension between lordship and people increased considerably. Earl Charles died in 1672, and was succeeded by his son William, a mere child. But when he came of age he persisted in his father's land policy. To his credit be it said that he appointed as bishop the great Thomas Wilson, who as a matter of fact was the chief agent in a peaceful settlement of the Land Question. He was succeeded by his brother James, a soldier with very little idea of ruling an island race, harsh and bullying, as befitted a soldier of his time. He died in 1736 without issue, and this branch of the Stanley family came to an end. The heir to the lordship would have been William, Marquis of Tullibardine, who had been attainted for his part in the '15 rebellion, so the succession went to his brother James, Duke of Atholl. He was a very good friend of his subjects, though not often on the Island. He was succeeded in 1764 by his daughter Charlotte, Baroness Strange, married to John Murray, son of Prince Charlie's general, who by right of his wife became Lord of Mann, and who was heir to the Dukedom of Atholl (third Duke) and the nearest male heir to the lordship. It was during this lordship that the British Parliament passed the Revesting Act (May 1765), buying the Lordship of Mann on behalf of the British Crown. This meant that the Atholls renounced their right to the lordship, and the new Lord was George III.

The Revestment Act, together with its accompanying " Mischief Act ", was the result of the smuggling " Trade " of the Island, which had become a menace to British trade and finance. This " trade " may possibly be deemed to have its origin in a comment of the seventh Earl in 1648. " This Island will never succeed till some trade be."

By the time Bishop Wilson reached the Island in 1698, a gigantic " trade " was developing. He soon found the Island was being used as a brandy-distributing centre. He saw it sadly in the effect it was having on his flock, where drunkenness was rife. He preached earnestly on the sin of drunkenness. His Vicars-General sentenced the drunkards with some severity. The bishop preached to the multitude of *nouveau riche* merchants, and they subscribed liberally to all his causes, but had no idea of cutting off their wealth at its source. The simple fact was that the Island, being an independent kingdom, could frame its own tariffs, and it resolved that in spite of Britain it was legal to import into the Isle of Man any commodities that could be re-sold. The Manx merchants (and any person with a few pounds to spare could become a merchant) were at liberty to buy brandy and silks from France, and rum from Jamaica, and bring them in to the Island free of duty. This they did, using fast Manx clippers to run cargoes. Cellars were constructed in houses of Douglas, Castletown, Port St. Mary and Peel, and stores of contraband maintained. All this was perfectly legal; it was not smuggling. Then with the same clippers skilfully handled by Manx crews who knew every mile of the Irish Sea, who were kept informed of the presence of revenue cutters, who used their coast-line with the greatest skill, ran cargoes to the quieter portions of the coast of Ireland, South Scotland, Lancashire, Cheshire and Wales. It was an adventurous business, and above all a highly paying business, and it was a perfect plague to the British revenue man. Many boats came into the harbours and paid a small " Lord's due " which was much appreciated, and increased the Lord's revenue magnificently. Much was run into the creeks and inlets of the coast, and landed free from Lord's dues. Everybody who could put a few pounds into the business was certain of a rich reward. The Lord's dues increased, but never so much as to cripple the trade. Douglas grew from a tiny fishing village into a considerable town and harbour. In vain the British Government increased its coast watchers and revenue men, in vain they increased their naval cutters, they were outwitted and outsailed. Many a Manx family owes its wealth and position to their forbears of those adventurous days of " trade " . . . not smuggling! The British Government, however, was determined to stop the trade. The Prime Minister, Greville, was ordered by Parliament to treat with the Atholls, who were obviously getting a wonderful income from this source. The Duke was asked in effect what it was worth to him, so that the British might buy out his interest. The Duke did not hurry to reply, but said he had only just arrived and such a question needed mature consideration. To hasten his reply Parliament passed what is known in the Island as the " Mischief " Act, giving the revenue officers the right to stop and search every boat arriving at or leaving Manx ports. This had never been legal on boats entering or leaving, only those entering English ports and under suspicion. The Act caused general consternation because it looked like ending completely the period of prosperity. The Duke, stirred by the Act, suggested that the lordship was worth to him £299,773, made up:

Regalities	£42,000
Patronages of Bishopric and vicarages	8,400
Customs dues, lands and manors	249,373

Parliament replied that they only wanted regalities and customs and suggested £70,000. Thereupon the Manx people took a hand. They had lost all hope of further profit. Moreover they had large stocks on hand which they had no chance of selling at a profit. The Duke was going to do well out of it. They were not. The Keys sent a deputation, George Moore, to Westminster to negotiate. He was treated with great discourtesy. The Revesting Act was passed. The Duke and Duchess were granted a joint annuity of £2,000 (Irish), and renounced all rights to the lordship.

The Duke died in 1774, and the Duchess in 1805. Their son, John, fourth Duke, on his father's death asked that the finances should again be revised, by means of an amending Act. This was objected to by the Manx, who had little enough of profit so far and looked like being called upon to pay a considerable sum into the Atholl coffers. The Keys put forward plans of many kinds affecting his manorial rights, and demanded new roads, new bridges and the draining of the curraghs. They abolished the hated herring tax, and the turf tax, they abolished his Great Enquest. He countered by asking Parliament to restrain all alienation of his rights, a deposition of all deeds with his seneschal, prohibition against building water-mills, the right to search houses, and to destroy dogs which might attack his game. A deputation of the Keys asked that such money as the Duke demanded be applied to their plans for improvement of amenities. The Commons refused the Amending Act, and the Duke asked for a Royal Commission to investigate. The Duke's chief allegations were:

i. His revenues had never been fairly collected by Island officials.

ii. He had the right of increasing duties without the consent of the Keys.

iii. His rights on Peel Island and the main ports had been curtailed.

iv. Tynwald passed laws in secret which he did not see, till he was asked to sign them.

The Commission "found for the Duke in general" but made no suggestions as to the setting right. Thereupon the King appointed him Governor of the Island (1794). As a result a large amount of patronage fell into his hands, and he started a campaign of nepotage, with "Murrays, Murrays everywhere". He appointed George Murray as bishop, who promptly demanded a tithe of twelve shillings per acre on potatoes. This caused a general riot all over the Island, and Bishop's Court narrowly escaped destruction (1817). The Duke realized his unpopularity. But he did very well at the end, for the British Government compounded with him for a total sum of £417,144, and he resigned, and left the Island. So the Atholl part of the Stanley régime ended in bathos. The purchase was completed in 1828. The price was very high, but the whole sum had been reimbursed out of the Island revenue by 1866. So ended the Stanley rule in the Island. It had been a long era in which the Lords had fostered Home Rule, while keeping a tight hold on personnel. On the whole the Islanders had been content, though from time to time they had been driven to desperation and rebellion, by attempts to change their land tenure, by harsh taxation, and especially by tithes, of which the Lords received a lion's share.

CHAPTER SEVEN

LEGISLATION: KEYS—COUNCIL— TYNWALD

O N E O F the best known facts about the Isle of Man is that it has its own home government. Not quite so well known is the fact that its Parliament differs considerably from the Imperial Parliament, and still less realized is that it is a Scandinavian form of legislature which has been established since the ninth century,

or possibly earlier, a long time before the Saxon witenagemot
had developed into the "Mother of Parliaments". The form of
its procedure is Norse, and can be directly traced from descriptions in the Sagas. The very name "Tynwald" is derived from
Scand: "Thing", an assembly, and "vollr", a field. Here be
it said that this word Tynwald is used in two senses, for the
assembled "parliament" of Governor, upper and lower chambers;
and also for the outdoor ceremony held on Old Midsummer day,
July 5th, on the Tynwald Hill at St. John's. The first record
of a Tynwald Court occurs in the *Chronicon*, and shows that by
the time the *Chronicon* was begun (eleventh century) the Tynwald
had been very long established. The first primitive Tynwald is
described in the Sagas, and explains that a chieftain raised an
altar to Thor, on a mound, and planted a line of trees, or constructed a fence made of tree-trunks, leading towards the mound.
On this mound, after suitable ceremonial and prayers, the chieftain would sit and listen to complaints from his subjects,
administer justice, and proclaim new laws. To these local courts
later was added a superior court of "Al-thing" presided over by
the king, the high priest of Thor and other prominent men.
Such a system seems to have been adopted in Mann under Scandinavian rule. There are known to have been Tynwald mounds
at Cronk Urleigh in Michael, and at Keeill Abban in Braddan,
besides the central mound at St. John's.

When in 1405 young John Stanley came to the Island to investigate conditions in his new kingdom, he was instructed by the
deemster of that time: "oure doughtie and gracious Lorde, this
is the constitucione of olde tyme, which we hadde given to ye in
oure dayes hoe ye shd be governed in Tynwald day. Firste ye
shall come hither in royal arraye, as ye Kinge oughte by ye
prerogatives and royalties in ys lande of Manne and upon the
hille of Tynwald, sitte in a chaire covered with a royal cloath,
and quishons, and yr visage unto ye east and yr sword before
you, holden with the point upward, yr barons in ye thirde degree
sitting beside you, and yr beneficed men and yr deemster before
you sitting, and yr clerk, yr knightes esquires and yeomen about
you in ye third degree and the worthiest men in yr lande to be
called in before yr Deemsters, if you will ask anything of them,
and to heare the government of ys landse and yr will and ye
commons to stande without the circle of the hill with three clerkes
in thr surplices. Then yr Deemster shall call upon ye coroner
of Glanfaba, and he shall call in all ye coroners of Mann, their
yardes in their handes with their weapons upon them sword or

ax and the moars that is, of every Sheading. Then the Coroner of Glanfaba shall make a fence upon pain of lyfe or lymme that no man make any disturbance . . . upon pain of hanging and drawing."

So it had been for hundreds of years before 1405, and so in almost exact detail it is carried out today.

On July 5th the Tynwald Court together with the officers of the Lieutenant-Governor, the clergy, the Captains of Parishes, the coroners and representatives of the towns are summoned. They assemble in the church, the Keys in their seats between the transepts, the council in the stalls in the chancel, the remainder of those summoned in the south transept, the general public in the nave, and a short service is held, at the close of which the procession starts for the hill along the pathway between the two "fences" over which have been strewn rushes which in bygone days had been brought hither from every parish, figuratively to cause the lawmakers to pass through every parish in which these laws were to become binding.

The procession leaves the church in reverse order:

Four sergeants of police and the coroners of the six sheadings.
The beneficed clergy from every parish, together with ministers and officers of the Methodist, Roman Catholic and free churches and the Salvation Army.
The Vicar-General and the Archdeacon.
The Mayor of Douglas and the chairmen of commissioners of the towns of Peel, Ramsey and Castletown.
The Chief Registrar, the Government Treasurer and a representative of the Commission of the Peace.
The seventeen Captains of Parishes.
Yn Lhaihder, the High Bailiff and the Second Deemster.
The members of the House of Keys, with their messengers, chaplain and secretary.
The Clerk of Tynwald.
The members of the Legislative Council and their clerk.
The Attorney-General.
The First Deemster and Clerk of the Rolls.
The Lord Bishop.
The Sword Bearer.
The Lieutenant-Governor and his officers attending.
The Government Secretary, the Chief Constable and the Surgeon to the Household.

Halfway down the path the procession halts and opens out allowing the sword-bearer with sword "holden with the point upward" followed by the Lieutenant Governor to pass through and ascend the hill, followed by his officers, the Legislative Council, the Keys, the Clergy, the Captains of parishes to follow on to the separate levels of the "hill".

The Governor and Bishop being seated, the Deemster calls on the Coroner of Glenfaba and *Yn Lhaihder* to "fence" the court. The Coroner proclaims: "I fence this Court of Tynwald in the name of our most gracious Sovereign Lady the Queen. I charge that no person do quarrel, brawl or make any disturbance and that all persons do answer their names when called. I charge this audience to witness this court is fenced. I charge this audience to witness this court is fenced. I charge this whole audience to bear witness this court is now fenced." This proclamation is then repeated in Manx by *Yn Lhaihder* (literally "The Reader"). The Coroners then ascend the hill and present their "yards" (batons of office) to the Governor. The incoming Coroners (usually the same men again) go up to the Governor, and are sworn by the Deemster: "By that Book and by the holy contents thereof, and by the wonderful works that God hath miraculously wrought in heaven above and on the earth beneath in six days and seven nights, you shall without respect of favour or friendship, love or gain, consanguinity or affinity, envy or malice, execute the office of Coroner. So help you God." The Governor then calls upon the Deemster to read the titles of all Acts of Tynwald passed by the Legislature since last July 5th, together with their dates of royal assent. These are then read out by the two Deemsters, one in English and the other in Manx. The laws being thus recited are deemed to be known by all. The Governor then calls for three cheers for the Queen, the procession descends the hill, and the legislative body returns into the church to transact such further business as is necessary. Tynwald Day is a national holiday. In times past the Manx folk used to leave their homes often in the early hours of the morning, since their attendance at Tynwald was of great importance.

Tynwald Hill is a four-tiered conical mound of earth; traditionally the earth was brought from each of the seventeen parishes, thereby symbolizing the whole island. The lowest tier has a circumference of 256 feet, the second 163, the third 102 and the top 60. The tiers are all about 3 feet in height. During the Tynwald ceremony the Governor occupies the top tier together with the Bishop and Legislative Council; the Keys occupy the third tier, the clergy and chairmen of local authorities the second, and on the lowest tier the Captains of Parishes. The public stands all around on ground level, and outside the "fenced" path on the green is St. John's Fair.

The church service is so arranged that the outdoor ceremony takes place about noon, which suggests that there may have been, hidden away in the past, some religious sun-worship basis.

THE HOUSE OF KEYS

The possible derivations of the word "Keys" are many and varied. There is a Scandinavian word "Keise" which means "elected", but it is never used in the political sense; nor have the Scandinavians any cognate word in political use. Professor Rhys suggested that it was a "portmanteau" Celtic word, made up of the two first words of "Kiare-as-feed" (twenty-four). This is most unlikely, for the Manx would not use part of a word for the whole, specially as the whole word is a precise number. In the earliest written account, the Keys appear as *Claves Manniae et claves legis* (Keys of Mann and of the law). Later they appear as "worthy men", "worthiest folk", "elders", "the twenty-four", "they of the land". Not till the fifteenth century do we find the word "Keys" applied regularly. Bishop Wilson wrote that the Keys were so called "for unlocking, as it were, or solving, difficulties of the law", a pleasant clerical parabolic explanation! but scarcely etymological. Again it must be remembered that when the cardinals in Rome are locked up in their palace in order to choose a new pope, they are said to be in "conclave" (keyed together). Incidentally the derivation of the English word "key" is not known! The number of the Keys seems to bear no special relation to any political division of the Island, where there are seventeen parishes in six sheadings. In 1422 Sir John Stanley called Tynwald together to advise him further about the constitution of his kingdom.

It is recorded that he was informed "The Keyes in King Orrey's dayes (also called "Taxi-axi") were xxiiij, videlicit viij in the out isles and xvj in your land of Mann". The "out isles" may reasonably be taken to mean the Sudreys or Hebrides. But such an explanation introduces further difficulties. However the number 24 is held tenaciously, and was insisted on at the last redistribution of seats. The Lord always kept a keen vigilance on the personnel of the Keys, and nobody was allowed to be elected other than his nominees. Indeed it was the Stanley method to make the folk believe that the Government was democratic when in fact it was autocratic. Bishop Meyrick in 1580 protested that the Island was in fact ruled by a caucus made up of Bishop, Deemsters and Keys all selected by the Lord, and he felt that in common fairness the twenty-four ought to be elected by the whole nation. "And," he continued, "all the officers held their positions *durante bene placito* . . . yet one was seldom turned out of office." Bishop Phillips, 1611, protested that Lady Derby should appoint two members of the Keys and in 1648 Blundell commented that with twenty-four Keys chosen by my lord it prevented justice being done. In Bishop Barrow's claim for the farm of Hangohill, the Keys twice returned a verdict that the farm was Lace's; the Lord threatened any who declared such a thing, as being unfit to sit in the Keys, and if they persisted would be deprived of all civil rights. Matters had improved somewhat by Bishop Wilson's time, for he wrote "The twenty-four Keys represent the Commons of the Island and join with the Council in making the law, and sit with the Deemster in difficult cases". But he goes on to explain that, when a seat is vacated, the rest of the Keys suggest two other names to present to the Governor, and he chooses one or other of them. Till 1862 the Tynwald Court was at Castletown, meeting in the castle, but later a new House was built in Parliament Square, Castletown, at present occupied by the Westminster Bank. The Act of Revestment found the House of Keys a self-elected body strictly controlled in the matter of "election" by the Lord, with life-membership, and sitting in camera. It left unaltered the matter of election, but demanded that the sessions should be in public. The Act did practically nothing towards making the Keys a democratic body. Petition after petition was made to Westminster, and one indeed direct to Queen Victoria, asking for reforms, but all were ignored, and it was not till 1864 that a quite unexpected attack on the House of Keys, brought about by the insular press, convinced the Keys that they must reform themselves. They themselves therefore bargained with the Imperial Government to submit to free election in return for being given some control over the insular revenue. Since 1866, the Keys have been elected as in Britain by secret ballot. The constituencies are the six "sheadings" and the four largest towns.

Formerly when the mode of life was mainly agricultural it was reasonable to have a mainly agricultural House. But with the rise of the visiting industry, and the increase in town population, and the decrease in rural population, it was found only reasonable to modify the representation so that it might be more or less on a population basis. At the redistribution of seats adopted in 1956 the representation is:

Castletown and Peel	1 member each
Ramsey	2 members
Douglas North	1 member
Douglas East, West and South	2 members each
Sheading of Michael	1 member
Sheading of Glenfaba	2 members
Sheading of Middle	3 members
Sheading of Ayre	2 members
Sheading of Rushen	3 members
Sheading of Garff	2 members

Members of the House of Keys are paid a salary of £2,180 plus travelling expenses and allowances for membership of the various Boards of Tynwald. There are at present about 45,000 voters on the Island. Women received the vote in 1881, well in advance of their British sisters.

There is no clearly marked party system in the House of Keys. Election candidates may adopt Conservative, Labour, Nationalist or Independent labels to indicate their political leanings, but there are no whips in the Keys and every vote is a free vote of the House. They debate in their own chamber, presided over by the Speaker, who has an onerous task in a non-party house. He is therefore responsible for the " business " of the Session. As at Westminster he is the " voice of the House ".

Differing from Westminster, the Keys also sit in company with the Legislative Council in the Tynwald Court. This is done in the Tynwald chamber where the Council under the Governor occupy the "gallery" and the Keys the "floor" of the chamber. The Governor presides over the debate, and the Speaker sits immediately below him. In the Tynwald Court the Speaker may speak and vote as an ordinary member, as well as represent to the Council the views of the Keys. In case of any disagreement between the Keys and the Council, any member of the Keys may move " that the Keys retire to their own chamber ". Any measure may be passed by a majority vote in the Council or in the Keys, but for a final reading there must be a clear majority of the Keys, viz. thirteen in favour.

Any measure may be introduced either into the Keys or the Council. It is read a first time without division. On a second reading it is dealt with clause by clause. It is then sent to the other chamber. Amendments may be accepted or rejected or further amended. Every effort is made, usually by conference, to reach an agreement on disputed points. In the case of a private bill, after due notice has been given, the Governor appoints a committee of both chambers to hear counsel for the interested parties, Counsel may be required to appear at the Bar of the Keys to elucidate points in the bill. At any time in any bill, the Governor may hold a conference or appoint a Committee to go into matters of disagreement, an exceedingly elastic and smoothly working system.

Other interesting points arising from the history of the Keys are, that the Keys have the right, once they have been assembled, to adjourn their sittings from day to day, and even from place to place; also from the closing words of Sir John Stanley's constitution of 1407: " And without the Lorde's will none of the xxiv Keyes to be " was interpreted as " without the Governor's will no session of the Keys may be held ". As a result, if the Keys adjourn *sine die*, they can neither recall themselves, nor be recalled by Mr. Speaker. They will remain adjourned till the Governor calls on them to re-assemble. Nor has the Governor any compulsion to call them together after any specified time, nor even at all.

THE LEGISLATIVE COUNCIL

The Legislative Council is the Upper Chamber. Its assent is essential for the passing of any Act. In effect the relation of Keys to Council is that of Commons to Lords, but with a widely different history. The House of Lords is in the main a Norman institution. The Norman régime scarcely touched the Isle of Man. The Manx Parliament as accepted by the early Stanleys followed the Scandinavian " Al-thing ". In this the " upper set " consisted of the chieftain, the arch-priest, and the law-men.

Under the Stanley régime we have seen that the Lord had complete control of the whole legislature. He appointed his council and picked the Keys. Today the Lieutenant-Governor represents the Lord. On arrival in the Island he is taken to Castle Rushen, there to be " sworn in " by the First Deemster. This oath demands allegiance to the Lord of Mann. " You shall truly and uprightly deal between the Lord and his people, and as indifferently betwixt party and party, as this staff now standeth, as far as in you lieth. You shall take the advice and consent of the rest of the Lord's Council of the said Isle, in all matters that concern the State and Government of the said Isle. These and all other things pertain-

E

ing to the Governor of this Isle, his office and place, you shall according to the purport and extent of your commission and the laws of the said Isle, do and perform as far as in you lieth." The reference is to the Governor's badge of office, the Staff which for the purpose of the ceremony stands erect before the Governor.

Under the Stanley régime there was no definite constitution of the Council. There appeared on the Council, from time to time. the Governor, Deputy Governor, Deemsters, Clerk of the Rolls, Bishop, Archdeacon, Receiver, Water Bailiff, Attorney-General and Vicar-General. The Governor appointed directly by the Lord was his direct representative, "whoso offended him should be punished as though he had offended the Lord". He exercised all the prerogatives of the Lord, he sat in judgment with the Deemsters, called and dismissed the Keys, nominated his Deputy for the Lord's approval, nominated to the Lord all posts of importance. Today, with all the reforms of the past embodied, the Lieutenant-Governor still summons and dismisses the Keys, nominates Justices of the Peace, and Captains of Parishes, controls the police and any military forces of the Island, can adjourn Tynwald, pardon criminal offences, advise as to nominations to all Crown livings (of which there are more than are controlled by the bishop). He has obviously a very responsible post.

The Lord Bishop of Sodor and Man is a baron in his own right, the only remaining Island baron, and is still a member of the Legislative Council. He is appointed directly by the Lord. That was always the right of the Lord, and the Duchess of Atholl, even after the Revestment, claimed as her right the appointment of Bishop Crigan (not a very satisfactory choice) in 1784. Today the Queen as Lord of Mann appoints the bishop, so that by the same "accident" that made her the Lord, the bishop is chosen on exactly the same lines as his brother bishops in England. The Bishops of Sodor and Man have been a very interesting line of clerics and really deserve a book to themselves.

The Deemster's title is always a matter of interest to visitors who wish to know as much as they can about the Island. Even the derivation of the word is uncertain. The *Oxford Dictionary*, ever prosaic, asserts that since the word does not appear in any document before 1611, it must be the Middle English form of the Norman "demestre" "to deem". In view of the fact that there is a Scandinavian "doomstaur", the "steersman of doom", who was almost certainly the "law-man" of the Sagas, this term may have been in very constant use, without being recorded. In any case, the "deem" or "doom" between them carry more or less the whole judicial function of "deeming" or considering, and "dooming" or punishing. Today the Deemsters are judges of the supreme court or "High Court of Justice". By courtesy a Deemster is addressed as "Your Honour". The Deemsters have complete control of what in England would be covered by the Queen's Bench, Chancery, Admiralty, Probate and Divorce divisions, as well as the Criminal Court (General Gaol Delivery). A Deemster may be called upon to sit as a Judge of Appeal against the decision of his brother Deemster, in which case he has a Judge of Appeal with him appointed from the English bar. It is customary to hold a Deemster's Court every week of term, in one or other of the four court-towns for cases requiring no jury. There is no regular assize, and General Gaol Delivery is held when required.

The office of Clerk of the Rolls has varied in importance with the passing of the years. At the beginning of the office, he was merely a clerk into whose care were committed all the legal documents. But the post increased in importance and to it were appointed lawyers of greater and greater ability and distinction, till judicial functions were attached to the post. But since 1920 the duties have been added to those of the First Deemster. The Deemsters no longer sit on the Legislative Council.

The Deemster's oath ends up with the words: "You shall execute the laws of this Isle justly between the Lord and his people, and betwixt party and party so indifferently as the herring backbone doth lie in the middle of the fish."

The position of the archdeacon, no longer a member of the Council in the Isle of Man, is of interest. Unlike his brother archdeacons in England, he is appointed by the Lord and not by the bishop. In the early days there were doubtless other archdeacons of the Isles, but the Archdeacon of Mann had no jurisdiction there and remains Archdeacon of Mann, not Sodor and Mann.

The Manx Church (see Church) is unique in maintaining the office of a Vicar-General. In former days each diocese had a vicar-general who was the lawyer and mainly the prosecuting counsel for a bishop. He also had a court for trying ecclesiastical offences. At the reformation the post was abolished in English dioceses, but the Kings of Mann maintained the national status of the Church with that of the people and retained the vicar-general. Indeed there were commonly two, who each held court, or held a combined court, trying all cases of church discipline, heresy and schism, offences against the canon law, non-attendance, brawling, drunkenness, fornication, adultery, illegitimacy, and all matters of wills and probate. But by degrees these matters were passed over to the civil courts; non-attendance died a natural death, and today the Vicar-General is the Church's advocate in all legal matters in which the Church is involved. He lost his seat on the Council together with the archdeacon when the Council was revised in 1920.

The Receiver-General was in effect the Lord's Treasurer, his officer, collected rents and dues of all kinds, received customs dues from the water-bailiff, attended to the repairs of the Lord's castles at Peel and Castletown. But with the Revestment the duties grew less and less, and in 1920 the Receiver-General was merged into the Chairmanship of the Harbour Board, and ceased to sit on the Council as Receiver.

The Attorney-General has powers approximating to those of the Attorney-General at Westminster. His main duty is to advise the Governor in matters of law. At present the Council consists of the Bishop and Attorney-General *ex officio* (but the latter having no vote) together with eight members nominated by the Keys. The powers of the Council to block the passage of new legislation have been curbed in recent years. Since 1946, the Governor has been assisted in legislative matters by an Executive Council, or " cabinet ", which comprises two elected members from the Legislative Council and five from the Keys.

Three other sets of officials taking part in Tynwald, but not in a legislative capacity, will arouse the interests of visitors to the ceremony. First the Captains of Parishes. There are seventeen ancient parishes in the Island. Under mediaeval law, each parish had to provide a rota of men for " Watch and Ward ", and the selection of men, and the rota, were controlled by one man in each parish chosen by the Lord. The post was therefore of a semi-military character. Each parish, too, in time past provided four horsemen nominated by its Captain to form a cavalry escort to accompany the Governor from Castle Rushen to the Tynwald Hill, and to any other function for which he might need them. Moreover the Captain of the Parish was a convenient person to disseminate through a parish meeting official information and orders. The Captain was responsible for general parish discipline. The post is one of dignity and honour. Indeed it is the highest honour that can be given to a Manxman *qua* Manxman. Today the non-military functions remain, but the Captains of Parishes appear at Tynwald as a sign of the law of the land reaching every parish in the Island. With the rise of the towns, captains of towns were appointed with similar functions, but today they are replaced by the Mayor of Douglas and the chairmen of the Commissioners of the other three towns.

The High Bailiff is the stipendiary magistrate of the Island. He also presides at inquests on deaths. There is the same system of Justices of the Peace as in England and magistrates' courts are held in the court towns.

The "coroners", who figure prominently at the Tynwald at St. John's, are not coroners in the English sense. The office is a very ancient one. As their name suggests they are "crown" officers. In ancient days they were responsible for order both in their sheadings and at Tynwald. They were armed with sword or axe, and stood by while the Coroner of Glenfaba (in which sheading Tynwald hill stands) "fenced" the court. Coroners were also empowered to arrest felons, to hold inquests, to serve summonses, to empanel juries, to act as bailiffs in case of debt, which services except for inquests and arrests they still perform. Each coroner has an assistant lockman in each parish whose duties in time past included those of administering whippings, duckings and probably hangings. His duty today is the delivery of court summonses. The coroner's badge of office is a short hardwood baton or "verge" about 15 inches long.

It is convenient under the heading of "Legislature" to give a short account of the financial system of the Island. In 1866, with the reform of the Keys, the British Parliament transferred the Manx customs dues to the control of the Manx legislature (Customs and Harbours Act), but at the same time it stipulated that the cost of law-courts, police, civil service, etc., should be first deducted before any money could be dealt with by Tynwald. These were the "Reserved Services". The remainder of the money was known as "Voted Services" Income. Its disposal was subject to a veto of the Governor, and needed the approval of the British Treasury. This in theory at least gave the Governor too great powers, for though there never was a severe clash between Governor and Keys, there was always the chance that there might be. In any case it gave the Governor far too great powers, as the civil service, police, and other services were under his complete control, and he could veto all other expenditure. However in 1957 the 1866 Act was repealed, and the Finance of the Island placed under the control of the Tynwald Court, with the proviso that the Voted Services Income should be a first charge and that a contribution of five per cent of the income should be paid annually to the Imperial Government as defence costs.

The British Treasury makes "Common Purse" arrangements

with the Island, covering both Customs dues and Value Added Tax. It pays to the Island a proportion of these dues, under an agreed system, modified from time to time as circumstances alter, and based on the " Fiscal Population ", which comprises the resident population (currently about 60,000) together with an agreed adjustment to account for the seasonal influx of visitors. Under the Common Purse agreement, the British Government undertakes the collection of Customs and Excise dues and VAT in the two countries, and pays over to the insular legislature the appropriate proportion of the total, after deducting the same proportion of the costs of collection. The Common Purse now yields over £12 million a year to the Manx exchequer, but as a proportion of the Island's total revenue, its contribution (now less than half) has declined as the revenue from income tax has increased.

In return for defence and common services provided by the British Government, the Manx Government makes an annual payment (known as the " Imperial Contribution ") which, although not a part of the Common Purse arrangement, is fixed at 5 per cent of the Common Purse receipts for the year (that is currently something over £600,000).

The insular income tax has remained stable at 21.25p in the £ for some years. Personal allowances are rather more generous than the British rates, and allowances for relief from double taxation for Manx residents who draw incomes from Britain are slightly complicated but available. Surtax was abolished in 1961. There are no death duties, stamp duties or estate duties. National Insurance contributions are paid at the same rates as in Britain and social services benefits are paid on a reciprocal basis between the two countries.

CHAPTER EIGHT

THE CHURCH

THE HISTORY of the Manx Church is in every way as fascinating as the rest of the Island story. In theory it is still an independent national church, in practice it is content to be the smallest diocese in the Church of England, and is included in the province of York. But that it still retains its independent

character is witnessed by these facts. It still retains its own Convocation. It is bound by no acts of the British Parliament unless
specially named in such an act. It still has its own canon law,
legalized (though hopelessly out of date in these days) by its own
national government. It still retains its own Vicar-General. All
its legislation is referred, not to Westminster, but to its own
insular legislature. It has its own tithe system, with a widely
different history from that in Britain. Its bishop has the right of
issuing marriage licences exactly comparable with those issued by
the Archbishop of Canterbury for marriages to be solemnized at
any time and in any place in the Island. Further, because he has
a seat in the insular legislature, the Lord Bishop of Sodor and
Man is debarred from sitting in the House of Lords even if he
is senior bishop. He has a courtesy seat only in the Lords, behind
the Woolsack, and may neither speak nor vote.

Traditionally Christianity reached the Island in the year 447
as a direct result of the Irish mission of Patrick's disciples. The
date is obviously uncertain, but internal evidence, in the form
of the keeills and their dedications, the Celtic crosses, and ogham
stones, supports the view that Christianity was strongly established
in the Island in the sixth century.

The Celtic missionaries arrived from Ireland, and built a multitude of small keeills or churches, the ruins of many of which are
scattered over the Island; some have been rebuilt as parish
churches, some remain as definite ruins, while others are merely
" map-sites ". These little churches were built on stone foundations with walls about 3 or 4 feet high covered with a steep
thatched roof. In plan they were rectangular, about 15 feet in
length and 10 feet in width. They had a western door, and
usually an east window, over the small stone altar-slab. Indeed
they were miniatures of the traditional architecture of Manx
churches all down the ages, which to this day are rectangular in
plan without chancel, side-aisle, or transept, with still the same
west doorway, and usually a bell-turret for one or two bells. They
have no architectural pretensions, no grandeur, nothing to com-
mend them artistically, plain, spotlessly white buildings with
black Manx slate roofs, dignified and homely inside, every whit
as well loved by their worshippers as the Norman and Gothic
village churches in England.

Adjacent to the keeills were usually small cells for the priests,
circular, low-walled and high-roofed single-roomed houses, of
typical Celtic design, now only to be made out by their circular
stone foundations. A typical keeill of this type is to be seen at

the Lag-ny-killey, a tiny ruin in the parish of Patrick, right below
the mass of the Cronk-ny-irrey-lhaa, on a small cliff almost over-
hanging the western sea, a position too beautiful for description.
To clamber down the slope of the Cronk is too dangerous for any
ordinary person to attempt, but the keeill is reached by a glorious
footpath starting from the spot marked 785 (O.S. 1-inch map) at
the head of the tiny Glen Mooar, from which point it wanders
down the cliffside through bracken and heather right to the tiny
enclosure, which was a garth and glebe for the lonely priest who
served the " culdee cell ".

Ancient Irish manuscripts supported by internal evidence in
the Island uphold the view that the Celtic Church of this period
was well organized and had bishops, of whom four were named,
Germanus, who brought the faith to the Island, Conindrus,
Romulus and Maughold. In the Book of Armagh the story of
St. Maughold is related. Maughold or McCuill, a native of
Ulster, had lived a very wicked life and had been guilty of a
foul murder. Brought for judgment before Patrick, that good
man felt quite unable to absolve him of his sins, but felt it would
best be left to the judgment of God. Accordingly he ordered
that Maughold should be placed in a coracle made of one ox-hide,
and be sent adrift, " with the Bishop's crucifix on the prow ".
" Now McCuill went to sea on that day, his right hand towards
Maginnis, until he reached Mann where he found two wonderful
men who had reached the Island before him, by name Conindri
and Romuil. Now when these good men met Maughold they
took him from the deep, and taught him the Word of God, until
he took the bishopric after them." Whether or not Patrick ever
visited the Island it is impossible to tell, but that his name was
highly honoured is shown by the fact that two churches (doubtless
founded on original keeill churches), namely those of Patrick and
Jurby, were dedicated in his name as well as seven other keeills
(Keeill-pherick).

Of Bridget, the same Book of Armagh says that she journeyed
to Mann to take the veil at the hands of Bishop McCuill, and
that she founded the Nunnery at Douglas which still bears her
name.

Tradition further says that the organized Manx Celtic Church
was founded by Germanus, nephew of Patrick, that he built the
first simple church on Peel Island which was later dedicated in
his name.

We have said that the existence of this Celtic Church is well
attested by its keeills and monuments. Of these monuments,

many are simple incised crosses from graves, and altars. In the Maughold collection is a very delightful stone of the sixth century marked along the edge with the whole Ogham alphabet (suggesting perhaps a Victorian sampler!) and on the face of the stone "BRIST UAN RAISTI TH RUNUR" ("The priest John, writ these letters"). Another interesting stone, known as the Itspli stone, was discovered built into Maughold Church. It bears a cross of hexagonal design and is inscribed on the circle ". . . NE ITSPLI EPPS DE INSUL . . ." referring apparently to a "bishop of this island by name Itspli", and along the edges . . . "ICI IN XRI NOMINE" and "CRUCIS XRI IMAGEHEM", or "*Feci in nomine Christi crucis Christi imaginem*" ("I have made in the name of Christ a copy of the cross of Christ"). Also in Maughold churchyard the "Juan" stone reading in runes: KRISTI: MALAKI: PATRICK: ADAMNAN, "BUT OF ALL THESE SHEEP IUAN IS PRIEST IN KURNA DALE". But most beautiful and valuable of all may be seen in the Museum the Crucifixion stone found on the Calf of Man. It is probably a portion of an altar slab, thought to be unique in Christendom. It depicts Christ upon a cross, fully robed, bearded and moustached. The hands are nailed with wide-headed nails through the palms, the feet nailed separately with similar nails. The robe is highly ornate and there is a large rosette upon the breast. The outer chasuble-like garment is worn over an equally ornate alb. Beside the cross stands a soldier with a long spear, about to pierce the Saviour's side. He is dressed in the traditional Celtic fashion with an outer tunic covering a skirt or kilt.

At a somewhat later date there seems to have been a missionary stream from Scotland, since there are dedications to the Scottish saints, St. Andrew (Andreas), St. Ninian (St. Trinian's), Brendan (Braddan), Ronan (Marown), Columba (Arbory). It is of interest that the Scandinavian word "Kirk" has been retained in place names rather than the Celtic "Kil-".

The first Christian King of Norway was Olaf I (Tryggvesson) (969-1000). He made Christianity the official religion, undeterred by the obstinate resistance of his people. The Faith did not spread far into his kingdom for he perished at sea in his great ship *The Long Snake*. It was the vigour of Olaf (II) ("the Fat"; or St. Olaf; St. Olave) that forced Christianity upon the outlying parts of the empire, though he was neither a saint nor even a Christian judged by his life. He realized the fact that it was much more satisfactory for his country to be classed as "Christian" rather than "heathen" in view of all his Christian neighbours. So it may be assumed that the Isle of Man as part of the Scandinavian Empire became Christian again about the middle of the tenth century or slightly later. The first recorded Scandinavian bishop of the Isle of Man was one Roolwer or Rollo consecrated 1069, as recorded in *Chronicon*. The first bishop of Mann and the Isles was Hamond, a Manxman, appointed by Godred Crovan when he separated Mann and the Isles from Norway to become an independent kingdom. The Isles were the Sudreys (Lat. *Sodorenses*), so that Hamond, a Manxman, was the first Bishop of Sodor and Mann (1079).

In the year 1134 Olaf I granted permission to the abbot of the Savignian Order in Furness Abbey to build a subsidiary abbey at the hamlet of Ballasalla in the parish of Malew. The Savignians were a strict Benedictine order. In 1147 it was placed under the control of the Cistercians. This order, also of the Benedictine mode, was founded in 1098 by Robert of Molesme. It was at first a very much more austere order than that of Savigny, though it was modified considerably subsequently. Rushen Abbey submitted to the change at once, but Furness held out for several years before accepting the Cistercian rule. The Cistercians made manual work, and particularly agricultural work, the key of their lives. It was as farmers, sheep-breeders, cattle and horse breeders that they made their names, and fame and fortune. They refused to accept tithes or revenues, and literally lived by the sweat of their brow.

By the middle of the thirteenth century their wool trade had assumed amazing proportions, and was their largest source of income. They ran their abbeys with two sets of brothers, the true monks or "monachi" and the lay brothers or "conversi". These two classes lived in different parts of the abbey buildings. The monachi had their own dormitories, refectory, infirmary and chapter house. The conversi had much humbler dwellings. The monachi were far from idle, and went out, many to work, others to supervise work done by the lay-brothers. In order to get more time for work, the monachi cut out and shortened many of the "hours" and even omitted the "Mass". The lay-brothers did not attend the week-day Mass. They were taught to say their "offices" at work. They lived very frugally, and meat was a rarity at their table. Their abbeys were almost always built in low-lying land beside a river. They were experts in land-drainage.

Rushen Abbey, small though it always was, was a good example of their prowess. Its chapter became the strongest force in the Island. It quickly became the controller of all the best farm land.

It took charge of all mining, and it also controlled the fishing. Its abbot was a baron in his own right, and held a court of "leet and baron". He had powers of life and death, and had a gallows on Black Hill, and in the North on Cronk Sumark.

The *Chronicon Manniae* is the record of the early history of the abbey, beginning with the laying of its foundation stone, and ending with John Donkan 1374. The abbey gradually became less and less important, and though at the dissolution it was the last of the British abbeys to hold out against the King's edict, it had then only its abbot and six brothers ejected on St. John Baptist's Day 1540. On the same day the nuns of St. Bridget's nunnery were similarly removed, one prioress and three sisters.

The pitiful little list of "treasures" from Rushen Abbey bought by the Lord for £38 8s. 4d. comprised: "Four challices, one crouche (crozier), one censer, one cross, two littel headless crosses, one navicula (incense box), one hand and one Bysshope's hede (presumably reliques), four cruets, eleven spones, two standing cuppes, two ale pottes with covers, one flat pece (drinking cup), one salt, two masers (wooden cups with silver mounts), one silver pyx."

The Kings of Mann always persisted in their right to appoint bishops, and it was a matter of great difficulty to decide where they should be consecrated. The church owed a loose allegiance to the Church of Norway and the earlier bishops were consecrated at Nidaros (Trondheim), which involved an unpleasant and hazardous journey. Indeed Bishop Lawrence (1248) with his archdeacon, returning from Norway, were lost at sea. The first bishop, Wimond, more or less forced upon Olaf by his new abbey, was at least a "character". Of lowly English birth, he was received by Fountains Abbey, where he impressed everybody by his charm and ability. He was transferred to Rushen Abbey and quickly won everybody's heart by his pleasant, friendly manner, his joviality, and his "silver tongue". Elected bishop by the abbey, he was duly consecrated at York 1135. But he flatly refused to return to his diocese, and instead assumed the name of Malcolm Macheath and laid claim to the earldom of Moray. He raised a troop of marauders which harried southern Scotland so fiercely that David the King accepted his claim to rule the border counties, whereupon he turned his attention to Northumbria. Here however he was less lucky and, defeated, captured, blinded, he was left to languish a prisoner in Byland Abbey, where he died.

In 1229 Olaf II pressed upon the Abbot of Furness a candidate whom the Abbot was unwilling to nominate, since he was from the clerical world outside the Furness influence. He was Simon of Argyll. Described as "*vir magnae discretionis, et in sacris scripturis peritus*" (a man of great discretion, and learned in ancient writings), he was consecrated at Trondheim, and came to the Island. He called all the clergy together in synod at Kirk Braddan, a synod which in effect initiated Manx canon law. Among other things, he placed tithes upon stock, grain, beer, and woven cloth. Further he began to build the cathedral of St. German, on the site of the earlier church, and he also built the tower of Bishop's Court.

Unfortunately, by 1275 the abbey had forgone its refusal to accept tithes and had placed very heavy burdens on the Manx country-folk. Bishop Mark, appointed by Alexander of Scotland, resisted the abbey, and brought some relief, but frightened by the Abbot of Furness he induced the clergy to pay to Furness the dues from Maughold—a considerable sum. The Manx drove him out of the Island, and the Pope responded by placing the Island under interdict. So they took the bishop back, and he imposed on every house in the Island a tax of one penny per fireplace, the "smoke-penny" which lasted until comparatively recent times. But Bishop Mark undoubtedly increased the authority of the Church, for he held a Synod at Braddan in which 34 canons were enacted, considerably reinforcing those of Bishop Symon. For the first time the church could claim a fish tithe, and a tax was placed upon merchants, traders, smiths, and artificers. The conduct of the clergy was raised to a much higher standard, and the nature of the vestments to be used was codified.

During the uneasy years (1250-1320) in which the fate of the Island was being determined as between Scotland and England the Bishop of the Sodorenses with Mann retained his control of the Scottish Isles and Mann. But when finally England retained the supremacy Mann was separated from the Scottish Isles, which were attached to Scotland. But despite the loss of the islands the bishop retained the title Bishop of Sodor and Man, which title he still holds today.

A new era for the church as well as the Island arrived with the lordship of the Stanleys. Always a staunch church-respecting family, they brought to the Island the ecclesiastical manners and customs that existed in England. They realized with many other noble families that the arrogance of the monastic houses must be curbed, in the interests of the people. Under their influence Rushen Abbey steadily decreased in power; the parochial clergy headed by the bishop became more influential, and the parish churches gained a place in the affection of the people.

After the reformation the Manx Church followed the norm of the Church in England. The bishopric was never of any great monetary value, and many of the bishops held cure of souls in England to augment their income. Many visited the Island rarely or not at all, but, on the other hand, many were faithful and devoted, and left their mark on the spiritual life of the Church. John Meyrick (1576) strongly opposed his patron in the matter of the spiritual position of the garrison troops, and opposed the method by which the Lord appointed the Keys instead of letting them be chosen by election. John Phillips (1604) was a strict disciplinarian and enquired minutely into the conduct of his clergy in their parishes. He, too, was the bishop who translated the Prayer Book into Manx. Being a Welshman he was keenly interested in the Manx language, and his manuscript Prayer Book, copied by hand by many of his clergy, was the first book written in Manx. Bishop Rutter was the chaplain and adviser of the "Great [7th earl] Stanley" and tutor to his children, and guardian of the family when his Lord was executed. Bishop Barrow, 1663, was able to redeem some of the purloined tithe from its wrongful claimants, raised a wonderful fund for the diocese to which even Charles II subscribed, started parochial schools, and raised a trust fund to send young Manx candidates to a university, a fund which resulted eventually in the founding of King William's College.

John Lake (cons. 1682), later translated to Chichester, after petitioning James II against the Declaration of Indulgence, and being tried, one of the "Seven Bishops" in the Tower, refused to take the oath to William and Mary. But the most famous of all Manx bishops was undoubtedly Thomas Wilson (cons. 1698), an able, forceful and good man. He had been appointed tutor to William [9th Earl of] Derby, who nominated him as bishop. He came to the Island and lived at Bishop's Court, which he restored from a ruinous condition. It was he, too, who beautified the grounds, planted numerous trees, and improved the farm and its working. Bishop Wilson started his episcopate very vigorously, demanding a great improvement in discipline, both among the clergy, who had degenerated very seriously, and also from the laity. From his clergy he demanded that the services of Sundays and all holy days should be strictly observed, that Communion should be administered regularly, and not merely three times in the year, and from his wardens he demanded that there should be strict presentments made of all offences against the ecclesiastical laws, profanation of the Sabbath, drunkenness, fornication and adultery, lying and slander, to the courts of the Vicars-General; and that all punishments should be sternly administered. This unfortunately caused considerable friction, since the bishop demanded the same high standards and discipline among the Lord's entourage as among the common people. Several appeals were made to the Lord against the bishop and his clergy. The constant differences of opinion between the Lord and the Church were brought to a head by Archdeacon Horrobin, who refused communion to a widow because of some slanderous comments made by the Governor's wife against her. For this, the Archdeacon was suspended by the ecclesiastical court. He appealed to the Governor, who demanded that the suspension should be retracted and cancelled. The bishop declined and was fined £50, and his vicars-general £20 each. These fines they refused to pay, so they were imprisoned in Castle Rushen. Such high-handed action almost produced a popular rebellion, for the bishop, in spite of his severe discipline, was loved by the great majority of the people. They came in crowds every day and stood outside Castle Rushen and called for the bishop to come to the window of his room and bless them. The bishop appealed to the Privy Council. After nine weeks in prison they were released, and their journey back to Bishop's Court was a triumphal procession such as never before had been seen in the Island. The Governor was dismissed, but his successor did not improve matters, for he claimed that although at the reformation Sodor and Mann became a diocese in the province of York, yet it remained a national Church, and the spiritual laws of York could not be applied, only the spiritual laws of the Island as approved by Tynwald. Further he decided that some of the Manx spiritual laws were in need of revision, and demanded the suspension of the whole code till they had been revised by the legislature. Appeal was again made to the Privy Council, but no decision was given. The tenth earl died and the Atholl régime began (1736), the ecclesiastical laws were reformed in a manner acceptable to Church and State, and though the number of presentments was much reduced, and the bishop's prison was less in evidence, there was much more general satisfaction. However the bishop still had stormy seas to navigate, for the phenomenal rise in smuggling brought him tremendous difficulties, moral and social, to combat. The bishop had increased his popularity among the Lord's tenants in the Island by the part he played in gaining the Act of Settlement (1704), the

great Land Security Law of the Island, which ensured the heredi-
tary descent of tenancy according to the ancient customs of the
Island, and not on the more or less "feudal system" that had
been desired by the Lords.

Among many other benefits the "good bishop" brought to the
Island may be noted parochial organization, in which he required
vicars to keep a register of every family in the parish, and the
dates of visiting them, and a statement of "what hopes he had
of reforming what is amiss in them". Further, he raised funds for
the improvement of the parochial schools, insisted on his vicars
visiting and teaching in these schools, and he restored the
Academic School at Castletown, and housed it in the old Chapel.
He also founded a Grammar School in Douglas, and put it in
charge of the Chaplain of St. Matthew's, a church he had established for the needs of the town, so far distant from its Parish
Church of Braddan.

The bishop's income scarcely exceeded £400, yet it was asserted
that he gave at least half of it away every year, in charitable
donations. He was without doubt a saintly, affectionate and just
bishop. He died in 1755 aged 93 and lies buried in Michael
Churchyard. He had been offered translation but declined with
the comment, "I will not leave my wife [the diocese] in my old
age, because she is poor".

Bishop Hildesley (cons. 1755) was a very worthy successor. He
at once began to learn the Manx language. He obtained a grant
from the Society for the Propagation of the Gospel to get the
Prayer Book and Bible translated into Manx. The Prayer Book
printed in Manx appeared in 1756. In 1771 the Old Testament
to the end of Job appeared, followed by the remainder of the
Old Testament in 1773, and the New Testament in 1775, the
translations being due to the hard work and earnest endeavour
of the more literary of the vicars of the Island.

It has been asserted that in Bishop Wilson's time there were
no Roman Catholics and no non-conformists. To a man the
population was one of churchmen. During the Cromwellian
period the Society of Friends was founded by George Fox, 1647,
a number of whom appeared in the Island, fugitives from persecution in England. But the Governor, Fairfax, made an order
that they were not to be received into any Manx house, nor were
they to "meet on the Lord's day in any field or outhouse". Those
who persisted in their faith were persecuted, thrown into the
bishop's prison, or returned to Britain. They were not re-admitted
but were brought back to the Island for further persecution.

Those who refused to pay Church dues were heavily fined, children were baptized against parents' wishes, the dead were refused Christian burial. At the Restoration Bishop Barrow persisted in the persecution. As Governor he confiscated all their property, a very horrible record. But his successor Bishop Wilson took great pity on them, refused to allow any persecution against them, released all those detained in prison, till, it is told, they "loved and respected him".

There are several points of interest in the Manx Church to which the attention of visitors may be directed. The Crown, as Lords of Man, holds the gift of eleven out of seventeen of the ancient parishes. The presentment papers, signed by the Sovereign, are sent to the Lieutenant-Governor, who in turn presents them, together with the incoming incumbent, to the bishop, requesting him to institute the Crown nominee. This duty is always carried out by the Governor in person. It is customary in the ancient parishes to elect four churchwardens, who need not necessarily be members of the Established Church.

The arms of the Manx Church as described in Keith's Catalogue of the Scottish Bishops are: "Azure, St. Columba at sea in a cockboat all proper in chief, a blazing star, or. On three ascents, the Virgin Mary, her arms extended between two pillars, dexter a church; in base, three legs." But it would seem that the name of St. Machutus should be substituted for St. Columba, while St. Bridget is usually depicted as carrying a church, and not the Virgin. This coat of arms is, as is customary, depicted on an ornamental shield surmounted by the mitre. It is customary for the bishop to quarter the shield with his own personal coat of arms. The very beautiful crozier carried by the bishop is made of Manx bog-oak, and Manx silver. The shape is natural, but the head has been beautifully carved. The scroll work was copied from the Scandinavian crosses. On a shield within the curve of the crozier are displayed the diocesan coat of arms on one side, and St. Machutus in his coracle on the other.

With the rise of smuggling the ease with which the fishing folk could amass wealth, the adventures of the young "Bucks" in running cargoes, the cheapness of spirits, the participation of the wealthier classes and tradesmen, and even clergy in "the Trade" brought about a general lowering of tone and behaviour, and the wretched state of the moral welfare roused in the pious Celtic breast an inspiration for a higher ideal of living. In 1758 John Murlin the "weeping Prophet" stayed a week in Ramsey, and his fiery preaching caused a sensation. In 1776 John Crook sent over a Methodist Mission from Liverpool. This was attacked with physical violence by a mob organized by the Curate of St. Matthew's. They sought protection from Governor Wood. But Bishop Richmond, one of the most unfortunate choices for a bishop, issued a most intolerant pastoral to his clergy describing the teaching of the Methodists as " crude, pragmatic, inconsistent, profane and blasphemous ". But the simple country-folk, still imbued with the teaching of Bishop Wilson and his vicars, found in the fervour of these itinerant missioners, who denounced the wickedness of the times, some message to their immortal souls, and were prepared to accept their teaching. John Wesley visited the Island in 1777. He found the new Governor, Edward Smith, a man who had a sound regard for Christian principles, and he was " received in a very friendly manner by a few persons of respectability and influence ". He found the people " loving and simple-hearted for they have but six papists and no dissenters " on the Island. Wesley of course was a clergyman of the English Church. In 1778 the Isle of Man was appointed as a definite " circuit " and two Ministers were appointed. In 1781 Wesley came again. He found in Bishop Mason a tolerant and friendly co-worker. Again he was struck with the simple and artless faith of the Manx folk. He was, too, much impressed by their singing, " as good as any I have heard in London ". By this time there were twenty Ministers in the Island, and their happiness in their work, their healthy looks and obvious welfare impressed him. He reported that " the Methodists of the Island still remain under the protecting wing of the Establishment ". Indeed the majority of the Methodists looked upon their Methodism as an extension and filling-out of their churchmanship.

At the present time, there are probably about the same number of nominal Wesleyans as nominal churchmen in the Island. Of the other Churches the Presbyterians have good congregations in Douglas and Ramsey, their presence being generally due to the immigration of Scottish and Ulster residents. There are Baptist and Congregational churches in Douglas. The Roman Catholics had no place of worship in the Island till 1813. In that year a small chapel dedicated to St. Bridget was built near Douglas. In 1826 the Castletown Chapel was dedicated, and the handsome Church of " St. Mary of the Isle " in Douglas was consecrated in 1859. Their numbers have increased considerably by the influx of tradesfolk and workers from Liverpool, and from Ireland, in addition to the Manx families. They have now churches also in Ramsey, Peel, Port Erin, Pulrose and Onchan.

F

CHAPTER NINE

BUILDINGS: DOMESTIC AND ECCLESIASTICAL

IN ALL parts of the country districts the original type of Manx cottage remains, sometimes still in its primitive form, but much more often enlarged, heightened, and modified.

In the north of the Island there still remain houses with the ancient type of clay-and-mud walls, and indeed mud-puddling for wall repairs lasted down into the memory of the older inhabitants of today. But in the country, on hillside and in the glens, large and small stones were utilized in building the cottage walls, rather substantial walls too, the interstices being filled up with clay, and as time went on, coarse mortar. Many such still remain inhabited though mostly enlarged. More often they appear in ruins, the roof collapsed and only walls and gable-ends remaining, "tholtans", never pulled down for fear the "good little people", who were their genies, should be rendered homeless. Blundell in 1656 describes Manx cottages as "mere hovels", compacted of stones and clay for the walls, thatched with broom, most commonly having only one room; very few have two, and further no upper room such as in their towns are called "lofts", nor any ceilings but thatch and bare rafters. "Yet in this smoking hut doth the man, his wife and children co-habit and in many cases with the ducks and geese under the bed, the cockes and hennes over his head, the cow and calfe at the bed's foot."

Thomas Quayle, in 1812, discloses a considerable improvement. "The walls are about seven feet high constructed of sods and earth. At each side of the door appears a square hole containing a leaded window. Chimney there is none, but a perforation in the roof, a fire beneath. The timber of the roof is slender, coarse and crooked. It is thatched with straw crossed chequer-wise at intervals of twelve to eighteen inches by ropes of the same material secured either to the walls by means of projecting stones or by stones hanging from the ends of the ropes. If the means of the inhabitant enable him to keep a cow an extension of the roof covers a similar hovel accommodating this valuable inmate. The floor of both portions is made of hardened clay. The embers burn on a stone flag placed on the clay earth . . . a partition

separates the two rooms. Over the chamber is often a loft
ascended by a ladder from the keeping room."

Every type of cottage may be seen still in use today. The
simplest type is still the thatched cottage with two rooms, though
alas! the art of thatching is all but lost. The doorway from the
road or garden opens into the living-room. The fireplace or
" chiollagh " has now been built in the end wall. The hearth
may still be mud, but is probably a piece of flag or limestone.
There is now an iron grate for the fire, and the smoke-hole has
been replaced by a " straight through " chimney. The roof room,
far too small and cramped, has necessitated the rising height of
the gable end. All that was needed to make the two " roof rooms "
sizeable was to take off the thatch, take down the rafters, build up
the gable walls to the necessary height, and then replace the roof
timbers and thatch. Meanwhile rafters across the living rooms
provide for flooring for the roof rooms, and a stairway opposite
the door, usually very steep and primitive, has replaced the earlier
ladder. It is most interesting as one walks or drives along the
Manx country roads to examine the gable ends of the country
houses, where the successive enlargements brought about by time
show clearly even through the whitewash of the ever-clean walls.

The small farmer had a rather more practical lay-out. His
house (and indeed most houses are the same in this respect) was
built somewhere near a stream or spring or " spoot " of running
water. The building was much more sturdy, the fireplace wall
usually recessed with wood-log or peat lockers, and a cupboard
recess for cooking utensils. The four-room type was the general
vogue, and outbuildings were commonly built round a rectangular paved yard or " street ". The enclosures included a good-
sized barn with an upper floor reached by outside stone steps, a
stable for at least two horses, a cow-byre or " bwane ", and a
pig-sty or " mucklagh " with lean-to roof. With ever-increasing
prosperity the farms became more and more pretentious, and
today the prosperous Manx farm (and there are many) differ in
no way from the average " north-country " farm. During the
Atholl régime, when smuggling brought much wealth to the
merchant classes, and when many wealthy folk exiled for various
crimes and misdemeanours from London and Liverpool and
Dublin came to the Island for refuge, these differing classes bought
farm houses in various parts of the Island, and rebuilt them on a
more convenient plan. This type was commonly a double-fronted,
but narrow type of house of two or sometimes three floors, each
floor with a central passage and rooms built on both sides.

Of the larger houses of interest to be seen in the Island, Bishop's Court is the most interesting. It stands beside the Peel-Ramsey road about a mile north of Kirk Michael. As a matter of fact the house stands in the parish of Michael while the chapel is in Ballaugh. It was traditionally built by Bishop Simon in the thirteenth century, as a fortress-tower. Parts of the tower (usually called King Orry's tower) are undoubtedly of this date. In its early days it was a moated tower, and the outline of the moat may still be seen. The old name for the locality was Ballachurrey, the "marshy" place. The first mention of its possession by the bishop occurs in a Papal Bull of 1231, which suggests that it was standing at least in some form before the arrival of Simon. Its locality is described as "Balicure" and at the same time it is stated that part of the estate was called "Knock-crogher" or "Cronk-ny-crogher", a name meaning Hangman's hill, identified as a small eminence beside the Orrisdale lane, once the site of a small chapel, and in former times the place of execution of criminals, for the bishop in his own right was (and is) a baron, with powers of *furca et fossa*, who in those early days had powers of life and death. So Bishop's Court was an outpost of law and order in the north, rather like the forts along the Welsh marches. The tower is a rectangular structure with very thick walls (in some places 12 feet). It has been greatly altered in course of time. There seems to have been a great deal done in the thirteenth century. By 1640 the tower had been roofed and the bell turret had been added. There was also an attached chapel but of very different appearance from the present. By this time, too, there was a low building running south-west in the line of the present house. This again is reminiscent of the Welsh border fortress castles, a pleasant place of residence in times of peace, and a refuge in case of trouble. After 1752, when Daniel King drew a picture of the court, there are few records of further building, but record after record of its ruinous condition. Bridgman, Levinz, Lake, Wilson, all complained that his predecessor had left it in shocking repair. Jury after jury was appointed to estimate the amount of repair needed; Bishop Wilson set on hand a scheme of repair. He too laid out the lovely grounds, and planted many trees, including the famous twelve apostle lime-trees which still stand to this day, less of course the one "Judas" tree which never would thrive, and disappeared. The present house was in part his contribution; other additions were made by Bishops Crigan and Powys. Bishop Crigan rebuilt the chapel, retaining the ancient Manx rectangular simple style, but it was extended and heightened to its present form by Bishop Powys, who added also two shallow transepts to make it cruciform. The chapel is today the " pro-cathedral " of the diocese, and contains the bishop's "cathedra", and the stalls of the chapter. It has the very unusual dedication to St. Nicholas. The chapel opens out from the ground floor of the tower, and this ante-room is the official place of meeting of the Manx Convocation on the Thursday after Whitsunday. Beside the tower stands an ancient yew. The original tree has disappeared, but the four basal branches that remain suggest that the tree is as ancient as the Simon portion of the tower.

Two houses in Douglas (now both hotels) are worthy of mention from a general interest point of view rather than for their architecture, Castle Mona and Fort Anne.

Castle Mona was the residence of the Governor, John Murray, later fourth Duke of Atholl, who must not be mistaken for his father, the third Duke of Atholl, the last of the " Derby Kings ". On arriving he found that Castle Rushen was wholly inadequate for a governor's residence, that Peel Castle was in ruins, and he complained bitterly, " I am consequently bereft of any habitation and thereby am compelled to lodge in an ale-house ". In 1801 he decided that, having looked round the Island to find suitable accommodation and finding none, he would build a house fit for his exalted state, and estimated that, built to his requirements, it would cost him £20,000. Manx stone was not good enough for his Scottish soul, so stone was brought by the ship-load from Arran. A piece of ground was bought on the shore just outside Douglas, and a long drive constructed along the shore, the present Promenade. The house was opened in 1804. He ordered that an account of the " baptism " should be inserted in the official *Liber Vastarum* (The Civil Records). All the high officials were there from Bishop Crigan to the " advocates and local gentry " and a whole host of Murrays! The poor architect George Stewart . . . Scottish of course! was too ill to do more than make a short appearance at the " sumptuous repast ". Today the house remains in a wonderful state of repair, but all the grounds have been swallowed up in the promenade boarding houses and the Palace Ballroom and concert hall.

At the other end of the Bay, up on Douglas Head, Fort Anne was built, overlooking the Harbour, by an Irish profligate, Buck Whaley, whose general bad conduct had driven him from his native country. He arrived in the Island in the Regency days, when many of the houses round about Douglas were occupied by

English Bucks and Corinthians living in quiet seclusion for various reasons mainly connected with the gaming tables. Buck Whaley, who was above all an eccentric, is said to have married a wealthy wife, whose fortune depended upon her living on Irish soil. So before building his house Whaley sent for a schooner-load of Irish soil with which he filled in the foundations of his house in order to ensure for his wife a safe basis for her income. Later the house became the home of the founder of the Royal National Lifeboat Institution, Sir William Hillary. It was he who suggested building the Tower of Refuge on the Conister Rock at the entrance of the harbour. Horrified by the number of wrecks, he with his lady resolved on building the tower where shipwrecked sailors could find shelter till the storm abated. The cost of the tower was £255. Of this £181 was obtained by public subscription, and the Hillarys paid the balance. The architect and designer was John Welch, who designed King William's College and the Smelt memorial column in Castletown. He had a famous partner, Hansom, who had to his credit Birmingham Town Hall and the "Hansom" cab!

In 1834 a great part of the Governor's House in Castle Rushen was included in the Court House, which left the residence too small, and provision of a suitable house became a major problem. At first the Governor was given a grant of £150 per annum, and told to find a house for himself. For Governors Ready and Hope, 1834-60, a lease was taken on Lorne House at Castletown. But when the lease expired and could not be renewed Governor Piggott rented Marina Lodge, the house of Henry Bloom Noble, the Douglas benefactor, a pleasant house now replaced by the Villa Marina. But Governor Loch was able to rent the present Government House, then known as Bemahague in the parish of Onchan.

Castletown sent in several suggestions of much more worthy houses in the ancient capital to house the Governor and retain the social status of Castletown. But eventually the Manx Government agreed to purchase Bemahague, which became *un fait accompli* in 1903 for the sum of £12,000. It is in no way an imposing house, but it has a glorious position overlooking Douglas Bay, and with very often a distant panorama of the English coast. It is pleasantly situated, except perhaps during the motor-cycle race period, at which time the racing machines pass right along the estate boundary before reaching "Governors Bridge" corner.

RUSHEN ABBEY

The Abbey of St. Mary, set up at Ballasalla, is very disappointing from an architectural point of view. Even in its prime it cannot have been in any way comparable with such abbeys as Tintern or Fountains. The land on which it was built, given by Olaf I, was marshy, and lay beside the Silverburn, which constantly overflowed, and does so to this day after heavy rain, in spite of the banks having been revetted and the bed deepened. At the dissolution of the monasteries, the abbey buildings and the lands went to the Lord. But little care was taken to preserve any of the buildings, and they quickly disintegrated. A picture, of date 1660, shows it as a ruin, but it is possible to make out the secular and the clerical buildings. Today there remain only the scanty ruins of the church, broadly cruciform in structure, without Lady chapel. There are no signs of there having been a central tower, but the foundations show that there was an earlier, smaller church on the site. The north transept was towered, and this tower still stands. Small parts of the south transept remain, but nothing of the nave, other than a very small west door with a small embattled tower. The chancel must have been very small compared with the width of the nave and aisles. The buildings were of undressed local limestone with little attempt at architectural design or decoration. There remains one good Norman arch in the north transept. Within the abbey garth are buried two Manx kings, Reginald II, murdered by Ivar the usurper at Rushen Church 1250, and Magnus (d. 1265, just after arranging the sale of the Island to Scotland). Of the secular buildings there still remain the columbarium, and beside it the guest house, now used as a museum of abbey relics. Near by are the remains of the abbot's house. About 1672 Bishop Bridgman bought the site from Deemster Moore, on behalf of Bishop Barrow's Trust, intending to set up a school, or possibly a university. But the site proved unsuitable and Deemster Moore generously bought it back at the same figure. He used the stones of the abbey ruins to build himself a house, which is now the hotel. The property has been in turn a farm, a market garden, and today a pleasure garden which has given the place a distinctly commercialized air. Across the river at the ford stands the abbey mill, disused since a heavy flood washed away the dam and mill race in 1830. By far the loveliest relic of the abbey is the beautiful little packhorse bridge, the Crossag bridge about 200 yards upstream from the mill. The bridge was sketched in Camden's

Britannia. In abbey days it was no doubt the abbey exit to the north, and the start of the Bishop's road, which can be traced direct to Bishopscourt. Whatever else in the Island has to be omitted by the visitor, everybody ought to go and see the Crossag bridge and its setting.

OTHER ECCLESIASTICAL BUILDINGS

Olaf I, who granted the lands for Rushen Abbey, was succeeded by Godred II. He gave a grant of land in Lezayre to the Abbey of Rievaulx to build a monastery. This monastery was duly built at Mirescogh, a site not certainly identifiable today, but from its boundaries given in *Chronicon* believed to be Ballamona, Lezayre. It was very small, and in course of time was given with its lands to Rushen Abbey. Today not a trace remains.

The origin of the Nunnery of St. Bridget, near Douglas, is not known. In the *Annals of Ulster* it is stated that Bridget in person went to the Isle of Man, founded there a nunnery and became its first abbess. But the *Annals of Ulster*, written about 1450, cannot be relied upon. If Bridget did found a nunnery it would have been destroyed by the Vikings. *Chronicon* tells of a nunnery in Douglas where Robert Bruce stayed on his way to breach the fort that preceded Castle Rushen, but to this particular convent the brothers from Rushen Abbey were transferred when their abbey fell into disrepair. This could scarcely be the nunnery of St. Bridget. At the Dissolution the abbess, Margaret Goodman, was expelled together with three nuns. The building and lands, from Douglas Head to Braddan Church, went to the Lord, who sold them to his Receiver, Robert Calcott, who married Margaret Goodman. She thus went back again as châtelaine where she had been abbess. The house was rebuilt, on a different site, and this new house was again rebuilt higher up the hill in its present form in 1830. Only the chapel of the old nunnery remains. It owes its preservation to the fact that it made a very efficient coach house. Entrance is by a Gothic door in the south wall. The general plan is that of the Manx style, a simple rectangle with no differentiation into chancel and nave. The windows have been well restored. The credence table was placed on a ledge on the south wall of the chancel. A recess on the north side contained the recumbent figure of an abbess, but nothing remains today except a part of an arm. Next to it is the piscina, evidently the original holy water stoup from the entrance. A rood screen has been introduced and placed upon the bases of

what were formerly cloister arches. Bones found in the stable-
yard outside show it to have been the " garth ".

Olaf II about 1230 granted a charter to the Abbey of St. Ninian
at Whithorn in Galloway, for a hospital at Ballacquiba (= Balla-
greeba), the Church of St. Ninian, and the Church of St. Ronan
(= Ma-rown), on condition that they say prayers for the souls of
Olaf's father, mother, brothers, sisters, and ancestors. The Church
of St. Ninian (now always called Trinian) is a well-known building standing beside the Douglas-Peel road under Greeba Hill.
This church was also built upon an ancient keeill, of which parts
of the walls and the outline may still be seen. Indeed two crosses
found beside the altar of the present church are sixth to seventh
century in date. Its walls are of undressed stone blocks in irregular
courses with good lime-mortar between. The position of a rood
screen may be seen. Unfortunately, in 1780, when Marown old
church was built on the hill to the south of Crosby station, much
of the stone work of St. Trinian's was removed to decorate it. St.
Trinian's Church was surrounded by a garth, of which the
boundaries may still be made out. The ruins of the church are
the scene of the well-known fairy story of the " Buggane of St.
Trinian's ", who persistently blew off the church roof as fast as
it was built. This sad state of affairs could, it was said, be prevented in future, if the village tailor could cut out and make up
a pair of breeches as soon as the roof had been completed. The
tailor undertook to do the work, and carried thither his roll of
cloth, his needle and thread, and all that was needed, and there
in the chancel he sat, solemnly stitching. The task was complete,
all but the last button, when he came to the end of his supply of
thread. He left his work, hurried down to his house to fetch a
new hank of thread, and was returning hot-foot when the buggane
arrived. With a mighty blast he blew off the roof once more,
and the tailor and the breeches and the roof were never seen
again.

The Franciscan brotherhood of minor friars founded a mission
in 1209 that swept across Europe like a forest fire. Strangely
enough it did not reach the Island (probably because of the
antipathy of the Cistercians) until 1373, when the Lord (William
Scrope Earl of Salisbury) gave permission and granted a piece of
land, in the village of St. Columba (Arbory). Of the buildings,
only the tiny chapel remains. (See " Arbory ", ch. 15.)

But the most important ecclesiastical building is the Cathedral
of St. German on Peel Island, and that too is in ruins. Its dedication is to St. Germanus, a nephew of Patrick, who is said to have

built a chapel there. The Irish hagiology was not known to the
English Church at the Reformation, and St. German was confused with St. Germain of Auxerre.

The earliest part of the cathedral is the chancel. It stands
upon the site thought to have been that of St. German's original
church. It is quite unlike any cathedral chancel in England.
It is built of slaty rubble with window and arch mouldings of
red sandstone. Traditionally it was built by Bishop Simon, 1230,
and the design is certainly of that date. The first written record
is to be found in *Chronicon*, " *ecclesia Germani quam ipse
aedificare ceperat* " (St. German's church which he (Simon) began
to build (or establish)). All its windows are lanceolate. The
chancel stands above the crypt, which shows no signs of ever
having been used as a chapel. Indeed for centuries it was the
episcopal prison. Moreover it was always in use, though how
anybody ever survived a winter in such quarters is difficult to
imagine. It is a huge cavern with no equipment of any kind, no
water, no drainage, and here were herded adulterers, fornicators,
brawlers, drunkards, profaners of the sabbath, alleged witches,
till they should ask for pardon and perform their penances. The
last occupant was Thomas Kneale in 1780, discharged " for that
he was of too weak a constitution to endure the severity of the
prison ". The poor Quakers lived here for years of unrelieved
misery.

The weight of the chancel appears to have been deemed too
great for the ceiling of the cave, which was reinforced by inserting
a series of thirteen arch-ribs, each one, because of the slope of the
floor, arising from a different level. At the same time the chancel
floor level appears to have been considerably raised, and probably
the transepts built.

The crypt has one splayed lancet window for lighting, and three
doors, one leading to the chancel above, another to a tiny walled
enclosure at chancel-level, but outside, and the third opens on to
the cliff face. The transepts are difficult architecturally, for they
are below the floor level of either chancel or nave, and indeed the
tower is raised on four archways based on piers which all arise
at different levels, a most baffling problem. The nave level is
approximately that of the chancel. In the year 1396 Sir William
le Scrope, treasurer to Richard II and Lord of Mann, received
from the Pope permission to build a castle in the place commonly
known as " Patrycks Holm near and belonging to the church of
Sodor whose church has been despoiled by his enemies ", on condition that " he put into repair the church to which the castle

will serve as a defence ". This accounted for the repairs carried out to the transepts and nave. At this date then the cathedral was about as complete as ever it was.

It must have been a very lovely sight, with its bright red sandstone walls. It has the traditional cruciform shape, and a rather squat tower. Its chancel, built on the very edge of the cliff, seems to rise straight from the sea. But its history has not been well recorded, and most references seem to concern its repair. Bishop Mark in his Convocation at Braddan ordained that priests must all " dress in a closed cloak and no other ". Should a priest possess any other, it must be seized and sold for the repair fund of the cathedral. By the time of Bishop Rutter's death it was so dilapidated that he was interred " under the uncovered steeple of the cathedral in ruins ". Bishop Barrow left the Island, leaving in his crypt prison certain parishioners of Patrick, who had failed to obey his order to repair parts of the structure. By the time Bishop Wilson arrived the chancel was in good repair and the nave re-roofed with blue slates, but the transept roof was in ruins. By 1710, however, the nave roof had again collapsed, and Bishop Wilson gave the lead from it to roof the new church in Patrick. In 1765 it was reported that only the chancel remained in repair, while by 1772 it was reported that " the chancel now has gone completely to ruin ". The dimensions of the cathedral are very small, 115 feet from east to west, small enough to be fitted into the choir of Westminster Abbey with plenty of room to spare. It is indeed less than half the length of Hereford, the smallest of the English cathedrals.

Several of the bishops were buried in the cathedral. Bishop Simon's grave was discovered in the chancel in 1871, during some work being carried out to prevent further damage to the chancel. The grave contained a complete skeleton wrapped in embalming clothes, and the skeleton of the bishop's dog was found alongside. The bones were re-interred and a memorial tablet set up: " In repairing the ruins of Peel Castle 1871 by the authority of H. B. Loch, C.B., Lieut.-Governor, the remains of SIMON Bishop of Sodor and Man, and the rebuilder of this cathedral, were here discovered and re-interred. He died 28th February 1247 in the 21st year of his episcopy."

Bishop John (d. 1154) was reported to have been buried in the cathedral, which must have been the original church of St. German. Bishop Mark was buried in 1303. John Phillips, died 1633, was buried in the cathedral and his successor Richard Parr left instructions that he should be buried in the same grave. The grave is not known. But the grave of Sam Rutter still bears his own epitaph. He had been chaplain to the "great earl" James, and tutor to the eighth earl. He had been present with the Duchess and her children during the time when the seventh earl was fighting for Charles II in Britain, where eventually he was executed. He was buried under the tower of his cathedral. Round his gravestone memorial is written in raised lettering:

SAMUEL RUTTER

LORD BISHOP OF SODOR AND MAN

1661

While his own self-written epitaph is on a brass plate:

In hac doma quam a vermi-
culis accepi confratribus meis
spe resurrectionis ad vitam
jaceo Sam. Permissione divina
Episcopus huius insulae

In this house which I share
with my brothers the worms,
in hope of the resurrection to
life lie I SAM by divine grace
Bishop of this Island

Siste lector; Vide et ride
palatium episcopi

Stay reader; look and laugh
at the bishop's palace

Obit xxx die mensis May
Anno 1662

He died the 30th May Anno
1662

The last bishop to be enthroned in the cathedral was Bishop Hildesley in 1755.

The question is commonly asked by visitors, "Why has the cathedral never been restored? " The restoration to the diocese would of course be a glorious event, and the position of the ancient cathedral is wonderful, and a restored cathedral would be one of the loveliest pictures imaginable. But there are diffi-culties. Worst of all is its difficulty of access. The causeway leading to the island is long and unsuited to motor traffic. The ferry across the harbour mouth is quite inadequate. The present condition of the ruins is such that they would have to be taken down stone by stone before rebuilding could take place. The cost would be gigantic. In these days of church activity a cathedral should be central to the population of the diocese, a place to which the clergy could get easily and quickly for diocesan conferences and services. If the present cathedral were restored very few services could be held therein, and the great sum of money spent for no practical result other than sentiment. The conventual buildings round the north-east corner of the cathedral are in a very bad state of ruin. Their stone has been used to repair the fortified wall, and construct the battery, and though they are collectively known as the Bishop's Palace there is no record of any bishop having lived there. Nor are there any records to show that there was ever a cathedral chapter. These buildings appear to have been built some considerable time after the rest of the cathedral, and very early they were taken over by the lords as an alternative dwelling to Castle Rushen. There is one large room, usually called the " refectory ". There is also a good well of fresh water.

THE ROUND TOWER OF PEEL ISLAND

No part of the Isle of Man has played so great a part in its history as Peel Island, or Peel Holme, or St. Patrick's Isle, by all of which titles it is called, for on it have been found Neolithic weapons and implements, a Bronze Age dagger, Celtic buildings, Viking fortifications and the mediaeval cathedral and castle. The monk Jocelyn (Jocelinus Furnesius monachus) in 1185 wrote an account of the Manx Church, which, however unreliable as history, was the tradition of his time. He says: " When Patrick had appointed one of his disciples, a holy and learned man by name Germanus, as bishop, he placed him at the head of the new Church of that people and established an episcopal see in a certain promontory which is now called St. Patrick's Isle because he himself used from time to time to preach there." So by the twelfth century it was a strong tradition that the Manx Church had been established in the fifth century based upon the missionary work of Patrick. The most outstanding feature of such a church is the Celtic Round Tower, which affords a striking witness to early Manx ecclesiastical history. We have noted already that the Celtic church buildings were, in general terms, small rectangular low-walled structures with thatched or wattle roofs. But quite early in the history of the Church important church buildings were more strongly built, and alongside was built a tower of refuge, in case of attack; for invaders were in the habit of the pillage and destruction of Christian settlements. So the Round Tower lies beside St. Patrick's Church, the ancient parish church of Patrick.

This church was of the invariable Celtic pattern, a plain rectangular building with west door (since blocked up), an altar at the east end. The building has been modified and enlarged in the course of time, but it has several well-marked " herring-bone " courses, suggesting a very early origin.

The Round Tower stands, as in the case of the Irish towers, at the west end of the church. There are twenty round towers in Ireland but only four outside Ireland, this one at Peel, and others at Brechin, Abernethy, and Egilshay (Orkney). In almost every case Neolithic weapons and objects of the Bronze Age are found, suggesting that the sites have been in continuous use for centuries.

The tower at Peel is 50 feet in height and has a circumference at the base of 45 feet. The entrance is seven feet from the ground, and as is customary is opposite the church door. The tower is built of the local sandstone with very hard mortar. It shows many signs of having been altered and repaired. Points of similarity with the Irish towers are:

    i. The tower is round in section.
    ii. The entrance is over a man's height from the ground.
    iii. At the top are four loop-holes facing the four cardinal points.
    iv. The door jambs incline inward from bottom to top.

Among marks of difference from the Irish type are:

    i. The tower is cylindrical and not conical.
    ii. The top of the tower is castellated instead of being covered with a conical roof. (But here be it noted the top of the tower has been rebuilt in mediaeval times.)
    iii. The walls are of almost uniform thickness, instead of being thick at the base and thinner at the top.
    iv. The tower is not so high as the average Irish tower.

KING WILLIAM'S COLLEGE

It is convenient under " Ecclesiastical Buildings " to give a short account of King William's College, which in spite of its name is in fact an ecclesiastical foundation. In 1663, when Bishop Barrow arrived on the Island, he was appalled by the low intellectual state of the insular clergy, and he took possession of two farms, Hangohill and Ballagilley in Malew in order to form the basis of a fund which would help to send suitable candidates to Dublin University to study theology. In his will he appointed trustees for this fund from among the leading men of the Legislature to control the lands and funds which were known as Bishop Barrow's Trust. The Trust Fund steadily increased, mainly because there appeared little desire on the part of young Manxmen to take advantage of it. Earl William, son of the " Great Earl ", had a strong wish to use the Trust in order to found a Manx University, though this was never put into action. His bishop, Bridgman, felt that a less ambitious and more easily accomplished plan would be to found a public school.

The Fund went on accumulating, while paying grants to certain deserving cases, till 1830, when the Governor, Colonel Cornelius Smelt, urged Bishop Ward to find some way of using the money profitably. The fund stood at about £5,000, not enough to build a school, though the bishop was determined to build. So he raised a fund in England, mortgaged the land, and asked for help in the Island. The response was very satisfactory, the people of Castletown giving gifts in kind, timber, bolts, screws and nails and free labour and stone for the building. A site was chosen in the Hangohill estate. The appeal was put before that astonishing King, William IV, who wrote that he was very sorry he had not enough money to subscribe, but that he would give something of far more value, his name, to the new College. So " King William's College " it is! Unfortunately in 1844 it was destroyed by fire, but again the public subscribed liberally for its reconstruction. It has been a great benefit to the Island, affording to Manx boys a public-school education in their own land. It has produced a magnificent list of old boys who have served Church and State alike in Man and in Britain, administrators, clerics, missionaries, soldiers, doctors, scientists, a list worthy of the best of public schools.

The college is a handsome building overlooking Castletown Bay, built of local limestone. At first it was in the shape of a T, the square central tower, which is an insular landmark, occupying a part of the stem of the T. But, in course of time, it has been built into a block of buildings surrounding two courts. The King's Court commemorates the visit to the college of King George VI and Queen Elizabeth in 1945. The detached chapel, standing awkwardly, has interesting windows in modern glass, illustrating persons who helped through the centuries to build up the Christian Church. A very fine dining-hall, the Barrovian Hall, perpetuates the name of its founder. The school has accommodation for 360 boys, rather less than half of whom are Manx. The science laboratories, originally among the first laboratories in the public schools, have been kept always up to date, and science teaching has always occupied an important part of its curriculum.

In Castletown there is an interesting little public school for girls, the Buchan School, founded by the bounty of Lady Buchan, a daughter of Colonel Mark Wilks, a Manxman who was Governor of St. Helena, for the East India Company, during the

time that Napoleon was prisoner there. Napoleon had a great
respect for Wilks, and was very fond of his small daughter. Lady
Buchan became a landowner of considerable property in the
Isle of Man, owning the estates of Kirby and Castleward in
Braddan. The Buchan School ensures for Manx girls a public
school education, on lines parallel to those of King William's
College.

CHAPTER TEN

THE CASTLES

Peel Castle. Whatever may be left to conjecture about
the origin of the cathedral, there is good reason for knowing that
the castle on Peel Island was built by William le Scrope, King
of Mann 1392-1399 and afterwards Earl of Wiltshire, and
treasurer of Richard II, who had bought the kingship from the
second Montacute. The Papal Bull allowing him to build the
castle in order to defend the cathedral which had been sacked by
Archembald, Earl of Galloway, in 1388, was dated 1396. There
are records of a garrison on the island in 1364, when Bishop
Thomas sought to recover his church and precincts from the
garrison of the second Montacute. This suggests that the garrison
had invaded the ecclesistical buildings, or may have held a small
fortress there. Indeed there are distinct traces in the gateway
of a smaller and earlier building. But the castle as it now is
seems to have been started by Scrope. It is a simple building,
consisting of a fortified gateway and a "keep", together with a
red-sandstone curtain wall, which together make a formidable
barrier on the landward side of Peel Island.

The island has only one accessible spot for any attacking force,
and that by no means simple, for one has to imagine the island
before the present causeway was built, with the rocks at the gateway falling sheer down to the water's edge. It was at this point
the gateway was built. The passage into it climbs up what are
steep steps even from the road level. The gateway wall rises up
sheer above, making a very formidable citadel. The castle
buildings seem today to be singularly small to have been used
by the Lord as a place of residence. But there is a mass of documentary evidence in the Museum concerning the domestic side

The Assembly
on Tynwald Hill

The Monks' Bridge, Rushen Abbey

Peel

Bradda Head,
Port Erin

Ramsey

Bishop's
Court,
Kirk
Michael

Castle Rushen

The Chapel, King William's College

of the castle life, which states, for example, that the main portion
of the garrison lived in Peel town. The garrison was divided into
seven sections and one section did night duty in the castle each
night. The castle was closed at sunset by the porter in presence
of the constable and the warders. The out-going garrison de-
parted; the in-coming detachment had already arrived. The gates
being locked, the porter spent the night in the ward-room and
on no condition except by express order of the governor of the

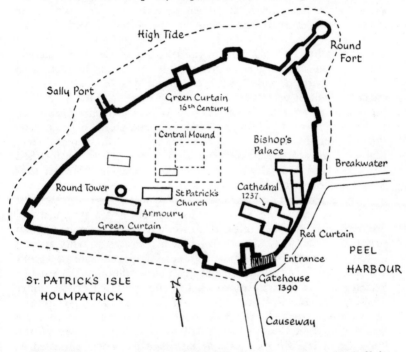

castle might the doors be opened till the porter rang the bell in
the morning "so soon as he could perfectly discover the land
marks at a mile and a half's distance". A ferry boat was kept
below the gate in the water all night. When the Lord or his
lieutenant was in residence there was a great retinue. For
example in 1600 "The constable, receiver (who controlled expenditure), steward, gunner, armourer, cook and scullions, butler,
launderer, plumber, brewer, miller, maltster, swineherd, cooper,
slater, carpenter, smith, ferryman, gardener, storesman, two watch-
men, two porters, drummer, chaplain, schoolmaster, surgeon, and
personal servants of the officers".

G

There must obviously have been a kitchen, dining-hall, wash-house, mill, brewery, malt-store, granary, bakehouse, butchery, smithy, which would seem very hard to fit into the available space. But that it was the case is supported by various inventories of the furniture and fittings of the castle. The " Bishop's Palace " on the opposite side of the cathedral, which we have already noted, was taken over at a very early date as the Lord's residence, and was used by him and his retinue during such time as he spent in the castle; while the gateway and keep were the military part of the castle, together with the armoury and other buildings later destroyed.

Of the other fortifications on the isle, one of the most interesting is the so-called "green curtain wall" in contradistinction to the "red curtain wall" on the landward side. The "green curtain" is built up of very large slabs of slate, with the interstices filled in with smaller pieces. Bishop Wilson attributed the work to Thomas first Earl of Derby, 1460-1504, and this is borne out by the architectural style. It is a remarkable wall, running completely round the isle, at the edge of the rocks. It has six fortified "towers" and two sally ports. Its date is fixed by the fact that it was a useless defence against artillery, so must have been set up before 1500. The defences would seem to have been against the Scots or the "Red Shankes" as they are called in a contemporary document. Historical tradition tells of two famous English prisoners. The first, Eleanor Duchess of Gloucester, who, alleged to have used witchcraft against Queen Margaret, wife of Henry VI, was committed to the care of Sir Thomas Stanley. It used to be alleged that she was imprisoned in the episcopal prison under the cathedral chancel, and was allowed once a day to go upstairs to the tiny airspace before mentioned. But it is known that she was detained in Chester Castle till she was handed over to the "Keeper of the King's Castle at Kenilworth" where she died in 1446. She never came to the island! The other was Thomas Beauchamp Earl of Warwick, who was banished to the Island in 1397 to the charge of Sir William Scrope. It was a tradition that he was imprisoned in one of the towers of the red-curtain wall which has ever since been called "Warwick's Tower", just as his imprisonment in the Tower of London gave the turret in which he was imprisoned the name of "Beauchamp Tower". As a matter of fact Warwick arrived in the island during the summer of 1397, and returned to the Tower of London in July 1398. For his lodging during this period, Scrope was paid £1,074 14s. 5d., a very generous allowance, though it seems highly improbable that he would have been lodged in a tower which was still in process of being built. The alternative name for the tower is the " Moar's Tower ", which suggests that it was mainly used as a civil prison. The first record of the name of the island being called " Peel " or " Pile " we have already noted in a bull of Pope Gregory to Bishop Simon in 1231. The word Peel or Pile refers to a " stronghold ". "Peels" were usually mounds of earth crowned with barricaded wooden buildings, and surrounded at the base by another stockade. By implication Magnus Barfod built three fortifications presumably to guard his ports at Peel, Ronaldsway and Ramsey. It was thought that the large mound in the middle of Peel Island might prove to be the "peel" from which Peel derived its name. But very careful investigation and excavation recently failed to show any sign of such a structure.

Other points of interest in Peel Castle are:

1. The sun-dial which can be read from any part of the town from which the gatehouse is visible. It is formed by the shadow of the bastion-wall of the red-curtain making a shadow on the wall on the other side of the ascending steps; and

2. The tower in the green-curtain on the directly opposite side to the main gateway. It is somewhat larger than the others, and forms the head of a sally port. It was this tower that Sir Walter Scott made famous as the scene of Fenella's leap after her lover Julian Peveril, who was leaving secretly by boat for London.

Beneath " Fenella's " tower is Fenella's cave, which runs well in under the Island but is only accessible at low tide with a smooth sea.

CASTLE RUSHEN gives Castletown its name (Manx Ballacashtal). It is a mediaeval building of outstanding interest. There is no better preserved monument of this type in Britain, nor even in Europe. It has formed the central axis of Manx history. It stands defiant of time, surrounded by the peaceful and imperturbable little township which seems to have altered very little all down the ages. One can walk through Castletown to this day, and almost expect to find a company of Derby halberdiers marching along its narrow streets, or a four-horse wagon load of beef carcases or beer barrels for the garrison, so peaceful does everything seem. At first sight the castle does not seem to be well sited. Castletown Bay is not easily navigable, and indeed all invasions of the Island took place by way of Ramsey or Derbyhaven. All the early settlements arose in the south. Even if an army landed at Ramsey, it would find very great difficulty in marching south over mountain or curragh roads. So that any king of Mann in the early days would make the defence of the south his first military aim. The early history of the castle is unrecorded. Its first mention is in *Chronicon Manniae* when it records the death of King Magnus in the castle, 1265, and his burial in Rushen Abbey. Many of his predecessors had lived on Peel Island. It seems almost certain that Godred Crovan must have placed a fortress here about 1090. It has been discovered in recent years that all round the Island Celtic headland strongholds had been further strengthened by subsequent Viking fortification. So it seems a certainty that over the headland above the entrance to the mouth of the Silverburn there would have been a Celtic fort, further fortified by the Vikings, which in course of time would have been converted from a timber and wall fortification to a stone tower-fort. This is borne out by architectural evidence, for in the castle, forming a considerable part of the inner keep-walls, may be seen the masonry of undressed limestone blocks bound together with good sound mortar, of style dating from the second half of the twelfth century. This would suggest the time of Godred II or his son Reginald—more probably the former. Traditionally the Manx people have always said that the castle was built by " King Orry ", which would be true, but not the " Orry " usually meant (Godred I, Crovan). There are signs that the south and west towers were added a little later, around 1200, so that the Scandinavian "castle" stormed by Robert Bruce 1313 would have been this smaller fort. After Bruce's assault it was repaired and rebuilt. With the coming of Edward III to the throne of England, the defeat of the Scots and the transfer of the Island to the care of England, the kingship was given to William de Montacute Earl of Salisbury (1333), who had the opportunity of choosing Peel or Castletown for his capital. He chose Castletown, and imbued with the Norman ideas of castle architecture decided to build a keep round the Viking fort. It was only to be expected that sooner or later the Scots would seek to regain their hold on the Island, so work no doubt began immediately, and it may be safely surmised that the castle keep was begun in 1333 or 1334. The work went ahead steadily. The Earl died in 1344, so the structural work was completed by his son. The finest and best dressed stone was dug in Scarlett quarry, set in a very hard white, gritty mortar. The keep now consisted of the original Viking fort, with its two flanking towers to south and west, enlarged and carried up very much higher, together with a new eastern tower, and a twin-towered gateway,

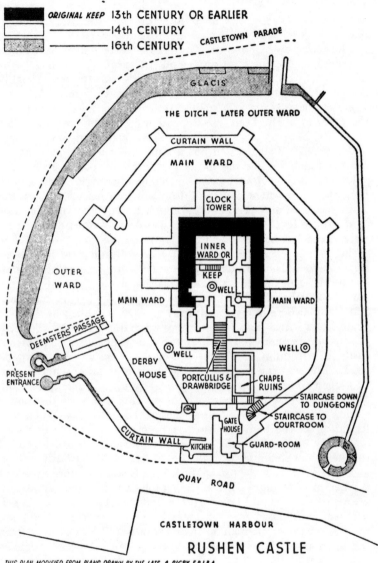

ORIGINAL KEEP 13th CENTURY OR EARLIER
——— 14th CENTURY
——— 16th CENTURY

CASTLETOWN PARADE

GLACIS

THE DITCH — LATER OUTER WARD

CURTAIN WALL

MAIN WARD

CLOCK TOWER

INNER WARD OR KEEP

WELL

OUTER WARD

MAIN WARD

MAIN WARD

DEEMSTERS PASSAGE

WELL

WELL

PRESENT ENTRANCE

DERBY HOUSE

PORTCULLIS & DRAWBRIDGE

CHAPEL RUINS

STAIRCASE DOWN TO DUNGEONS

STAIRCASE TO COURTROOM

CURTAIN WALL

GATE HOUSE

KITCHEN

GUARD-ROOM

QUAY ROAD

CASTLETOWN HARBOUR

RUSHEN CASTLE

THIS PLAN MODIFIED FROM PLANS DRAWN BY THE LATE A. RIGBY F.R.I.B.A.

a most imposing building comprising the lower three-quarters of the present "keep". The architecture and details are much like the castle keeps at Carnarvon and Beaumaris.

The keep now being a very formidable fortress, steps were taken to complete the fortification by putting around a strong "curtain" wall, and external gateway. This curtain was roughly octagonal and distant from the keep about 15 yards. At every angle of the octagon is a small strong point. Directly opposite the gateway of the keep was the gatehouse of the curtain. This gatehouse has on the ground floor an unusually large guard-room and kitchen. The kitchen has a sink, a corner fireplace and a buttery hatch for serving meals to the guard-room. Below the gatehouse is a vaulted basement chamber wrongly said to have been the vault where Bishop Wilson was imprisoned. When the castle was used as a prison and also as a lunatic asylum, this vault in its upper level was used for intractable and violent cases, who were manacled here. The lower parts of the vault were below spring tide level, and even now, after a wall and road have been constructed outside, water still percolates through at high tides. From this vault too runs a passage leading to the tidal mill, whose sluice opened through the space now filled up by the road outside. Somewhere along the sluice was an undershot wheel. The beam holes which held the grinding mechanism can still be seen. It must be remembered that, at the time when this stage of the castle construction had been achieved, there was no quayside road. The sea came right up to the castle foundations, and flowed in a deep trench at least part of the way round each side of the gatehouse. The passage which now leads down to the police station was not there, but from the gatehouse a draw-bridge was let down on the bank on which now stands the castle doorway. The only entrance to the castle was over this drawbridge and through the gatehouse. When the curtain wall was built, it took away the view from the top of the keep. It was therefore necessary further to raise the walls lest the whole of the inside garrison in a state of siege should be unsighted and therefore useless. When the keep was raised to its present height its garrison could fire over the heads of the men on the curtain wall. The passage from the outer drawbridge to the gatehouse had a "dog-leg" angle so that it would be difficult to get a battering engine across, and would make fighting in the passage very difficult for an invading body.

Between the gatehouse and the inner keep was the great drawbridge of the keep across a very deep trench. This drawbridge is unique, in that it normally stood erect in the magnificent arched recess in which it is fixed, and there was a lowering mechanism used when egress from or ingress to the keep was necessary. The keep gateway, too, is guarded by two very strong portcullises, one each side of the very strong door, and the usual "murder" holes through which could be dropped red-hot stones and molten lead. Inside are two guard-rooms. The gateway opens into the inner court. Access to the rest of the castle from this point was limited to one very narrow spiral staircase in the thickness of the wall, its entrance just inside the gateway, on the right. In the courtyard too are the inner well about 20 feet deep and a stone staircase leading up to the buttery. This is an old staircase, but not the original. There is a possibility that in the old castle there was no outside staircase, but that food and materials were hauled up by block and pulley, so as to prevent any invaders from having any approach to the upper storeys save by the spiral staircase. The side rooms of this ground floor were store-rooms. Today the way to the upper floors is by means of an iron-railed staircase put in in the nineteenth century when the castle was used as a prison. It was for many years labelled "Grand staircase of the Kings of Mann".

The first floor of the castle is best entered up the buttery stairs from the inner courtyard which leads to the kitchen, a small vaulted room in the east tower, with a large fireplace. The sink has disappeared, but the sink outlet is open. The kitchen opens across the stair-landing into the hall, a very small and originally dimly lit room, with the dais at the west end, away from the kitchen. It has no fireplace. Leading from the hall on the south side is a "dog-leg" passage leading to a small room with two pleasant window seats. There were two other rooms flanking the hall, the more distant the withdrawing room, the other now occupied with the head of the prison stairs. From the kitchen end of the hall a second spiral staircase leads to the floors above. On this floor too, over the gatehouse, are the rooms that contained the portcullis chains and mechanism. There are three stairways to the rooms on the second floor. But here the "hall" is fitted up as a museum and contains many interesting objects and pictures. The roof is modern. The rooms on this floor over the gatehouse contains further accommodation for the portcullis mechanism, and tubes communicating downward suggest extra ropes and possibly windlasses. The actual portcullises rose considerably higher than this floor, so that the ropes must have gone down to the lower ends of the portcullises.

The third floor is reached only by the spiral staircase. There is a room in each of the east, west and south towers. The room in the south tower is an oratory chapel. There may still be seen the altar supports, the aumbry and piscina. It now houses the famous clock whose dial outside has only one hand. Traditionally the clock is said to have been given by Queen Elizabeth I. Indeed her monogram appears in gold on the black dial. The design of the dial is such as may have been set up in her reign, but the mechanism of the clock is certainly of very much more recent date. The date of the mechanism is about 1720-40. There were clocks before the time of the pendulum, and it is thought that the Derby family had a clock which was not satisfactory. Elizabeth took the lordship from Earl Ferdinando. It is presumed that she replaced the Derby clock with more efficient " works ", and that about 100 years later a pendulum clock replaced hers. The clock is maintained by a falling weight, raised by a windlass attached to the opposite wall to that which carries the dial, but the pendulum " drop " is so small that the clock needs winding daily. The clock " strikes " on a bell given by Earl James, 1729.

The fourth floor, also reached by the spiral staircases, is the roof, from which the most delightful views may be seen over the surrounding country and sea.

Returning again to the ground level, space between the curtain and the keep was occupied with a host of buildings built up against the curtain wall with lean-to roofs; stables, bakehouses, a smithy, a mint for making coins, and a brewery.

The duplication of the rooms on the first and second floors is interesting, and it was due to the fact that the Lord on those occasions when he was in residence preferred to have his meals, and keep company only with his more honourable officers. In the castle were three grades of society apart from the domestic servants, namely the garrison, who had their own dining-room and kitchen in the gatehouse, the garrison officers and junior officials, then the Lord and his Governor, and the higher officials. Those dined with the Lord " who received a gentleman's wage, and the Comptroller ". He, poor fellow, seems not to have received a gentleman's wage! With my Lord dined, *en famille*, the Governor, the Attorney-General, the Water Bailiff, the Receiver-General, the Captain of the Guard and the Comptroller. It is not certain which set used which rooms, but the dais in the lower hall suggests that the Lord dined there. Probably when he was not in residence, there was less ceremony, and all dined below to ensure that there was no carrying of hot dishes upstairs.

About the year 1536, during the lordship of Edward the third Earl, the outer glacis was built. There was a great advance in the use of artillery and the new gun, firing from a distance too great to be put out of action easily, could fire cannon balls to break down the strongest door, so castles were protected by a high mound of earth, stones and rubble. This glacis was constructed outside the moat all round the castle except where it was protected by the sea. It is not certain what was the condition of the moat at Castle Rushen. It was formerly very deep, but it has not been excavated. It may well have had water in always, even when the tide was out, though more probably it was a deep ditch and only the portion near the harbour was filled with tidal water.

The glacis extended right round the moat, but today it has been sadly cut down. Houses to the west have cut into it for their gardens; to the south it has been set back to make more room for the market place and to set up a gateway into the "moat", now filled in, for social gatherings of the governors; and on the east, to allow of road widening. But it still remains a remarkably fine sample of the military glacis.

In the outer courtyard, just inside the gatehouse to the left, stands what is called the Derby House. This was a house built in 1582-3 by the fifth Earl, Henry, who found the gloom of the castle interior too depressing, and who preferred to live more in the light. At the same time he built a small oratory chapel, the ruins of which lies beside the pathway to the drawbridge. Here the family could worship without climbing up into the castle oratory. The house is now used in part for the caretaker, and in part for the withdrawing rooms of the deemsters, high bailiff, and justices, who sit in the courtroom over the outer gatehouse.

When the moat was filled in, the outer drawbridge was taken down, and a passage-way with loop-holed walls and barbican constructed, and the passage closed by the present entrance. Inferior stone was used, and now the entrance passage looks the oldest part of the castle and not, as it really is, the most recent.

OTHER FORTIFICATIONS

On St. Michael's Island, Malew, or to use its more common name "Fort Island", stands a circular fort. This fort was built probably about the same time as the glacis of Castle Rushen, in the reign of Henry VIII, by Edward the third earl. He had a good knowledge of the power of artillery, and it was probably he who built also forts at Douglas and Ramsey. There was a great fear in his time of invasion from Scotland, and France, and possibly Spain. This fort was repaired and rearmed by the Great Earl, James, for the defence of the harbour of Ronaldsway. It was then armed with "one whole culvrain" (11 feet long and firing a 17 lb. ball) and a "demi-culvrain" (11 feet long and firing a 4 lb. ball). The fort at Douglas was also of the same round shape in hard stone and armed with "four pieces". But of this not a trace remains except the name "Fort Street".

Of the same period is the large earthwork at Ballachurry, Andreas, in the form of a large rectangular structure about 40 by 48 yards. The earthen walls are about 20 feet thick, with a bastion 48 feet square at each corner, the whole surrounded by a fosse. It was ordered by the Earl to be constructed "in the very middest of the island".

CHAPTER ELEVEN

PEOPLE—CUSTOMS—FOLK-LORE

THE MANX of the country districts have remained markedly isolated in manners and customs. To this day Manx weds Manx almost exclusively.

There were never any divisions of the people into aristocracy, thanes and serfs, as in the Norman areas of Britain. The Lords and their retinues were English, but there were no "titled folk" among the Lord's followers, and no Lord ever conceived the idea of creating a local insular roll of honour. The high officials, lieutenant governors, comptrollers, and such like, were English, and returned to England at the end of their term of office. The insular officials, deemsters, attorney-generals, captains of parishes, were all Manx and were on the whole from the families of the landowners, and here again it must be remembered that there were no big estates comparable with those in Britain. In general terms the largest farms were little larger than "small holdings", so that society has always been purely plebeian. When "the trade" brought large fortunes to some of the families there were efforts to buy up the small farms to make larger estates and some families began to have "ideas beyond their state" and there was a distinct trace of snobbery (though nothing more) which tried to ape the exclusiveness of the Regency court in a very minor fashion. But, in a small island such as this, everybody knows everybody's family antecedents and ancestry, so that snobbery is impossible, and the whole atmosphere is one of friendly bonhomie. If perchance anybody should consider himself "somebody", the dissection of his character and the characters of his own family and his wife's family right back for a century or more is an entertainment that it is a pity to miss. It is typical of Manxmen to refer to their acquaintance in terms of their parents' occupation. "Uan of Tom the Pot" is John, son of Tom the potman; or "Harry—the Coffin", a system of genealogy that causes very much joy when used in recording the ancestry of a V.I.P. of not very friendly character.

In character the true Manx are careful and thrifty. They like to see the way ahead, and even in these State-assisted days they like to lay up a respectable nest-egg. There are very few even of the wage-earners who "die under four figures". The appearance in the Island press of lists of "Other People's Money" (and wills are very quickly proved in the Island) is a constant source of interest.

The caution of the Manxman is seen in many walks of life. He is a good listener, but is reluctant to talk in strange company. Even if one has lived in the Island a long time, direct questions may beget a stony silence. When induced to express an opinion they give it with the greatest latitude, leaving themselves a good way of escape. They describe themselves as "Jes the shy", but "cautious" would be a better word than "shy". Another less commendable trait is the tendency to put off making decisions, which often leads to unnecessary delays in performing work or duty. "Traa-dy-liooar", they say, "There's time enough".

In his humour, too, the Manxman is cautious. Although thoroughly humorous-minded, his type of humour is vastly different from English, Irish or Scottish humour. The English sense of humour is "broad", the Scottish "dour" and the Irish sense of humour is all-embracing and catholic. But Manx humour knows none of these qualities. It is "gentle" humour, ill at ease with "innuendo" even of the innocent or pleasant type. It used to be said that you should not joke with a Manxman until you had known him at least thirty years, but here, as elsewhere, customs change with the passage of time, and such observations are perhaps less generally relevant than they once were.

Another obvious trait in the Manx character is his innate modesty, specially as regards his own achievements. He is no braggart. One of the most noted traits of the Manx is their simple religious background. They have all the Celtic mysticism and fervour in their make-up. They are very fond of words and oratory, and will listen to a fervid preacher with far more interest than to an intellectual. But they are not carried away as are the Welsh. They are still strongly sabbatarian, and it is only in recent years that public houses have been permitted to open on Sundays.

They are a musical nation, and music plays an important part in their lives. They sing readily without mock-modesty. There is a high proportion of tenor voices among the men, a tenor soft and gentle in contrast to the ringing volume of the Welsh tenor. In the Manx Music Guild, held just before the holiday season begins, there are classes for all ages and combinations of voices, and the standard of artistic ability is high. *Per contra* there is little instrumental music on the Island. The general reason given is that practically every person can sing, and learning to use the voice is simpler and less difficult than learning to play an instrument. On the other hand they take very kindly to the drama, and there are many dramatic companies to compete in the Guild with great skill and artistry.

The Manx language is no longer used in everyday life. There are evening classes for those who wish to learn or improve their knowledge of the language, and these are well supported. But it is a language without literature and its future is the less certain for its lack of a strong literary base. Many Manx sayings and proverbs are still quoted and remembered, but alas their number becomes less with the years. Church services in Manx are held from time to time and many children can repeat the Lord's Prayer in Manx, but the number of men who can speak extempore Manx is very few. The titles of the Laws are read in Manx on Tynwald Hill every year. The Manx speaking voice is soft and musical in the vast majority of cases, though there is the occasional non-musical voice. The general intonation is distinctive and impossible to mistake. Many stories are told of recognition of Manx men and women who have met abroad quite unknown to each other. In speaking, the Manx have the Celtic uplift of the voice at the end of their sentences in contrast to the Anglo-Saxon method of dropping the voice.

Family life and family pride are strongly marked even in the

humblest families. Genealogies are all known for many generations, and intermarriages all followed back. There is in so small
an area a great amount of intermarriage locally, so that each
family seems to have intermarried with every other family and
it is never safe to make derogatory remarks to one Manxman
about another lest that person be quite closely related. Strangely
enough there is less likelihood of people of the same name
being closely related. There is a common quip in the Island,
" Same name, no relation. Different name, probably a cousin."

Typical Manx farms are run on a family basis. Sons and
daughters all help in their several ways, and in work never spare
themselves. Like many other British people, the Manx refuse
to be driven. There are certainly no other people who more
quickly become obstinate and embittered under arbitrary treat-
ment. History throws many a light on this side of their nature.
It might be lord or bishop, vicar or employer, but beyond a
certain point there lay bitterness and rebellion. The Manxman
is not at heart a fighter. The Celt in him is stronger far than
the Viking. He prefers to live in peace, and indeed he will
sacrifice a great deal for peace, more perhaps than his counterpart
" across the water ". But drive him, and he can be a nasty enemy.
He never wished to fight, but he never failed as a fighter.

A prime example of how the obstinacy of the Manx nature
can still prevail occurred in very recent years, when a new
Lieutenant-Governor was appointed by Her Majesty the Queen,
Lord of Mann. The people looked forward expectantly to his
arrival, until they heard that his wife was not intending to
accompany him to the Island, but would remain in England.
This was too much; the Governor's wife was expected to look
after the Governor's house and to participate in the social life
of the Island. The wave of reaction which swept the Island was
sufficient to ensure that the gentleman withdrew from the post
without ever setting foot in the place. In due course, a successor
was appointed, and his wife came with him.

Great hospitality has ever been a trait of the Manx. No trouble
is too great for the Manx housewife to honour a welcome guest.
From the very humblest one gets an invitation for " a bite and a
sup ". Always still in the isolated farmhouse in the hill-country
there is a glass of milk or buttermilk and a soda scone and butter
for the weary pedestrian walking over the mountains with an
invitation to come in awhile for a rest. The natural instinct is
toward thrift and economy, but nobody could be more generous

toward a good cause. The Manx part of the Island community is contentedly prosperous. These points among many others are the virtues that have made the Manx such excellent and successful colonists. There are large Manx communities in Canada, the United States, South Africa, Australia, and New Zealand, where Manx manners, customs and sayings abound, where still their thrift, reliable hard work and "carefulness" have made them popular and wealthy citizens. Generations that have never been within a thousand miles of the Isle of Man are steeped in Manx lore, brought up on Manx proverbs, eat Manx dishes, and know full well where lies their spiritual home. During the two World Wars young Manxmen from every part of the Empire visited the Ellan Vannin of their fathers, in their thousands.

In all parts of the country it is very difficult to get countryfolk to tell their old "folk stories" to strangers. But the Isle of Man like all other Celtic areas has a wealth of folk-lore.

In days long since gone by the perforate St. John's wort, Bollan feall-Eoin (*Hypericum perforatum*), common in all parts of the Island, and approved by the Church, was worn on St. John's Day, which is also Tynwald Day (O.S.). This indeed was the custom over the whole Christian world. In the early nineteenth century members of the House of Keys were reported to have adopted the mug-wort, *Artemisia vulgaris*, a somewhat localized plant in the Island. It seems difficult to account for this change round. It might be quite fortuitous, except for the fact that Artemisia carries the name of Artemis, or Diana, and is a familiar plant of witchcraft. Diana was the goddess of fertility, and her festival was held on Midsummer Day, which is also St. John's Day. There seems therefore to have been a change over from St. John and the Church to the summer festival revels of midsummer night, which still persisted well into this century. Many stories remain, for example around Castletown, of wild frolics and dances in the heather on Barrule, revels too shocking to be told, suggesting that the Church, in its invariable attempt to swamp the heathen feasts with Christian (Christmas for Yule, Easter for the Spring ceremonies, St. John for Diana), may have failed to dispose of Artemis as thoroughly as they had hoped, and her obscene flower eventually ousted the blossom of St. John in the button-holes of the sober legislators.

The elder tree (Trammon) is widespread over the Island and may be seen still in front of the great majority of old cottages. Its virtue is that it is intolerable to witches, who will not come near it. The hawthorn, illustrative of the crown of thorns, is to be seen growing by many sacred wells. Daffodils must not be brought into the house. The Manx name "Lus-ny-ghuiy" (goose flower) is given because if there are daffodils in the house the goose passing by will see them and mistake them for goslings and refuse to go on hatching her eggs. Primroses are lucky flowers. They are "sumark" in Manx, and are picked on the eve of May-day and scattered in the farm street, and in front of the houses, because they are loved by the "little people". Many plants of course have medicinal qualities and are still keenly sought by the many herbalists who still ply their trade in the Island. The water violet *Pinguicula vulgaris* (Lus-y-steep, the rennet flower), apart from its rennet properties, is good for weak eyes, and tooth-ache. The ragwort, *Senecio Jacobaea* (Manx "Cushag"), the "Manx national flower", is potent against infection.

With reference to animal superstitions, there is a singular shortage of native mammals in the Island, but of these the hare is, as is usual in Northern Europe, an alternative for a witch. The pygmy shrew is alleged by folk-lore to be poisonous, and is correspondingly harshly treated by country-folk.

It is difficult to assess the amount of belief in ghosts. The Manx are ever cautious, and very few will deny the possibility of the existence of ghosts. Probably very few even of the well-educated Manx would imagine that the existence of a ghost is fanciful. Many honest and reliable people claim to have seen "The Grey Lady" of Castletown. Many folk still, to this day, can tell of friends and relatives who visited Peel Castle, saw the "Moddy Dhoo", and died within a few months. The "Mauthe Dhoo", be it said, of Peel Castle was alleged to be a black dog presaging death and quoted by Scott in the *Last Minstrel*.

Among fisher folk there is a very curious superstition, that the "third boat" to leave harbour with the fishing fleet will have no luck. To prevent such a misfortune, even in recent times, the second and third boats would put out to sea lashed together. But today, with the Manx boats heavily outnumbered by Scottish vessels, any Manxman who still believes the super-stition need not be long delayed in waiting for a Scot to take the third place. Another superstition still held is that of the "third day", i.e. that the spirit still haunts the body for two full days after death, and to have a funeral before the third day might cramp the freedom of the spirit after death, which might stay and haunt the house.

In the Museum may be seen a "swearing stone", a stone used by men making a sale, specially of land, or any statement of fact. They would place one foot in the foot-shaped hollow in the stone and bear witness that the sale or statement is genuine. Till quite recently any claim against the estate of a deceased person could be justified by the claimant putting his foot on the head end of the grave of the deceased, before witnesses, and thereby verifying the claim.

Charms are still in very popular use, in many types. One peculiar to the Island is the " bollan " charm. The bollan is a sea-fish which carries in its gullet a triangular-shaped set of pearl-like teeth. These, dissected out and suitably mounted, make a very bonny brooch charm, which given to one's sweetheart ensures her fidelity, while if carried loose by a fisherman or farmer, or indeed by anybody, when thrown into the air points to the direction one should take to obtain a good catch, or make a journey, or find fortune. The possession of a " caul " is still sought by fishermen and sailors and demands a high price, running into pounds, on the belief that no one who has a caul can drown.

The shedding of blood has mystical significance. Special penalties were inflicted by Church and State on those who caused a " blood-wipe ". Today there are many folk who believe that there are people (whom they can and will name) who are blood-stanchers, and whose presence in a room will arrest the flow of blood.

As in Britain, and indeed in most European countries, warts are susceptible to many and varied " charms " and incantations. They usually need as a subsidiary aid some substance that will quickly decay. The usual procedure is to take a small piece of raw meat, rub it over the warts, mutter the incantation, wrap up the meat and throw it away or bury it. When the meat has decayed the wart will disappear.

Another superstition in the Island is the superstition that attaches to a white stone, or " clagh bane ". Fishermen carefully go through their ballast and throw out any piece of quartz or other white stone, whose presence may bring disaster. It is thought that this superstition has come down from Neolithic times, when the graves were paved with white pebbles.

Funerals have their customs. In a Manx funeral, when the coffin is taken from the house it is placed on two chairs, and the friends gather round with the vicar and a hymn is sung suitable for the occasion. The coffin on the bier or hearse is taken to the churchyard slowly, followed by close and distant relatives and friends. Till quite recent years a funeral dirge was sung all the way to the church. No new roads must be traversed by the coffin of a true Manxman, however much further the old road runs. In church the relatives near and distant occupy the front pews and remain seated all through the service, and they commonly attend divine service on the following Sunday dressed in mourning, and again sit through the service.

Of seasonal customs, the harvest is, as in Britain generally, a great Church festival accompanied (again note the religious and the pre-Christian celebrations) by a parish tea. This tea has largely replaced the "harvest home" celebrated on each farm separately in days gone by, known as "mhellia". The word means a "doll". This "doll" is the last sheaf garnered, made specially small, and known as "moidyn" or virgin, and this is fashioned like a doll, and becomes the central decoration of the well-laden tables.

With the rise of non-conformity, and the strong Scottish and Irish influence, Christmas has always taken second place to New Year's Day so far as the festal spirit is concerned. Christmas Eve was until about fifty years back the day of "Yn Oei'l Verry", the eve of Mary's Feast, and was marked by a singing of carvals in church. In bygone days the vicar turned up and said Evensong, and then left the church to a kind of parish singing competition. The carvals, which were not even of a Christian or religious nature, contained some very ancient folk music, but the words were often profane solo verses about bishops, vicars, wardens, cess, and tithes! New Year's Day is a very important day. The cat must be kept indoors all night before, for to have the cat cross the threshold first on New Year's Day would presage a disastrous year. The first visitor is called a "qualtagh". If the qualtagh is a woman it is next worst to being the cat. An old woman is even more disastrous than the cat. A dark-haired man is lucky and shades of darkness reduce the degree of good fortune till a red-headed man is practically worthless. On New Year's Day, too, the Manx housewife sweeps her floor from the door to the fireplace lest she should sweep out her good fortune. In Peel it is asserted that if the sun doesn't shine on Peel Hill on New Year's Day it will be a bad year for the herring. Of the parish fair-days all have died out during the past century with the exception of Arbory, where the dedication of the church to St. Columba gives its name to the festival "Lhaa Columb killey", the festival of St. Columba's Church. The fair-day at St. John's has recently been revived, and the Laxey fair is a great attraction.

Witch superstitions have survived very strongly in the Island, and have left a dark mark on its history. Cronk Sumark is the

H

traditional scene of the witches' dance. All the Island witches assembled here and lured the young unmarried women to join them in a lewd Bacchanal dance, forming a ring around the hill.

In the Kirk Maughold area many strange tales of witchcraft linger. The most famous of all Manx witches lived here, Berrey by name, who organized a "chapel" of witches. These delectable females had the power of disappearing into the side of North Barrule, under which mountain on stormy nights their shrieks could always be heard as they danced at ever increasing speed. There is a record, too, of their dance round Maughold Church in a vain attempt, like, but less successful than, the witch of Endor, to call up St. Maughold from his grave. Another famous but far less aggressive witch was the little Red Lady of Garraghan, Ben-Veg-Carraghan, often seen by visitors walking across that lonely mountain and described as wearing a tall steeple hat and a dark red cloak, to catch sight of whom was to run into difficulty or misfortune.

Best known of all the "witch" areas is Slieu Whallian, the steep slope frowning down above St. John's and Tynwald Hill. This traditionally was the place of punishment for witches, and is best known as the "Witches' Hill". Down this hill tradition says those suspected of practising the Black Art were rolled in barrels through whose walls spikes had been driven. The unfortunate suspects were placed in those barrels and rolled down the hill. If they arrived at the bottom dead they had obviously incurred the judgment of heaven. If they arrived alive they were obviously witches, and suffered a witch's doom at the stake. But it must be admitted that there is no contemporary record to support the story.

The Isle of Man shares with Scotland the ancient quarter days, which are not those of England, but occur about half-way through the English "quarters". They are linked with the seasonal festivals which are "witches' sabbats", at which times wild orgies might be expected. May Day-even is the witches' high festival, and even within living memory it was customary to drive all cattle into the farm "street" to protect them from the baleful influence of the "evil eye" or witches' curse, while, all around, the gorse and heather were fired to drive off all evil influences.

Among other "black" accomplishments was the custom of reciting pieces of scripture and specially the Lord's Prayer and the Invocation to the Trinity backward. Folk living today tell of children being taught secretly such "backward" repetitions as would entitle them to join a witches' chapel.

Most terrible of all the horrors of witchcraft, of which more than a trace remains today, is the witch's curse, a "gigantic" curse, a terrifying, horrible experience. The witch went openly and unashamedly to the home of her victim. She carried with her her broom, and she swept the dirt up the path towards the house, while she uttered her curse on bed and board, on flocks and herds, on crops and fruits, on happiness and success, on child and property. She was a terrifying sight, and her very fluency carried conviction and horror to her hearer. She meant to convey terror, and she succeeded. There is no doubt that, to the Celtic mind, the curse and the "evil eye" were very real, and up to recent times there were many people who retained a belief in the witch's power. Manx Church records have countless accounts of trials for witchcraft. Bishop Barrow made great efforts to subdue the practice of witchcraft, which of course was an offence tried at the Vicar-General's court. The guilty were made to do penance with sheet and candle at one or more or even at all the parish churches on Sunday mornings. Bishop Wilson, who was a man of much kindlier nature, appears to have made a study of the "craft", and seems to suggest that it was well organized, and not merely haphazard. In 1741 he wrote to his clergy "witchcraft . . . is a cursed practice carried on secretly by Satan and his instruments". He urges his clergy "to terrify those who practise it, and confirm their parishioners' faith that God is more powerful than Satan or his wretched instruments". There is every reason to believe that craft secrets were passed on from mother to daughter.

The most interesting "folk-custom" in the Island, which has survived till this year of grace, and is unique, is the St. Stephen's Day December 26th custom of "Hunt the Wren". On that day a party of boys and girls (sometimes, though rarely, both) arrives outside one's house singing a quaint little carval, and bearing with them a casket prettily decorated, and containing a bunch of feathers. Until recent years this bunch of feathers was a dead wren. The "casket" is commonly made up of two wooden hoops tied at right angles, containing a bright cushion, and strung with coloured ribbons, paper streamers and evergreens. The actual words sung vary from parish to parish, and probably from year to year. One old version runs:

> We'll away to the wood says Robin to Bobbin
> We'll away to the wood says Dickon to Robin
> We'll away to the wood says Jac o' the land.
> We'll away to the wood says everyone.

Countless verses describing the chase and slaughter of the wren, with vivid details usually ending up with "He's ate, he's ate, says Robin to Bobbin".

The origin of the custom is hidden in mystery. Many suggestions have been made but none seems satisfactory. The commonplace suggestion would be that it was a miracle play concerning the stoning of Stephen, but since all Manx customs and festivals are timed for the Old Style Calendar this doesn't seem probable.

"The White Boys" (common as mummers in many parts of Britain until quite recently) went round the villages with their buffoonery during the Christmas season, with a play closely resembling St. George and the Dragon, but with the Dragon providing much of the "slap-stick", ably assisted by a blackamoor.

Another purely insular custom is "Hop-tu'naa". All Hallowe'en, October 31st (O.S. November 11th) is a date of some importance and interest. It is known as "Hollantide" (Hallowe'en-tide). It was formerly counted the first day of winter. The Celtic races looked upon the day as "witches' sabbat", when all the witches and warlocks careered around and held high festival. The days of darkness had arrived. But later in history it was counted a "half-quarter day" and the main hiring-fair of the year was held. In the evening of the hiring-fair, children and young people ran from house to house, carrying turnips or swedes, carved in the likeness of a human face and lit internally with a candle, singing the song "Hop-an-naa Trollalaa Hop-tu'naa Hollantide eve, the moon shines Dance tonight". Today the turnip-and-candle survives, often exceedingly realistically carved, and just the one remaining line "Hop-tu'naa".

The folk-music of the Island has been very well collected and recorded by Miss A. G. Gilchrist in the *Journal of the Folk-Song Society*, vol. VII. Two famous songs of the Island life, "The Sheep under the Snow" and "The Loss of the Herring Fleet", have ancient folk tunes, and are well known as harmonized part songs. Another, "Mylecharaine", about an old Jurby miner, was noted by George Borrow when he visited the Island in 1855.

Several shorter love-songs have been re-written as concert songs. They all have plaintive, pleasing melodies. But by far the greatest number of Manx airs are the old "carvals".

One of the best known tunes is the so-called "Manx Fishermen's Hymn", included in some hymn-books of the Anglican Church. The tune is an attractive one, a variant of an ancient traditional tune set to very different words, which has been adapted to fit modern and somewhat sentimental verses. But neither words nor music had any connection with the ancient custom of the sixteenth century, when one of the duties of the vicars of the parish was to go down to the port every time the fishing fleet set out, and hold a service on the quay with prayers for a blessing on their labours, and a safe return to land.

FOLK-LORE

In a country in which the prevalent culture has been Celtic deeply tinged by Scandinavian, one must expect to find the unseen world peopled by a whole menagerie of "fantasticals". In Man there is a multitude of quaint creatures and beings to be found in all parts and localities. At the miniature end are the "little people". Quite frankly the reputation of these small folk is puzzling, and undoubtedly recent years have added apocryphal accretions to their characters. The Manx little people, like their angelic counterparts, are divided for some cause or causes unknown into two main divisions, the "good little people", or "mooinjer-ny-gione-veggey", who retained their primeval goodness; and the wicked little people, or "phynnodderee", who "fell" and are responsible for much mischief and evil.

Not many years ago, the legends of the Norman-French "fairies" reached the Isle of Man and they were in Manx given the manufactured name of "ferrish", a name that displeased the "little people" very severely, and no true Manxman with any feelings for them ever calls them "fairies", with whom they have nothing whatever in common. The "fairy" of French origin is an insipid feminine character, the "l'il folk", both good and bad, are sturdy, virile little people who scorn being called "fairies", and what they think of their favourite haunt along the Santan-burn at Ballaglonney being called officially "The Fairy Bridge" no human can imagine. Their correct title is "the little people". In appearance and habit they follow the Celtic pattern with more than a trace of the Scandinavian "troll". They usually dress in green with red caps. They are mainly outdoor folk, but come indoors on cold or stormy nights. They are benevolent except to those who do them insult or injury. They live around the homesteads and farms through the day, and in the sunshine they dance in the valleys and glens, and on hot days love to splash in the water, especially under the waterfalls. In winter the fire must be kept in all night for their comfort, and scraps of food and basins of water or saucers of milk are left for their food.

But in the case of the malevolent type, the fallen folk, the "phynnodderee", things are very different. They are degraded little folk, with harsh, hairy faces, and bright, shining eyes. They are guilty of every conceivable act of malicious wickedness but fortunately they are afraid of any suggestion of Christianity, and church bells and holy music expel them from any place they haunt. It is amusing to note that when the Bible was translated into Manx, and it came to the translation of Isaiah "satyr shall call to his fellow", it was translated "phynnodderee gyllagh da e heshty". Of the other folk-lore creatures appearing in the tales told by generations of the Island folk, the "ben-varrey" (woman of the sea or mermaid) occupies a prominent place. Mermen and mermaids are the common heritage of all maritime nations in the North Atlantic, and almost certainly owe their description to the seals that are commonly to be seen on such coasts. One of the earliest descriptions from the Island annals describes them as "playing on the beach, combing their locks, popping into the water silently, disappearing and reappearing in a different place". In the Manx tales they live in wonderful palaces beneath the sea.

The "cughtagh" is a sea monster who inhabits caves and uses his tremendous voice to shout above the storms. But when it is calm, his breathing can be heard in the caves and chasms, a shy creature! He is never seen. *Vox et preterea nihil!*

The "Keimach" (prancer) is the guardian of churchyards and burial grounds, a swift-running creature who sits on the tombstones when nights are quiet, but runs swiftly toward any trespasser, and appears quietly to those whom Death is about to claim.

The "glashten" or "glashen" is a particularly unpleasant breed of phynnodderee guilty of most of the evil deeds that are done in farm and home, and the name is sometimes also used for the "gabbal-ushtey" or "tarroo-ushtey" (water-horse, or water-bull). This seems to be a modification of the almost universal "Europa" story of the horse or bull that consorts with the common herd and by its ingratiating ways encourages some beautiful maiden to ride on his back, and then abducts her.

The "buggane" or frightful one is the Manx giant. He has a voice almost as mighty as that of the "cughtagh" on a stormy night. By nature he is malevolent to man, and he uproots trees and throws down buildings.

It is interesting to note that the giant legends are nearly all based on the north or Scandinavian portion of the Island, and the little people mainly in the southern, or purely Celtic portion, a fact that supports the theory that giants and little folk were respectively names used for Viking and Celt.

The "lhiannan-shee" is a guardian spirit of a family. Concerning such is the legend of the Ballafletcher Cup, which may be seen in the Museum. Ballafletcher is the estate upon which Kirk Braddan church is built. The cup is a glass goblet rather larger than the ordinary tumbler, alleged to have belonged to St. Olaf, in whose shrine it was placed at his death. It was stolen from the shrine by Magnus, his successor (1093). For 300 years it disappeared but was ultimately found in the possession of the Fletcher family at Kirby, who returned it to Rushen Abbey. After the dissolution of the abbey the cup eventually came into possession of Robert Caesar of Malew, whose family gave it to the Museum. There are said to be only three such cups in existence.

Mention must be made of the Manx wells or "chibbyrs" that occur in every parish of the Island, all traditionally having some useful properties. They are not deep wells, but usually small hollows, often in grotto form, which remain full of water at all seasons. Even in these enlightened days there is ample evidence that the wells are "used". For example many of the "wishing wells" may be seen to bear on their basins bright metal objects, coins, and ornaments thrown in as votive offerings, while the curative wells still show in the bushes round them pieces of cloth hanging, suggesting that to this day men and women haunted by fear of disease have used the waters, and placed the cloth in the bush believing that, when the cloth disintegrates, the disease will have fled.

Many wells have church connections, for example St. Ann's well (wrongly so-called) at Santan, St. Maughold's well, many Chibbyr-phericks (Patrick's wells) and several Chibbyr-katrineys (St. Catherine's wells), all of which have eye- or sight-improving powers. Many have "fertility" powers, as for example the well on Maughold Head, difficult of access, but still visited; and many wells whose waters alleviate the pangs of child-birth. Of less romantic value is the water of the well at Glencrutchery, the waters of which were taken by the farmers' wives of Onchan, who would pour a few drops into the churns to ensure a quick "coming" of the butter, even on a cold morning. While in Lezayre was a spring popular with the fisher folk, who went thither, and took handfuls of its waters and threw them toward the sky in the direction of what they thought would be a good wind for their venture, and never in vain.

CHAPTER TWELVE

FLORA AND FAUNA

DURING THE glacial period, the whole original flora of the Island had been demolished. Such plants therefore as exist today have been re-established either by those which followed the recession of the ice and snow before the level of the Irish Sea rose and cut off the land bridge; or those whose seeds were transported by wind; or those that were introduced by man, officinal and such-like plants. In any case the duration of the land bridge was not sufficient time in which an extensive flora could return from the surrounding continental mass. Viewed in terms of plant associations the Island flora can be classified into:

1. A coast series with three main types:
   (*a*) The shingle beach.
   (*b*) A very small salt marsh series.
   (*c*) A sand-dune series.
2. An upland moor series of two types:
   (*a*) A cotton-grass association.
   (*b*) A heath-moor association.
3. A marsh series:
   (*a*) The submerged and semi-submerged curragh flora.
   (*b*) A marshy-meadow formation.
4. A poorly represented siliceous (slate) series.

The comparative absence of woodlands is a sad fact, specially in view of the fact that in time past the Island was well-wooded. Bishop Wilson recorded that during the draining of part of Ballaugh curragh masses of tree trunks were found, oaks and firs in great numbers, all lying in the same direction as though thrown down by some gigantic S.W. gale. Hensley (*Trans. Geol. Soc.*, vol. 7) examined this " curragh-timber " flora and recognized ash, walnut, black-alder, holly, oak, and fir. He also described a submerged forest in Poylvaish Bay.

Of plants of more than usual interest may be cited the Manx cabbage (*Brassica monensis*), first recorded in Ramsey Bay by the great biologist John Ray in 1662. It is still to be found all round the coast on sandy shores.

Some plants are only found in restricted areas, e.g. the black horehound (*Marrubium vulgare*) only in Bride, while the most elusive of all plants, the "Dodder" (*Cuscuta epithymium*) is reported spasmodically, and always on Langness.

Of other flowers the bluebell (*Scilla non scripta*) covers the glens in spring, but confuting the general idea that it is only a woodland plant covers large unshaded areas on the Calf! Its close relative, *Scilla verna*—far less common in Britain and apparently another of the western coast series of Europe—is one of the glories of the Island flora and is to be seen in profusion on Langness. Both British water-lilies, yellow and white, are to be found (*Nymphaea lutea* and *Castalia alba*) but only sparsely in the northern "dubs". The lovely horned sea-poppy (*Glaucium flavum*), formerly very common, appears less common of late, but the sea holly (*Eryngium maritimum*) still flourishes, together with the sea-rocket (*Cakile maritimum*) and the sea-convolvulus (*Calistegia soldanella*) in company with the marram-glass.

In the autumn, the mountains are purple with heather. Ling and bell-heather occur in about equal quantities, and there is a good sprinkling of cross-leaved heath (*Erica cruciata*). Holiday-makers in the mountain country are always delighted to find white heather or ling, and a walk across any of the mountain areas will always give this reward to those with seeing eyes. In summer the outstanding sight on the moorlands is the wealth of cotton grass (*Eriophoron angustifolium*), whose white, hairy "heads" are called by the Manx "clooie-hunnag" or "duck's down". There are a few orchids, *O. pryamidalis*, *latifolia*, *maculata*, *Habenaria virescens*, and *Listera ovata*.

The so-called Manx national flower is the Ragwort (*Senecio Jacobaea*) (Manx Cushag), which certainly forms a magnificent splash of colour on the mountain, but in the lowlands is a per-nicious weed. It is a common gibe of the "come-overs" that the national flower is Thrift (*Armeria vulgaris*), which occupies every nook and cranny on the rocks above the splash of the waves, accompanied by masses of scurvy grass (*Cochlearia*) and sea-campion. The country lanes in summer are a mass of foxgloves and ferns, while on hedge-wall and "tholtan" may be seen a wealth of pennywort (*Hydrocotyle*) and ivy-leaved toadflax (*Linaria cymballaria*). On the summit of South Barrule (and only there so far as report allows) grows the cow-wheat (*Melampyrum montanum*), reminiscent of the isolated flora of many of the Scottish mountain peaks.

Every botanist (and for that matter ornithologist and entomologist) should spend some time in the curragh-lands of Ballaugh and Jurby. Their position at the foot of the mountains is in itself glorious for any lover of nature. They form a lonely area, quite unnoticed by the thousands of folks who drive their cars or occupy the motor-coaches which in summer pass in a ceaseless stream along their border, never realizing (*Laus Deo!*) the glories they are passing by unknowing and unheeding. One may take one or other of the almost unknown paths that run in from the main road, and within a short stone's throw be in a new world entirely alone in quiet and peace. The area is occupied by extensive meres or "dubs" fringed by borders of scrub, willow, honeysuckle, and bog-myrtle. The dubs are covered with a profusion of bog-bean (*Menyanthes trifoliata*) and other less-showy aquatic plants, and the royal fern (*Osmunda*) adds its own special glory. But the area is not without its dangers, and exploration should not be made far from the pathways, for much of the bog is reputed to have quagmire qualities, while many of the "dubs" have deep holes of fantastic depth which are very dangerous to wading folk.

It may be added that examination of the Manx mountain peat layers which were deposited upon the glacial drifts has proved quite a scientific romance, and has disclosed the seeds, pollen-grains, fruits and leaves of plants of the greatest interest in the origin of the Manx flora, and especially of the plants that crossed the "land bridge" as the snows of the glacial period retreated.

Of plants other than flowering plants the wealth of ferns has been noted. There are three club mosses (*Lycopodium selago, clavatum* and *alpinum*) on the northern mountains, and a mass of Sphagnum moss all over the mountain tracts.

THE FAUNA

The fauna of any island cannot help being of interest, whether it be an "oceanic" or a "continental" island. The British Isles are continental, broken off from the land mass of Europe, so that the animals of today and yesterday are roughly those common on the main land mass. But during the glacial period all animals were destroyed, and in post-glacial times only those quadrupeds arrived that were able to get across the land bridge.

Until the appearance of myxomatosis the Island suffered from a plague of rabbits, a plague that was the worse for the absence of foxes from the Island. But it seems highly probable that even the rabbit was introduced by man. Tradition says that it was brought over by the Derby family retainers. There is no Manx-

Celtic word for the rabbit. The name "conning" is a modification of the Norman-French *connog* from the Latin *cuniculus*,
and in old English "coney".

The hare seems to be a genuine Manxman. Its Manx name is
Mwaag. The common species is *Lepus timidus*, although it has
many points of similarity to the Irish hare *L. hibernicus*. As
elsewhere in Celtic country folk-lore it is always associated with
witchcraft. In the eighteenth and early nineteenth century packs
of beagles were kept for "the chasing of the hare".

Two rats are common. Both probably have been introduced
by ships. *Mus decumanus*, the brown rat, was introduced first.
But since it arrived in Britain no earlier than the fourteenth
century, it could not have been indigenous in the Island. The
black rat (*Mus rattus*), which reached Britain before the brown
rat, reached the Calf consequently upon the wreck of a Russian
boat in the early nineteenth century. For many years it remained
in the Calf, but during the past fifty years it has appeared over
the whole Island. There are no water-rats, although the brown
rat swimming is commonly reported as such. The house-mouse
(*Mus musculus*) is uncomfortably prevalent, and the long-tailed
field-mouse (*M. sylvaticus*) is also abundant. There are no
squirrels.

There are two insectivores present. The pigmy shrew (*Sorex
arenaeus*) may be native. It is found all over the Island. Its
Manx name is "Thollog faiyr", the "grass louse". The hedge-
hog is the commonest wild mammal, judged by the number of
corpses to be seen on the roadways (car casualties). But it is an
introduced animal, brought over by the schooner *Hooton* sailing
from Whitehaven and wrecked on Rue Point, Andreas, about 1805.
A box containing several hedgehogs, the property of a passenger,
was rescued from the wreck, and the owner gave a pair to the
farmer at Cronk-y-dooiney whither the survivors had been taken
from the wreck. Eventually all the hedgehogs were given to local
people. From this boxful all the insular hedgehogs of today are
descended. Of moles there are none.

Of the carnivores, the stoat (*Mustela arminea*) is established,
though not common. It is most often seen on the eastern side
around Lonan. It has a far happier time in Man than in
Britain, for there are no game-keepers' boards over here, and the
farmers, knowing its enmity to the rat, look upon the stoat as a
friend. There is a superstition that if one kills a stoat all the
whole stoat family will wreak their revenge on the slayer. The
stoat does not as in Scotland change its colour to white in the

winter, presumably because of the more temperate climate. The Manx name for the stoat is "atthag" and the Manx saying "Daney as atthag" . . . "bold as a stoat" bears witness to its distinctive character. There are no foxes. When the Bible was translated there was no Manx word for "fox", and the translators of the Bible agreed to translate it as "shynnagh", a hawk or kite, and "shynnagh" it remained, and in the Gospel "the foxes have holes and the birds of the air have nests" appears literally as "the hawk has a hole, and the other birds of the air have nests".

The seal must be counted as a Manx wild animal, for rarely are all its beaches and rocks free from the presence of seals. The seal in question is *Phoca vitulina*, the grey seal. The Manx name for the seal is "raun" and many rocks round the coast have names incorporating this word, e.g. Gob-ny-rauna near Ramsey. From time to time very young seals are seen, which suggests that they actually breed in the Island.

Included among occasional mammals must be the porpoise, very often seen leaping and frisking in the larger bays, or near off-shore. The name porpoise is a corruption of the Norman-French "pors-pice" or pigfish. The Manx name is the analogue "muc-varrey", "pig of the sea".

Three bats appear to be indigenous, the pipistrelle (*Vesperugo pipistrellus*), the long-eared bat (*Plecotus auritus*) and Natterer's bat (*Murina nattereri*). The pipistrelle is the most common, and is well spread all over the Island. The long-eared bat is much less common, while Natterer's is a species confined to a few colonies only in the north of the Island.

BIRDS

In any island of the size of the Isle of Man there must be considerable bird interest. The Island is happily placed in the very centre of the British Isles, so that it may be expected to have a very fair selection of birds which are normally residential in the British Isles. But it is surrounded by a considerable breadth of sea, so may be expected to have interesting sea-birds, while its position in a more or less north-south direction lines it up with Iceland, the Faroes, the Hebrides, Biscay and the Iberian peninsula, a convenient guiding line for bird migration. Moreover the Island itself, with its varied surface character of dune, moorland, farm-land, glen and small wood, makes a very usefully differentiated habitat for a large and diverse bird population. It is not surprising, therefore, that bird-watching is a popular recreation in the Island, and that bird-lovers find it an ideal place in which to pursue their observations. It is impossible, of course, to classify birds into regular inhabitants and migrants. There are at each end of the scale some invariable long-distance migrants, and some rare visitors, as well as some ever-present species. The magpie is always with us, in amazing numbers. Bishop Wilson records (*History of the Isle of Man*, 1722): " It is not long since a person more fanciful than prudent or kind to his country brought in a breed of magpies which have increased so rapidly as to become a nuisance ", and that is true today. The blackbirds, thrushes, robins, remain in the same vicinity of the same houses generation after generation.

Two unusual features are (i) the buzzard, which is very common in Lakeland and Northern Ireland and is a superb flier, is only rarely reported here, and (ii) Mother Carey's chicken, or the stormy petrel, which originally gave its name to the Chicken Rock, is only occasionally seen from the steamers.

Further, the woodpecker, reported about seventy years ago as being a visitor, is never seen today. The Island affords good raven territory, and at all times of the year these wonderful birds may be seen. There are at least fifty nesting sites, mostly on inaccessible cliffs, and inland crags high up on the mountains in Sulby Glen. Rooks are abundant, and rookeries well distributed. Carrion crows are very few, but " hoodie " crows are very common and do untold damage among the young lambs on the mountains. Carrion-hoodie hybrids are numerous. The jackdaw is very common, and one of our most beautiful residents is the chough. There was a fear that it was being ousted by the jackdaw, but it still remains one of the most-watched of birds and its numbers are increasing. Jays never come here, but starlings come in great flocks and use the Island in migrating periods. The strident note of the corncrake, formerly frequent, is now rarely heard.

The golden oriole is a rare visitor. Of the finches, the chaffinch and greenfinch are common. The goldfield has increased of late, more specially in the north. The hawfinch and bullfinch are rare. The siskin is not uncommon and the lesser redpoll breeds in the curraghs. Linnets are common, and the twite is often found in the hills. Crossbills are reported from time to time. The yellow bunting is very common, the corn bunting less so. During the winter months composite flocks of linnets, bramblings, siskins, yellow buntings and sparrows may be seen. The snow-bunting is an occasional migrant. The tree-sparrow is rarely seen but the reed-bunting breeds here. The skylark grows less common, and seems largely to have forsaken the farm lands for the heather lands. Meadow and rock pipits are well spread over the Island. Four wagtails, grey, white, pied and yellow, all add greatly to the interest and amusement of the watcher.

Tree-creepers are more often heard than seen; goldcrests are widespread though never abundant. There are four tits, the great, blue, cole, and long-tailed. Waxwings have been reported. A steady stream of migrants passes across the Island from March onwards; chiff-chaff and wheatears lead the way, closely followed by the warblers, willow, sedge, and grasshopper garden and wood, the blackcap, whitethroat, and lesser whitethroat, swallow, house-martin, sand-martin, swift, nightjar and cuckoo. Large numbers of all these, except perhaps whin-chat and redstart, stay to breed. To listen to the " migrants' chorus " in the curraghs during the nesting season is indeed a wonderful experience. The perky little stone-chat is in evidence throughout the year, nesting in any gorse-filled spot. The hoopoe makes an occasional appearance. Kingfishers are reported from time to time on many of the rivers. There are a few black redstarts; and large numbers of field-fare and redwing come in the winter. Missel-thrush, blackbird, and song-thrush occur abundantly. The ring ouzel and dipper are occasionally seen; both have been known to breed on the Island. Robins, wrens and hedge-sparrows are widespread but the gold-crest wren is not common. The long-eared owl and the barn owl are residents, and though the short-eared owl is found there is so far no record of a nesting place. Of the hawks, the peregrine falcon is commonly seen. It is the first bird to appear in Manx records, for in 1406 Henry IV gave the Kingdom of Mann to Sir John Stanley "on the service of rendering two falcons on his paying homage, the same to be repeated to his heirs on their Coronation day". This was continued till 1821, when the Duke of Atholl made the service to George IV. Kestrel and sparrow hawk are common, the merlin falcon less so. The common buzzard and hen-harrier have been reported.

There are two well-filled heronries whose inhabitants are in-creasing. An occasional bittern sometimes may be heard and seen in the north. The spoon-bill is very rarely reported. The mute swan is a resident, and the whooper, and Bewick's swans are regular winter visitors. Geese also are winter visitors, grey-lag white-fronted, bean, pink-footed and barnacle geese all appear. Ducks of varying species may be seen in the sanctuary on Langness most of the year round in their season, mallard, widgeon, teal and shelduck. Gadwall, pintal, shoveller, pochard, tufted scaup, golden-eye, eider, common and velvet scoter, goosander, smew and red-breast merganser all are reported from time to time. The cormorant and shag have several breeding places in the Island. In summer, the gannet can be seen diving and fishing close inshore. Francis Willoughby in 1676 gave the shearwater (Puffinus) the name "Manx" after examining birds nesting on the Calf. Camden in 1586 mentioned the colony, and Challoner again in 1656. In the fifteenth century the tenant of the Calf paid a yearly rent of 500 puffins to the Lord. This practice obtained till the eighteenth century. But, about 1786, rats, from the Russian ship previously mentioned wrecked upon the Calf, completely exterminated the colony, which hasn't returned since. The fulmar petrel was first reported as nesting on the Calf in 1936, and has now become well-established. The great-crested, Slavonian and black-necked grebe are irregular winter visitors. The little grebe is common and nests in various "dubs" in the north. The winter-visiting divers are represented by the northern, the black-throated and the red-throated divers. Wood-pigeons are very common, but stock-doves are not. The rock-dove, formerly common, has disappeared. On the sandy beaches are to be seen many waders. Bar-tailed godwit and whimbrel are seen frequently, black-tailed godwit rarely. Immense flocks of curlew are a common sight, and breed on the moorlands and curraghs. Woodcock and common snipe are plentiful, while the jack-snipe is a winter visitor. Turnstone, knot (infrequently), dunlin, sandpiper, purple sandpiper, little stint, sanderling, ruff, and common sandpiper are all visitors but do not breed here. The redshank is frequent and breeds here, the Iceland redshank is a rare visitor, and the greenshank is occasionally seen. Ringed plover are plentiful and nest here, as also does the lapwing. The golden plover is frequent, the grey plover less so. The oyster-catcher is one of the commonest shore birds. There are several colonies of tern on the northern shore, including the common, Arctic, sandwich, and little species. There are eight species of gull commonly to be seen, the herring gull, great black-backed, lesser black-backed, kittiwake, black-headed, common, and glaucous. The first six breed here. The great skua and Arctic skua are rare visitors. Razor-bill and guillemots breed in large colonies, and also less numerously the black guillemot and puffins, specially on the southern cliffs. The little auk is a less frequent visitor. Red grouse are mostly introduced and are preserved. The pheasant is very rare, but flights of partridge are common. Quail are very occasional but have been reported nesting here.

REPTILES AND AMPHIBIANS

The reptile distribution in the Island follows closely that of Ireland. There are no snakes. The viperine snakes never reached Ireland or Mann. The colubrine snakes represented by the green grass snake in England (not Scotland) did not reach the Island. Of the British lizards, two reached these shores, the common and the sand lizards, and in this respect Mann differs from Ireland, for the sand lizard never reached Ireland. Amphibians are similarly very poorly represented, for there are neither toads nor newts, and the frogs (for which there is no Manx word) are said to have been introduced comparatively recently and are very ill-established.

FISHES

Freshwater fish are singularly specifically few. Only perch occur in some of the northern "dubs" and it is suggested that they are the progeny of the abbey of Mirescogh of Lezayre. The fishes that have arrived by sea are in good supply. Salmon run up the Santan, Glass, Dhoo and Sulby rivers in plentiful numbers, and the Board of Agriculture and Fisheries have a breeding station at Maughold from which these rivers are re-stocked. The brown trout, too (generically indistinguishable from the sea trout, and from which doubtless it is derived), is found in goodly quantity in all the streams, and though it never reaches any great size it affords, at half a pound, a very pleasant exercise of skill for the fly-fisher. The two-spined and three-spined sticklebacks (*Gastrosteus aculeatus* and *G. pungitius*), indifferent to fresh- or sea-water, are common everywhere, while the eel finds its way here in quantities, from its West Indian breeding ground and as the larval sliver crosses the shallow water on the beaches, gives great joy to the children.

Of the land invertebrates very little interest has ever been taken in the mollusca, or the spiders. After ornithological interests, probably those of the entomologists are of the next importance. Of the insects, there had been little work recorded other than for the Lepidoptera and Coleoptera. The beetles recorded were published in the *North-western Naturalist* (1945-46). The number is few compared with those of Ulster, Galloway, Cumberland and North Wales. The Lepidoptera, too, are disappointing. 340 species have been recorded, but some are very doubtful. A careful survey is needed. In the British Isles there are about 2,000 species. Of these there are 68 species of butterfly; only 16 have been recorded in the Island. This is very probably due to the fact that there is no calcareous soil formation in the Island, and therefore no calcareous flora, while in Britain a large number of butterfly caterpillars depend for their food on such plants. Among the moths the Island appears to have two peculiar species, the grey and tawny shears *Dianthaecia caesia*, and *D. caphsophila*.

Of the extinct mammals, the red deer was once very common and was transported to the Calf. Its history goes back to the Neolithic era and its bones are found frequently in the kitchen-middens of Neolithic and Celtic house sites. But of much greater interest is the occurrence of many skeletons of the giant Irish deer, *Cervus gigantaeus*, formerly more picturesquely the Irish " elk ". It appears to have been a giant fallow deer, which spread across Western Asia, central Europe and the British Isles in Pleistocene times. Its fossil remains suggest that it arose in the far north, was driven south by the glacial period, and then followed the vegetation north again as the ice receded. It was a magnificent creature. A good sample stood about 6 feet high at the withers and had a horn span of about 12 feet. The Museum specimen should be seen, as a good example, by all interested visitors. The first record of the finding of one such deer is that of Feltham in 1798 (*Tour of the Isle of Man*). He mentions there the " bones of elks or segns found near St. John's ". The most famous skeleton was that found at Ballaugh curragh in 1815. It was assembled by Thomas Kewish, the local blacksmith, temporarily employed to dig marl at Ballaterson. There was some trouble, since the skeleton in part lay under the boundary of Thomas Corlett's property, and he had a conscience about allowing any skeleton being dug up on his side. However, he was prevailed upon to allow the digging to proceed and, as a result, parts of several skeletons were found. Kewish was able to assemble a complete skeleton from these *disjecta membra*, all but the pelvis. However, being a man of resource, he bought the carcase of an old farm horse of approximately the same size and so completed the skeleton! The carcase of the old horse was burnt, in order to achieve the dark brown tint of the remainder of the bones. The skeleton was then exhibited as a " peep-show " in Ballaugh.

At this juncture the Duke of Atholl heard of the find, and claimed the skeleton as his property. Kewish ignored the claim in sturdy Manx fashion and announced that he meant to exhibit the peep-show in Douglas. He procured two carts; one, ostentatiously carrying a mass of bones and antlers, he sent to Douglas, pursued by the Duke's henchmen, while on the other he loaded the covered skeleton, which he sent aboard a boat in Ramsey harbour, and dispatched it to Whitehaven, where it was for some time on show, but the Duke had considerable local influence in Whitehaven, and Kewish had to close down. He compromised with the Duke for £70, and certain " expenses ". The Duke presented the skeleton to Edinburgh Museum, where it was exhibited with the inscription:

EXTINCT IRISH ELK
Megaceros Hibernicus (Desmarest)
of post-Pliocene Age
From Kirk Balaff, Isle of Man
Presented by His Grace the Duke of Atholl

The specimen aroused the interest of the famous French Zoologist Cuvier, who had a plate made (*Ossements fossiles,* vol. ix, plate viii), in which the horse's pelvis is painfully obvious. The Edinburgh skeleton has since been corrected. There is a good specimen in Leeds Museum found near Peel, and that in the Manx Museum was found at Close-y-garey, Poortown, German. The skeletons are usually found in Marl layers, in hollows which would seem to have been the beds of " dubs " and Reid suggested that the creatures with their terrific overweight of horn had approached the treacherous edges of these pools, fringed round with soft turf, and the water covered with a mass of potamogeton, chara, and other weeds; they must have plunged in head-first with no hope of escape.

Mention must be made too of the famous Manx tailless cat, now so famous the world over. The true Manx cat has only a tuft of hair in the place " where his tail belongs to be ". It is certainly not indigenous but is very well established. It has important skeletal differences from the normal domestic cat. The hind legs are considerably longer in proportion, giving the stance a hare-like appearance. In fighting it springs over its opponent and attempts to use all four sets of claws simultaneously. Continuous inter-breeding with the domestic cat has produced a race that is not truly tailless, and inter-breeding of two tailless specimens always produces tailed, part-tailed and tailless specimens. The true Manx cat has always a much reduced coccyx of vertebrae, completely covered and not showing externally. Tailless breeds of cats occur all across the Asia-Europe land mass, and seem to have arisen in the East Indies. It seems very probable that the breed was introduced to the Island by some sailor who brought home a couple of kittens as domestic pets.

The Manx sheep or Loghtan is a very distinctive and distinguished creature. The male is a handsome fellow with four long recurved horns. The female has two somewhat shorter. The wool is reddish brown in colour, and of excellent texture. For generations it was made into Manx homespun cloth of very good wearing quality, left undyed. In shape the sheep is somewhat lean and has a narrow section of somewhat goat-like form. It is exceedingly active and agile, almost impossible to keep in fields, and hence presumably unpopular as a farm animal. These sheep, formerly very generally distributed over the Island, are now reduced to a single flock of very modest dimension. There is also connected with the Island a breed of tailless fowls. In these days of competitive egg-production they are in danger of extinction, although they are often to be seen in the old-fashioned farms. They are apparently the remnant of a Scandinavian species also found in the Scottish Isles.

CHAPTER THIRTEEN

TRADE, INDUSTRY AND COMMERCE

THE structure of the Manx economy has changed greatly over the past hundred years. Before about 1870, as far as most of the population was concerned, the Island subsisted on the two staple industries of agriculture and fishing, and the land and sea were not always bountiful in providing for a growing population. Mining was an insular industry from early times; it reached its zenith during the second half of the nineteenth century but was already in its death-throes by the early decades of the twentieth. But, by the 1870s, changes were already stirring, as workers in the industrial midlands and the north of England found, for the first time, that they were able to save sufficient from their wages for an annual holiday, and once the steamers were operating, many visitors found Douglas to their liking. In the succeeding decades, the Island was vigorously promoted as a holiday centre to such good effect that tourism was the Island's chief money-earner for many years. The fact that the industry no longer holds that position today is not so much due to that industry's decline (although it has declined to a certain extent) as to the rise of another—the financial sector.

Through the 1950s, despite a post-war revival in its tourist industry, the Island suffered a difficult time. Due to a lack of alternative employment, the 'off-season' eight months from September to May was annually a time of high unemployment. Many Manxmen spent the winters away from their families, working on English farms, and more than seven thousand people actually emigrated from the Island during that decade. To alleviate this situation, the Manx Government instituted its policy of low direct taxation and incentives for new industries. This policy has had three main consequences:

(i) an influx of new residents, with a consequent expansion in the building trade;

(ii) a growth of light manufacturing industries, providing a further diversification of employment;

(iii) a large increase in the number of company registrations and the establishment of the Island as an offshore financial centre, to the extent that this sector now produces a far greater revenue than tourism.

Inevitably, this train of developments has wrought changes, both on the Island and on its community, and all of the changes have not found favour with all of the people. But, undeniably, the Government's policy has been beneficial to many people. The new diversity of employment has brought a year-round stability which was not there before, and the Island's economy has never been stronger.

In order to appreciate the present diversity of the Manx economy and the way in which it has evolved, it is perhaps best to consider each main sector of Manx industry and commerce in order of antiquity.

AGRICULTURE AND FISHING

Agriculture is the oldest of industries, having been pursued in the Island since Neolithic times. In the Neolithic graves of the Meayll Circle were found grains of wheat and barley closely akin to modern crops, and of a similar size and weight. The Celts, as we have already noted, had their prosperous farms and cattle pens, and smaller holdings. The Scandinavian invaders came to plunder but stayed to farm. The arrival of the Cistercian monks, too, we have seen, improved the Island's farming out of all recognition, and we have noted the great value of Cistercian wool. Bishop Meyrick (1590) left it on record that "the Island is rich in flocks and corn and more through the industry of man than kindliness of the soil", and this after the closing of the abbey.

Less than fifty years later, Blundell wrote that "the Island grows large areas of hemp and flax". Many of the old farms still have remains of the flax-retting ponds, where the soft tissues were rotted away to leave the flax fibres. Challoner in 1660 reported that the Island produced good crops of wheat, rye and barley, and especially oats, this providing the chief "bread-corn" of the people.

Root crops do not appear in the Island records till the latter half of the seventeenth century but are widely grown today. So far as can be ascertained, the system of farming during the seventeenth and succeeding centuries was to grow corn crops for several years on the same ground until the soil became exhausted, then to put the land to a "grass fallow" for several years and graze it, before once more ploughing up for corn crops. The first sound farmer after the days of the Cistercian seems to have been Bishop Wilson, who set his own farm at Bishopscourt in good order and then helped his people to carry out such reforms in their methods as he had found beneficial.

There was always a great mass of land impossible to cultivate —the sandy stretches in the north, the wetlands of the curraghs, and the acidic, peaty mountain lands. The upland farms were taken very high into the hills, well above the 600-foot contour which is about the limit of successful farming. But today these farms stand as abandoned "tholtans", surrounded by pitiful little fields to which gorse and heather have returned. Many were deserted around the middle of the nineteenth century, when their holders left to seek their fortunes overseas.

During the last century, much curragh land has been drained, and the sandy soils of the north have been improved by modern agricultural methods. A great step forward was the formation on the Island in 1807 by John Christian Curwen of a branch of the Workington Agricultural Society, which later in the century became the Royal Manx Agricultural Society, whose annual shows encouraged the competitive spirit and have brought the industry right up to date. After World War I, the former prisoner-of-war camp at Knockaloe Farm, Patrick, was taken over by the insular Board of Agriculture to become an experimental farm under government control. This has been most successful, and the establishment now provides the Manx farmer with the most modern and scientific advice and assistance.

The history of the Island has resulted in a large number of small farms of about 50-100 acres, and this has remained so until very recent years, when there has been a tendency towards amalgamation to form larger units. During the past three decades, there has been a steady reduction in the proportion of cultivated land devoted to arable crops, and a corresponding increase in the acreage of permanent grassland, to which the soil and climate of the Island are particularly suited. The farming industry today is inevitably linked with the tourist industry. It provides milk, cream, butter, eggs, flour and meat to feed resident and visitor alike, and there is a steady demand for Manx cheese of the Cheshire, Cheddar and Gloucester varieties. Manx honey is a popular and well-established product, probably due to the vast areas of heather-land.

In bygone times, fishing in the Island went hand-in-hand with farming. Observers of Island life down the centuries have emphasized fish as a principal constituent of the staple diet. Many of the men divided their time between the boats and the farms, depending on the season and the jobs to be done in each sphere, and usually spent the winter months on the land. The first record of the industry in 1610 demanded that all "Scowtes" going to the fishing should be of four tons burthen. Bishop Wilson says that the boats of his time were smaller, of two tons. The last Derby record gives their number as 200 in 1797, while in 1839 the Duke of Atholl estimated that there were 490 boats of about eight tons. At that time the boats were mostly single-masted craft carrying a full-length square sail. They were followed by " Dandy-rigged " boats, and later still by the Cornish-type " nickeys ". The boats gradually increased in size till they were half-decked and could stay out for longer periods and extend considerably the fishing areas. The boats were locally built, mainly at Castletown and Port St. Mary, though all the port towns had their yards.

But, as the years passed, and both fishing and farming developed and became more complex and more demanding of its labour force, the descendants of the old-time crofter-fishermen were forced to make a choice between working on the sea and working on the land. And when Manxmen were faced with that decision, most chose the land. Consequently, the Manx fishing fleet today is greatly depleted, compared with what it once was, and at the height of the herring season the Manx boats are heavily outnumbered by those from Scotland and Ireland. In the time of the Derbys, Derbyhaven was the chief fishing harbour, but today the industry is fairly well divided between Douglas and Peel, with a good number of boats still using Ramsey. Strict conservation measures are now applied to the Manx herring fishery, with a seven-week closed season during the autumn spawning period and a strict quota system for the rest of the year.

The kippering industry, once centred on Derbyhaven, has now long been established at Peel, and the Manx kipper retains its justly earned fame. It is illegal to apply any dye in the Manx kippering process, and the curing is still done over smouldering fires of oak wood chips. The work of the kippering houses is a sight which all visitors should see. Recent years have seen the rise of a new shellfish industry, especially for escallops (tanrogans), of which there are several colonies around the Manx coast. This industry is also based at Peel and there is a steady demand for its products. But the fishing industry, like farming, now provides a very small part of the Island's income.

MINING AND QUARRYING

It is not known when mining started in the Isle of Man. However, it was the first *recorded* industry, for in 1246 Harald Olaffson granted a charter to the monks of Furness Abbey, allowing them " the full use of all mines that may be found within my kingdom ". (Incidentally, this charter is the document that shows Harald's seal to have been the ship emblem, and not the " three legs of Man ", thus making 1246 the earliest possible date for the adoption of the three legs as the king's emblem. *See* " three legs of Man ".)

In 1292, Edward I granted to John Comyn, Earl of Buchan, leave to dig lead on the Calf for the purpose of " covering eight turrets of his castle of Crigelton and Galloway ". In the title deed of the gift of the Kingdom of Mann to Sir John Stanley, Henry IV " gives all into hys hande, royalties, hundreds, wapentakes, sea-wrecks, mines of lead and iron ". Captain Edward Christian reported to the Great Stanley that the lead from Bradda cliffs contained much silver, and Blundell prophesied that " it will be experienced hereafter that Mann is far richer underground than above ".

A fruitless search for coal was begun in the sixteenth century, and further borings were made in the nineteenth century in various parts of the northern and southern plains but nowhere were there any seams approaching workable size. During this search for coal, salt was discovered in the Triassic marls underlying the glacial drift of the northern plain. The salt was dissolved in water at an extraction site near the Point of Ayre and the brine was piped along the shore to the salt works (which is now a shipyard) at Ramsey. But the end product was more expensive than imported salt, and so the enterprise did not survive beyond the middle of the present century.

The Manx mining industry entered its heyday towards the middle of the nineteenth century, when operations at the two main centres, Laxey and Foxdale, were in full swing. The Laxey mines were opened about 1750 and were entered from the surface by adits, and not from shafts. They proved to be so productive that, in 1852, £80 shares in the Laxey Mining Company were selling at £1,100. In 1854 the great wheel-pump known as the " Lady Isabella " was built. The wheel of this pump, still one of the " sights " of the Island, achieved fame as " the largest wheel in the world ". It was designed by a Manxman, Robert Casement, and its purpose was to pump water from the lead mines. Its axle was ordered from the Mersey Iron Works, but the rest of the wheel and its assembly and erection were the work of Gelling's Iron Foundry of Douglas. The wheel has a diameter of 72½ feet, a width of 6 feet; it is a back-shot wheel, its water coming from a cistern on the hillside and passing through a circular stone tower to the top. Its crank worked a long rod, driving a piston pump working at a depth of over 1,000 feet and raising 250 gallons of water per minute. Today the wheel serves no useful purpose but is maintained in working condition as a tourist attraction.

The Foxdale vein runs almost due east and west, crossing the Castletown–St. John's road in the village of Foxdale. The derelict shafts run for three miles along this vein which, like the Laxey intrusions, yielded lead and silver. In all, thirteen shafts were sunk. The most westerly was Beckwith's, above Glen Rushen, sunk in 1881 following the discovery by a man driving a haycart of a mass of galena in the heather. The shaft reaches to a depth of 1,100 feet, which is 500 feet below sea level. Between Beckwith's and the main road are three more shafts, " Cross's " (only sunk 600 feet) and two " Dixon's ". The most productive mine, which remained open till 1910, was that in the village of Foxdale. Here there are four shafts with cross-galleries and the workings reach to a depth of 2,000 feet. Next in order comes

" Hodgson's shaft " (also known as " Faragher's " or " Louisa ") and further east, near the Eary Dam, the East Foxdale group, which marks the end of the lode. Foxdale lead contained a good admixture of silver. In 1894, for example, 4,800 tons of ore were raised, which produced 85,522 ounces of silver of value £39,000.

The Manx mining industry went into its fatal decline when the richer lodes had been worked out and operations became uneconomic in the face of competition from the richer ores being mined elsewhere. But now that those ores are themselves becoming depleted and metal prices have risen, renewed interest has been shown in the Island's metal deposits. Prospecting licences have been issued and surveys carried out but, to date, there has been no move towards a revival of actual mining. If such a move does come, it is to be hoped that some method is found of avoiding the unsightly waste tips such as still blot the landscape around Foxdale.

In bygone days, all building stone was quarried locally, and each type of stone gave its characteristic colouring to the various localities; the grey-blue limestone to Castletown, the rich red sandstone to Peel, the light-coloured shale to Douglas and the darker type to Ramsey. The limestone quarry at Scarlett produced the stone for Castle Rushen, King William's College, numerous other buildings, and for the pier extensions at Douglas and the quays of all the other fishing ports. Further west is the quarry producing the black " Poylvaish marble ". There is no building stone quarried today but the quarry at Ballasalla still produces limestone for the making of agricultural lime. Over the years, the Highway Board has obtained roadstone from four main quarries, working the granite outcrops at the Dhoon, Foxdale and Santan, and the intrusive gabbro at Poortown, near Peel, where the modern crushing plant now provides for most of the Island's needs.

TOURISM AND TRANSPORT

The development of the Island as a tourist centre has been remarkable and has naturally been linked with the development of shipping services. At the end of the eighteenth century, the only way to get to the Isle of Man was to enquire at one of the north-country ports if there were any merchant about to transport merchandise to the Island. There was no regular service until, in 1819, a weekly steamer service was begun between Douglas and Whitehaven, but the vessel was small, uncomfortable and slow. About this time, the *Robert Bruce* ran a weekly return route, Greenock–Portpatrick–Douglas–Liverpool, but by 1830 James Little of Liverpool had started a thrice-weekly service to Douglas. Of his boats, the *Superb* was the most interesting, and later achieved fame by becoming the first steamboat to reach Australia. In 1832 another Liverpool company began operating the *St. George,* which was a marked improvement over any previous boat. But when she had driven all other boats from the route, the company replaced her with the *Sophia,* a miserable little steamer running twice a week only.

Douglas merchants, appalled by this service, encouraged Mark Cosnahan, member of a well-known Santan family, to build a boat. He built the *Victoria,* ran her for two months as a private venture, then offered her to the Douglas merchants in £50 shares, with each shareholder having the right to three free return trips to Liverpool. Unfortunately the merchants did not rise to the occasion, so Cosnahan sold her to Sir John Ross, who needed a strongly built steamship to explore the Northwest Passage. and she was ultimately abandoned in the Arctic. Thereupon a Manx company was formed, eventually to become the Isle of Man Steam Packet Company, and with capital of £7,000 they built the *Mona's Isle,* with accommodation for fifteen first-class and seventeen steerage passengers and cargo. Her funnel was red, with a wide black band at the top, and these were the company's colours thenceforth, to be copied much later by the Cunard line. Return fares of 5s. (cabin class) and 3s. (steerage) were steadily reduced to 2s. 6d. (with lunch) for cabin class and 6d. for steerage. To compete with the *Mona's Isle,* the former Liverpool company brought back the *St. George* but, fortunately for the Manx company, she was wrecked on the Conister Rock in a gale. Her crew was saved by the Douglas lifeboat, in whose complement was Sir William Hillary, founder of the Royal National Lifeboat Institution.

Thenceforth, the growth of the Steam Packet Company and the growth of Douglas went hand-in-hand. As more boats were added to the fleet, so more hotels and boarding houses were added to the town. Over the years, as older boats were scrapped and replaced by new ones, several of their names have been used over again. Thus five ships have now borne the name *Mona's Isle. Ben-my-Chree, Mona's Queen* and *Tynwald* have also been used five times each, *King Orry* and *Mona* have been used four times, and *Manx Maid, Manxman* and *Lady of Mann* twice. The notable exception from the list of duplications is *Ellan*

Vannin, which was the name of the little steamer overwhelmed in a storm near the Mersey Bar in 1909, lost with all passengers and crew, and about which there is now a well-known folk-song. Obviously the name could not be used again. The present passenger fleet consists of four side-loading car ferries of up to 3,000 tons and three passenger vessels operating services to Liverpool, Fleetwood, Ardrossan, Llandudno, Belfast and Dublin. In 1977-8 Douglas harbour was converted to handle the modern "roll-on, roll-off" car ferries, and a new company announced plans to begin a service to Heysham.

The early rise in passenger traffic was spectacular. From 25,000 visitors a year in the 1830s, the number of arrivals had reached 90,000 by 1873 and attained the record total of 634,000 in 1913. There followed a decline between the wars but annual arrivals again exceeded 600,000 in the years 1947-9. Since then, there has been a decline in the numbers arriving by sea (due perhaps to fundamental changes in holidaying habits and to the cost of bringing a car to the Island) followed by a levelling out to a plateau of about 350,000 summertime arrivals. When airline arrivals are taken into account, the total number of visitors to the Island in the season is around half a million. Air travel did not really begin to influence traffic patterns until after the war. The modern Ronaldsway airport was developed from the war-time Royal Naval air station, and today there are regular services to and from London, Liverpool, Manchester and Belfast.

At the time of the Island's discovery as a potential holiday centre, Manx roads left much to be desired. Outside the towns and larger villages, the scattered components of the Manx community were served (if that is the word) by a network of unsurfaced pack-roads that had scarcely changed in centuries. Consequently, road travel was slow and uncomfortable. And so the arrival of increasing numbers of visitors wishing to see something of the Island, together with the potential for bulk goods traffic from the still-flourishing mines, brought just the right conditions for the development of the railways.

There were two railways in the Island. The Isle of Man Steam Railway had two lines, one from Douglas to Peel (with a later branch-line from St. John's to Ramsey) and the other from Douglas to Port Erin via Castletown, but only the Port Erin line now exists. The Manx Electric Railway connects Douglas and Ramsey, with a branch-line from Laxey to the top of Snaefell. Both railways are of narrow gauge and both are now operated by the Manx Government. The steam railway is of great historical interest. The company was the first in the British Isles to employ automatic coupling and the first to use electric lighting in the carriages. The locomotives were 2-4-0 tank engines by Beyer Peacock and Company of Gorton, Manchester.

The initiative for forming the company was taken in 1870 by twelve Island businessmen, who brought in Sir William Pender, M.P., from London to organize it. He said he could not succeed without capital of £300,000 and of that only £30,000 was forthcoming from the Island. The remainder, however, was subscribed from Britain, mainly by the Duke of Sutherland. The Peel line was opened in 1873, the Castletown line a year later, and the first three locomotives were named *Sutherland, Derby* and *Pender.* When the subscribed capital began to run low, the proposed line to Ramsey was abandoned, and the southern line continued to Port Erin instead. This aroused anger in the northern town, whose inhabitants resolved to build their own line, which they did in 1879, linking up with the Peel line at St. John's. The Ramsey line ran as a separate venture till 1904, when the two companies amalgamated. A branch-line built to serve the Foxdale mines could not survive the collapse of the mining industry. The growth of road transport dealt a serious blow to the Isle of Man Steam Railway and, since 1965, only the Douglas-Port Erin line has been retained.

The Manx Electric Railway runs through spectacular scenery and is never far from the coast. The line from Douglas to Laxey was opened in 1894, the branch to Snaefell summit in 1896 and the northern line reached Ramsey in 1898. In 1956 it was realised that the line could not be run at a profit. The shortness of the season, coupled with the high costs of maintenance, motive power and wages, made a wind-up of the company inevitable. The insular Government has managed the operation ever since, but not without repeated threats of closure.

Another " archaic " form of transport is provided by the horse-drawn trams of Douglas, which still run along the promenade in summer and celebrated their centenary in 1976. The only Island-wide system of public transport today is provided by the bus services of the Government-owned Isle of Man National Transport Ltd.

MANUFACTURE AND COMMERCE

The composition of Manx industry has become greatly diversified over the past twenty years. Some of the older crafts survive, though now in modernized form, and newer industries have become established as a result of the Manx Government's policy of attracting suitable light industries to the Island. Thus one of the oldest cottage industries, weaving, still continues but is now centred on the two highly mechanized mills at Laxey and St. John's. The formerly water-driven mills are now electrically powered, and products in the Manx tartan are particularly popular. Brewing continues to be based on two breweries at Castletown and Douglas (though there were twenty-three Manx breweries operating in 1837) and Manx *jough* (beer) remains a popular beverage. The building trade, responding to the influx of new residents and new industries, went through a marked expansion phase in the late '60s and early '70s but this has now levelled off. Closely allied to this trade are brick manufacture at Peel and gravel extraction on the Ayres.

Of the newer industries, the largest field of employment is in engineering, much of which is based on specially built industrial estates at Douglas, Union Mills, Ronaldsway and Jurby, the latter occupying buildings of the former R.A.F. station. The largest single employer on the Island is the Ronaldsway Aircraft Company, which employs more than five hundred people and exports aircraft ejector seats to most of the developed countries of the world. However, most concerns are much smaller than this, and products include shoes, carpets, hosiery and general engineering products.

This diversification of industry has been encouraged by the Manx Government's policy of maintaining a low rate of income tax and providing incentives, in the form of grants and low-interest loans, for the establishment of new industries. Indeed, as has been pointed out, the policy of attracting new residents and new industries was specifically devised to revive the Island's depressed economy of the 1950s, to relieve its high level of unemployment and to reverse the marked decline in population experienced during that decade. In these aims, the policy has been successful but the Manx Government has not been without its critics, such as those who feel that the Island's population (currently about 60,000) may increase further to an undesirable extent and that the indigenous Manx population may be swamped by a renewed influx of new residents.

But, paradoxically, the sector of the economy which now produces the biggest contribution to the Manx exchequer is one which is totally invisible to the casual observer. This is the financial sector and is the direct result of the Manx Government's policy to establish the Island as an offshore financial centre. Attracted by the Island's low taxation, there has been a phenomenal rise in the number of company registrations in recent years, and the growth of commercial banking, finance and insurance services based in the Island has been such that this sector now contributes more than a quarter of the Island's total income and raises almost twice as much revenue as the tourist industry itself. And today the tourist industry—for so many years the Island's main source of wealth—must vie with manufacturing for second place in the league of Manx revenue sources.

CHAPTER FOURTEEN

MISCELLANEOUS MATTERS OF INTEREST

THE THREE LEGS OF MAN

VISITORS TO the Island are always much interested in the national badge of three legs, and always ask how it came to be. The question cannot be definitely answered. The design is obviously derived from the so-called Greek cross or "gammadion", a cross with equal arms each bent at right angles. It occurs frequently in India, where it is an anti-Brahmin sign, known as a "Swastika" or "lucky cross". It is also a well-known heraldic sign, in which case it is usually a "fylfot" or design used to "fill the foot" of a shield, window or panel. In its three- and four-armed form it occurs in Neolithic, Celtic and Scandinavian stone carvings. It was frequently used as a decoration by the Romans, and many Roman ornaments discovered in Britain bear the device. But the country which very early incorporated the three legs into its national badge was Sicily.

In the Scandinavian design a three-armed device of this shape was used to depict Thor's thunderbolt, while in the Sicilian legend it represented the wheel of the sun, for the Greeks, and indeed Sicily was the "land of the sun". This is almost certainly why the Sicilian device was booted and spurred, with the feet "following the sun". The vexed questions are "How, why, and when, was it adopted as the national badge of the Kingdom of Mann?" There are two alternative possibilities, (1) that the source was Sicilian and (2) that the source was Scandinavian. In this respect the date of its appearance might be helpful. It is known that the seal of Harald Olaffson on his charters of 1245 and 1246 had the device of a ship as his seal-sign. The three legs therefore must have been adopted after that date.

The earliest representations of the three legs occur (*a*) on the Manx Sword of State and (*b*) on the Maughold Village Cross. Unfortunately neither of these can be definitely dated. The Manx Sword of State is traditionally the sword of Olaf Godredson, used by him in his fighting against the Moors in Spain, which would require a date of about 1230. Experts at the British Museum give the sword date as about 1250. This very sword, incidentally, is carried before the Governor in the Tynwald procession at St. John's on Tynwald Day. The first definitely dated representation of the three legs as the national crest occurs in the shield of Henry de Bello Monte, Lord of Man (1310), and again by the Earl of Moray, in 1313. If the date of the sword is accurate (and it must be allowed that sword dates are often as romantic as the swords themselves) then the "three legs" appeared from some unknown Scandinavian source by way of Godredson. The other theory is that it came through Alexander III of Scotland, who before winning Mann from the Vikings in 1266 had been in attendance at the English Court, where preparations had been going on for the enforcement of the claims of Henry III's son Edmund as King of Sicily. Edmund had already adopted the badge, and when Alexander came into possession of this new "Island Kingdom", he may quite possibly have used the badge of the Mediterranean Island. The evidence of the Maughold Cross is indefinite. The "three legs" are there, but the cross itself has been several times repaired. The lower part of the shaft is older than the upper part, which is adjudged to be of the fourteenth century. The upper part is decorated with a "Tudor" rose pattern. But this was not necessarily of Tudor period, for many double rose designs were known much earlier. If therefore the upper and lower parts of the shaft were of the same age, the somewhat later date of Alexander III might be the more satisfactory period. The motto *Quocunque jeceris stabit* (It will stand wheresoever you throw it) made its first appearance on Manx coins dated 1668, but here the word "jeceris" appears as "gesseris", an obvious phonetic misprint.

The description of the armorial bearings is given as:

"Gules, three legs armed, conjoined in fesse at the upper

part of the thighs, flexed in triangle, proper, garnished and spurred, or."

Unfortunately it has never been laid down which way the three legs are supposed to be running, but it is always assumed that this is a sun sign, and the three legs are "following the sun", from left to right.

THE MUTINY OF THE "BOUNTY"

The Mutiny of the *Bounty* (1787) has very close and interesting relation with the Isle of Man. Three of the chief characters of the drama had Island connections, Fletcher Christian, leader of the mutiny, Peter Heywood, very unjustly condemned to death as a mutineer, which he certainly was not, and Captain William Bligh, whose stern, harsh discipline was the prime cause of the mutiny.

Peter Heywood was Manx by birth, son of Deemster Heywood, and born at the Nunnery June 6th, 1773. He was baptized at Braddan, where his name is to be seen in the register. He was only fourteen years old at the time of the mutiny. He was not allowed to travel in Bligh's boat, and was not taken on to Pitcairn Island by Christian, but was left in Tahiti, from where he was arrested by the Navy. He was described by Bligh in the indictment as . . . "fair complexion, much tattooed, on his right leg by the 'three legs of Mann', as on the coins". After his trial and condemnation his sister Nessie made her epic journey to beg the life of her brother through Queen Charlotte. She was successful and her petition was granted. Peter was reprieved, forgiven, and taken back into the service, in which he rose to the rank of Captain, with a very honourable record. His only part in the drama was the complete inability of a mere boy to alter the course of events set in motion by his seniors Bligh and Christian. Captain William Bligh by a curious coincidence had been married in 1781 in the Island at Kirk Onchan to Miss Betty Betham, daughter of the first Customs Officer under the newly established British Excise in the Island. The marriage register reads:

Mr. William Bligh and Miss Elizabeth Betham of the town of Douglas were married in this church by licence this Fourth day of February anno predicto, by me Thomas Quayle, vicar. This marriage was solemnised between us, William Bligh: Elizabeth Bligh, late Betham.

In presence of Alexander McNaight; Chas. Colven.

The Inner
Harbour,
Douglas

The Legislative
Building,
Douglas

The fourteenth-century Maughold Cross

Port St. Mary
Harbour

Contorted strata on the east coast

The Laxey Wheel

Langness Lighthouse

The northern
hills under snow

The Blighs' daughter was baptized in St. Matthew's Church, Douglas, in 1784. Bligh met the Heywoods when he visited Douglas for his wedding and offered to take Peter as midshipman, under his wing.

Fletcher Christian, the master's mate, was a young man of good education, a member of the famous Christian family of Milntown, Lezayre, who also owned estates in Cumberland. His father, Charles Christian, of Brigham, Cumberland, was third son of John Christian of Milntown. A man of rugged character, Bligh's oppression drove him to desperation. After setting Bligh and his party adrift, Christian took over the command. He left some of the mutineers, and Heywood, at Tahiti, while he himself, the rest of the crew, and some Tahitians set sail and reached Pitcairn Island where they scuttled the *Bounty*. He was murdered some years later.

THE MANX LANGUAGE

The Manx language is allied alike to Highland Gaelic and Irish. Anyone versed in either of these three languages can reasonably well follow the others. Until the eighteenth century Manx was an entirely spoken language. The only known printed text before 1700 appears to have been the ballad "Manannan Beg Mac-y-leirr, my slane Coontey jeh Ellan Vannin", to which Train had access, in an ancient copy. Even in the eighteenth century there were only the Bible and Prayer Book in print. Dr. Kelly's (the first) Grammar was published in 1804 and Cregeen's Dictionary in 1835. From time to time ballads and stories have been written down and printed, and a few English poems have been translated and published.

As in other Celtic tongues there is a system of mutable consonants, e.g. "ch" changed to "h" and "j": "Chiarn" a lord: "ehiarn" his lord: and "nyn jiarn" our lord. Nouns are masculine or feminine, never neuter. Adjectives follow the nouns and are declined with them, e.g. for plurals "dooiney mooar" the big man, "deiney mooarey" the big men.

It seems unlikely that the Manx language can now be anything more than a subject for students and scholars. The Manx Language Society, *Yn Cheshaght Ghailckagh,* is active in promoting the language by means of publications and the sponsoring of bilingual street signs. The language is perpetuated in personal and place names, and many proverbs are used by the Manx folk. Many Manx children can recite the Lord's Prayer in Manx, and greetings are often exchanged in the country in Manx. From time to time Divine Service is said and sermons preached in Manx, but this is almost entirely "read Manx". Manx was the official language of·the Law Courts till the early nineteenth century. John Cosnahan is recorded in 1800 as the first Deemster who could speak no Manx, yet he came of a long line of vicars of Santan and Braddan who for generations had preached fluently in Manx. The S.P.C.K. in a pamphlet published in 1764 said: "Of a population of 20,000 the greater part speak no English." In 1875 there were 190 who spoke no English, and 12,340 who spoke both Manx and English. Since 1901 there has been none who speak only Manx.

MANX LAW, AND LAND TENURE

As the Island has its own legislature, it will have points of difference from the laws of Great Britain. Such differences may be theoretical or practical. The Land Tenure system, though virtually the same as that in Britain, has a very different history. When in 1422 Sir John Stanley became "king" he allowed the lands to remain in the possession of all landowners who swore fealty (which was the thin end of the feudal wedge) while confiscating the lands of those like the abbots of Whithorn, Furness, Bangor and Saball who failed to appear. Their lands he converted into "lord's land", a still more feudal action. However, the allodia of the resident Manx were allowed, though through the ages constant attempts were made to trespass on their rights. Still, every Manxman hung on to his quasi-customary freehold. He could sell his land without any scrip, by attending a Court Baron and resign his claim by handing over a straw as token of the sale. Various lords imposed various "customs" on the landowners. There was the ancient custom of Watch and Ward for example; lord's tithes were imposed as well as those of the church; work in fencing and road-making were demanded; nobody might leave the Island without the lord's leave; the eldest sons of farmers might be detached to work on the farms of those in arrears with their customs. The lord demanded that farmers should plough and manure their lands (good husbandry, but bad "freehold"!). All such moves were obviously attempts to make free-holders into tenants.

In the Act of Revestment when the Crown took over the lordship, all lands were freed from lord's rents. The lord still claims ownership of the land, but grants complete freehold. As a result transfer of land is a cheap and easy process, compared with

Britain. All original deeds affecting real estate are lodged with the registry of deeds, where they are always readily accessible. Some interesting facts are extant with regard to mines, minerals and quarries. On such the tenant must pay royalties. He may use a quarry without payment for his own immediate use, or for giving stone to his friends. But he must allow the lord to quarry on his land, should the lord so desire. Moreover he must allow anybody to use his quarry free of charge for their own personal use, free of all charge other than payment for damage. Metals have much higher royalties.

Deeds in the Island must be signed, but not sealed. Interest above the rate of $12\frac{1}{2}$ per cent is illegal and the Island's history of low interest rates undoubtedly accounts for the complete absence of pawnbrokers.

Some interesting old laws remained unrepealed until recent times. Among such may be quoted a law of 1577: " If any man take a woman by constraint or force, against her will, if she be a wife, he must suffer the law; but if she be a maid, the Deemster shall give her a sword, a rope and a ring. Then shall she have her choice to cut off his head with the sword, to hang him with the rope, or to wed him with the ring." Tradition has it that another ancient law gave Manxmen the right to shoot any Scotsman on sight. Needless to say, such laws have not been invoked in living memory, and much of the ' dead wood ' on the Manx statute book was pruned out in 1977.

SPORT

Little has been recorded as to mediaeval sport. There are records among ecclesiastical papers suggesting that bear and bull baiting were indulged in. During the Atholl régime purr-hunting was a popular sport with the lord and his retinue. The " purr " was a wild pig of the domestic variety. Herds of purrs were protected and the Manx folk had to suffer their attacks on crops and stores without redress, a matter which was a very sore affair with them. Hare-beagling has been mentioned, and there was always hare-coursing.

To the Derby family also must be ascribed the honour of starting horse-racing in the Island, a race quite probably the precursor of the Epsom Derby. The date of its inauguration is uncertain, but there is evidence that it was in being in the time of the "great earl " (1627-51). The race was restarted by his son

the eighth earl Charles after the Restoration. The object of the
race was for the encouragement of "a breed of good horses". The
race was to be run on Langness in an area beside Derbyhaven,
still known as "the racecourse", and some of the "rules of the
race" are still preserved in the Rolls Office.

> "It is my good will and pleasure yt ye 2 prizes formerly granted
> for hors runing and shouting shall continue as they did be run
> or shot for and so to continue dureing my good will and
> pleasure."
>
> Given under my hand at Lathom ye 12 of July
>   1669"   "Derby 8th Earl)

The course is described as: "Every rider shall leave the first
two powles in Macbrae's close, one on his right hand, the other
on his left; the two powles by the rocks on his left hand, the
fifth powle in the coney warren also on his left hand and so turning next to Wm Looyre's hose on his left, the next two powles,
one on either hand and the distant distance powle on either hand."
This course is not exactly known, but evidently began and
finished on the Castletown end of the present golf course with a
turning point just short of the ruined Langness farm.

The races were discontinued after the end of the Derby regime
and, for many years, horse-racing in the Island was illegal. However, it was resumed in 1974, but without on-course betting,
which remains illegal.

Shooting and Fishing

As to game-shooting, there is practically none. There are no
organized game preserves and the ideas of the average Manx
countryman are free and easy in matters of poaching. There are
no large estates, so that game preservation is scarcely possible.
There are from time to time small flocks of red grouse on the
mountain lands, and of partridge on the farm lands. The hare
has been almost completely annihilated. A good number of
people enjoy rough shooting by courtesy of the small farmers.
Angling in the Island can be very good, and is steadily improving.
The streams are well stocked with very game, small trout. Fishing
is preserved, but the licence costs only half a guinea. But the
stream banks are not free, and permission must be obtained from
the landowners. Good salmon (and the rivers are stocked with
fish bred at the government hatchery at Maughold) may be taken
in the four rivers Dhoo, Glas, Santan and Sulby, though fishing
in these is dependent on the amount of water and is not in any
way comparable with salmon fishing on Welsh, Irish and Scottish

rivers. The skill of many of the local inhabitants in netting and gaffing salmon is too well known to please the angler. Sea-fishing is a very popular pastime, and grand results can be enjoyed from boats, from the rocks, and from the harbour piers.

There is good yachting all round the Island.

Golf

The Langness links are superb, an eighteen-hole course almost completely surrounded by the sea, almost good enough for a national championship, well known and well loved by thousands of north-country and midland enthusiasts. There are two good courses near Douglas, and pleasant links at Port Erin, Peel and Ramsey.

Motor-Car and Motor-Cycle Racing

The reason for the Island's long association with motor racing is simple. In Great Britain, no road may be closed to the public except by Act of Parliament, and it would provoke great opposition if it were suggested that any circuit of roads should be closed. But in the Island, there is a difference. The Tynwald Court is never so busy as not to be able to consider amending the Highway Act, so as to allow the roads to be closed, at certain times and under certain conditions; and further opposition is very unlikely to be stern in an Island which desires to attract as many visitors as possible. In the early days of motor-cars, with their primitive machinery, fittings and accessories, it followed that progress would be very slow unless there could be some sort of competitive performances which would try the machines under strenuous conditions. Such a race was inaugurated to be held in France to compete for the Gordon-Bennett Cup, presented by James Gordon Bennett, proprietor of the *New York Herald*. In order that there might be chosen a British team to compete in this race, the Royal Automobile Club of Great Britain sought leave in 1904 to practise on the roads of the Isle of Man. A special Tynwald Court was held, which gave permission for the Highway Act to be amended so that such a course could be taken, with suitable time for practising.

The race had to be run over a closed circuit on roads free from all traffic, the " course " running practically the full length of the Island from Douglas to Castletown, thence by Foxdale and Kirk Michael to Ramsey, Ballaugh and Ballamooar and St. Jude's and from Ramsey back to Douglas over the mountain road, a lap of about 50 miles. Drivers were required to do five laps of this course. The five laps had to be completed on a strict time-table. There were stopping and re-starting tests on a steep hill. This had to be accomplished, not on the perfect Manx roads of today, but upon roads not macadamized, dusty, ill-made, steeply cambered, with broad grass verges and deep ditches, with the main roads often hampered by grass and weeds, and the mountain road for over half its distance a three-track road of wheel-ruts and hoof tracks, making overtaking absolutely impossible.

In 1905 the trial was in reality a race, and morning practices were inaugurated, beginning at 4 a.m. The race was run in September; it was of four laps (209 miles) and allowance of petrol was made for 22½ miles per gallon. There were 14 starters. The winner was J. P. Napier in an 18 h.p. Arrol-Johnston at 33.8 m.p.h.

In 1906 another course was chosen, Douglas, Peel, Kirk Michael, Ramsey and the Mountain Road, four laps of total 161 miles. The winner was the Hon. C. S. Rolls at a speed of 39.29 m.p.h. In 1907 a division was made into heavy and light cars, run simultaneously. The race was run in a downpour of rain so that the speed in both classes was reduced to around 28 m.p.h.

In 1909 a radical alteration in the regulations was made limiting the h.p. of any machine to 25.6 and having not less than four cylinders, together with a minimum weight of 1,600 lb., exclusive of driver, petrol, oil, spare parts and tools. This made for diversity of form, and tremendous improvements. Thirty-eight cars started. The course for this race was a fresh one, Douglas, Ballacraine, Kirk Michael, Ramsey, and the Mountain Road to Douglas. Ever since 1909 this has remained the standard course, the "T.T. Course" for all races.

There was a pause till 1914 before the race was run again. The first World War then intervened, and the next and last race was run in 1922, this time again for heavy cars. The races had proved their value in producing a small engine of very great power, reliability and efficiency, and the British light car led the world's production. At the same time tremendous advances were made in ignition, carburation, braking devices, and metallurgy in the construction of chassis and engine parts. The races were purely experimental and the Isle of Man may be proud of the part it played in developing the car and car engine.

And what is true of the car is even more true of the air-cooled internal combustion engine of the motor-cycle. In 1907 the Auto-Cycle Union, that branch of the R.A.C. concerned with the motor-cycle and its rider, sought permission to run a race in the Island. Permission was granted and a " short " course selected and running " widdershins " from St. John's via Glen Helen to Michael, thence to Peel by the coast road, and back to St. John's. The course, devoid of any fantastic hill climb, though with a mass of corners, was as much as the motor-cycle of those days could negotiate. Engines were of one or two cylinders. The single-cylinder machine race was won by C. R. Collier on a Matchless at 38·23 m.p.h. and in 1908 by J. Marshall on a Triumph at 40·49 m.p.h. The small engines were dropped in 1909, in which year H. A. Collier won on a Matchless at 49 m.p.h. In 1910 C. R. Collier won on a Matchless at 56·63 m.p.h. The speeds and reliability, as will be noted, rose steadily. In 1911 the " Mountain Course " covered by the car race was adopted, and has remained ever since. This race on this course has attracted riders and machines from every part of the world and is recognized as the leading international meeting to compete for the blue riband of motor-cycle racing, and the map of the Isle of Man with the Tourist Trophy course marked on it, with the Manx " three-legs ", is a badge known literally on every continent. The races bring over thousands of spectators every June. The week before the race week is given over to practising. There are various categories of machines: the Junior (for machines of up to 250 c.c. cylinder capacity), the Senior (up to 500 c.c.), the Classic (up to 1,000 c.c.) and the Sidecars. A new innovation in 1977 was the introduction of the T.T. World Championship for Formula 1, 2 and 3 machines.

A race or practising period is inaugurated by sending round a car carrying a notice " Roads Closed ". After this has passed nothing is allowed upon the roads, no cart, cycle, human being, or animal, under severe penalty. The roads remain closed until a similar car runs round after the race with the notice " Roads Open ".

In general terms these races are run as an experimental competition for the information of the manufacturers. Machines are brought from many countries, with new ideas to be tried out. The information gained by their success and probably even more by their failure to stand up to the gruelling conditions have guided the evolution of the air-cooled engine, which it must be remembered also became the engine of the aeroplane. It must be agreed that the permanent inhabitants of the Island suffer many things during the period of practising and racing. The pande-monium of the engines racing fill the Island " with strange noises ". The majority of the roads are out of use except in the south between Douglas and Port Erin, and in the north between Ramsey and Bride. Nobody in the centre of the Island can get outside the circle of the course; the greatest care must be taken of animals, lest they stray on the course.

About 180 different makes of machine have been on the course during the same period, and the improvement in the strength, reliability and speed of the machines has been remarkably steady. It was not until 1920 that the "long course" was won at an average speed of over 50 m.p.h. Speeds climbed to 60 m.p.h. in 1924, 70 m.p.h. in 1929, 80 m.p.h. in 1935, and to 90 m.p.h. in 1950. In the Jubilee year, 1957, the course was lapped at over 100 m.p.h. with a record average speed of 99 m.p.h. Today's winning averages are consistently over the 100!

It has often been said by critics that the races have done a disservice to motoring by magnifying the value of speed on the roads. The accusation is unjust, for the races are run on traffic-free roads with "nothing round the corner". Speed is merely the testing factor, to which the inventions and designs of the factory are submitted to prove what is good and worthy, and to find out where there is unreliability.

So popular did the Tourist Trophy Races prove to be that it was suggested in 1923 that a purely sporting race, for the average young motor-cyclist, might be popular and well supported. A band of Island enthusiasts started such a race. At first it was known as an "Amateur" race, but unfortunately a satisfactory definition of "amateur" was impossible. However by the kindly co-operation of the manufacturers the race was resolved into a race for young men who had never ridden in the manufacturers' race, who would not be able to obtain experimental machines, but who were members of the hundreds of clubs from all over the British Isles, and indeed of the British Empire and foreign countries. They took to the race immediately. They came to a very happy place and were looked after by a party of Island enthusiasts who set themselves to make the meeting a great success so that it is attractive to the competitors, and a good thing for the Island. Speeds achieved are reasonably comparable with the speeds of the trade machines, and the young folk who do well in the September race go on to achieve fame in the June race. For all practical purposes it is a race organized by sportsmen for sportsmen. This race is known as the "Manx Grand Prix".

The ordinary cyclist has taken the opportunity of getting a closed road for a series of cycle road races, which attain inter-

national fame. This meeting, held in mid-June, started as a race
for insular clubs. It consists of two laps of the T.T. course, a
very gruelling course considering the long six-mile climb up the
mountain of nearly 1,400 feet altitude. The competitors adopt
a mass start and their first half mile gives them a run down Bray
Hill *en masse*, affording a wonderful and sparkling sight. The
race of about 75 miles is won at speeds up to 24 m.p.h., which,
including as it does two climbs of hills of average gradient 1 in 10,
is truly remarkable. Moreover it is purely an amateur event with
no cash prizes. Marathon runners and walkers also race round
the course each year.

CHAPTER FIFTEEN

TOPOGRAPHICAL

B EFORE EMBARKING on a tour of the Island, it may
be instructive to note the uniqueness of the Manx system of local
government, and to realise that all administrative processes are
not centred in Douglas. The day-to-day administration of civic
affairs in the towns, and even the larger villages, is controlled
by relatively small local authorities. Thus, just as the borough
of Douglas is administered by its town council, so the towns of
Peel, Castletown and Ramsey have their boards of town commissioners, and the villages of Laxey, Onchan, Port St. Mary,
Port Erin and Kirk Michael have their village commissioners,
who administer the byelaws in their respective areas. In the
country districts, each parish has its board of parish commissioners whose powers are somewhat more restricted. Turning
first to the towns:

DOUGLAS is the present capital of the Island, having ousted
Castletown from that position in 1869, a fact that the old capital
will never accept, forget or forgive. Douglas is the only town in
the Island with a mayor; the others all have " chairmen ". The
rise of Douglas was due to its deep-water harbour. Its only
rival could have been Peel, but that was on the wrong side of
the Island for traffic, and its harbour has a silting floor while
that of Douglas is based directly on the shale. The harbour
works have grown steadily with increasing trade and prosperity.

In early Victorian days the harbour was the inner portion only, between the Red Pier and the Tongue, bounded by the North and South Quays. A stone jetty was built out from below Fort Anne more or less to cover the harbour mouth. But the Red Pier, now almost obliterated but still the chief cargo-handling quay, was in those days the pride of Douglas, its fashionable promenade and social parade ground. Nobody in clogs was allowed to defile its pavements; workers had to carry their clogs in their hands! The North Quay had all the warehouses, and merchants' offices, many of which remain to this day. The Victoria Pier was opened in 1871, affording excellent deep-water berthing. At the same time the Battery Pier was built out for a protection to this new outer harbour, which still was very difficult in a south-east gale. Local opinion called for an outer breakwater, but the Admiralty insisted upon an extension of the Red Pier known as the Edward VIII pier, into the centre of the outer harbour, with deep berthing on both sides.

That Douglas had no church was a grave concern to Bishop Wilson, who encouraged the building on the North Quay of the chapel-of-ease of St. Matthew. This church has been replaced by a much more ornate church not far from its former foundation. It has a Flemish-style reredos, and a lady-chapel, separated by a good hand-wrought iron screen. As the town grew and prospered houses were built over the hills to the north and in 1761 St. George's Church was built as another chapelry of Kirk Braddan. It is a handsome, roomy building. In its churchyard Sir William Hillary (founder of the Royal National Lifeboat Institution) and his wife are buried. Sir William lived at Fort Anne (q.v.) but lost most of his money in a local bank failure, and spent his later years in proud poverty; a sad and little-known story. St. George's has always been used as the pro-cathedral of the diocese (though officially this should be the chapel of St. Nicholas at Bishopscourt) and here all services at diocesan level and all national services are held, the bishop enthroned, and national thanksgivings celebrated.

The House of Keys, the Tynwald Court room and many Government offices are situated on the east side of Prospect Hill, quite unworthy buildings for such an ancient assembly. The old Douglas streets, Duke Street, Strand Street and Castle Street retain their eighteenth-century narrowness, but still form the main shopping centre, in spite of the newer, better constructed Victoria Street, which with its continuation forms the main traffic artery of the town.

Everybody with an interest in the Island should see the Museum on the bluff above St. Thomas' Church. It has been carefully and capably built up as a National Museum. It has an art gallery and a very fine archaeological section showing the pre-history and early history of the Island. There are good models of a typical Viking ship, and of a Celtic manor-house. Here may be seen the Cronk-yn-How pictures stone, the Calf Crucifixion, a fine collection of Manx dresses and uniforms, the interior of a Manx cottage, a wonderful relief map of the Island, a collection of Manx birds and animals, a skeleton of the Giant Irish Deer already mentioned, a wonderful collection of Manx historical documents and a gallery of archaeological treasures and casts of all the Celtic and Scandinavian crosses.

The Promenades of Douglas extend for well over two miles around the bay, towards the north end of which the modern Summerland sports and leisure complex has risen from the ashes of the disastrous fire of 1973. The town has a fine hospital, built originally from the bounty of Henry Bloom Noble, a wealthy timber merchant who left a large fortune mainly for charitable purposes in Douglas. Manx Radio, which was the first authorized commercial radio station in the British Isles, occupies a prominent position on Douglas Head.

CASTLETOWN is naturally dominated by its castle. The town lies around this wonderful building. To its inhabitants it still remains the centre of fashion, breeding and learning, of culture and politics, of justice and society. Its church is far from attractive, but it has one glorious advantage: from all its south windows, which are plain glazed, may be seen the glorious sweep of sea forming Castletown Bay. The centre of the Parade (for Castletown was till quite recently a garrison town) is occupied by a giant Doric column in memory of Colonel Cornelius Smelt, Lieutenant-Governor 1805-32, a man whose term of office filled a very difficult time when the Duke of Atholl was Governor, and this he filled with tact, great courage, and kindliness. He was at the end of his days the only official not appointed by the Duke, who did his best to get rid of him, or at least remove him from the castle where he lived. Almost his last official act was to lay the foundation stone of King William's College, whose architect John Welch designed the column. A very interesting sundial with thirteen faces stands on the castle glacis beneath the castle clock. The old Grammar School, a very small building, seems to have formed a part of the old St. Mary's Church, which stood at the east end of the present church. It still contains two arches of a similar type to those in the ruined church of Rushen Abbey, and a good timbered ceiling. The church was in pre-Reformation times served by the brethren of Rushen Abbey, and after the Restoration was subsidized from Bishop Barrow's Trust. In 1681, it is recorded by a document from the Castle Rushen papers that the Earl of Derby . . . "paid a schoolmaster the sum of sixty pounds a year salary for reading prayers in the castle at 11 and reading logic and philosophy with four academic scholars who were to wear black wide-sleeved gowns and square caps; the schoolmaster to have free lodging in the Castle".

The tall, gaunt building overlooking the harbour is Bridge House, the home for many generations of the Quayle family, a family that served the Island well, as lawyers and bankers. Of great interest is the Nautical Museum, a part of the outhouses of Bridge House, and presented to the nation by the Quayle family. This Nautical Museum was originally the boat-house of Captain George Quayle's boat, the *Peggy*. She still stands at the top of a runway, down which she used to slip into Castletown harbour. But the exit was, after the death of her owner, bricked up, and the *Peggy* imprisoned. So far as is known she was built about 1790 in the local ship-yard, and was commissioned by the British Admiralty in 1793. The surrounding seas were not safe, for French privateersmen sailed right up to the Island to attack light shipping between Liverpool, Bristol and Belfast. This accounts for the *Peggy*'s armament of eight small cannon. She is a schooner-rigged clinker-built boat with two masts, a gaff mainsail and a jib. Her keel is of elm, and her timbers of pine. Frames and floors are of oak. Her spars and mast are still intact, though much of the bolting is badly rusted. Her length is 26 feet 5 inches, her depth 4 feet and her burthen $6\frac{1}{2}$ tons. Her owner, Captain George Quayle, served his country well. He was captain commandant of the Manx Yeomanry in the uneasy Napoleonic days. He was a member of the House of Keys and, with his brother Mark, he founded the "Isle of Man Bank", opened in 1802 and closed in 1818. Its "notes" were considered "as safe as the Bank of England". When the bank closed its doors in 1818, he sold his large estate, the Barony of St. Trinian's in Kirk Marown, in order to have sufficient ready money to buy in all the "notes", which he most honourably did. The upper storey of the boathouse was fitted up like the stern quarter of a ship, the wall facing over the harbour containing small "cabin" windows, with a miniature "promenade deck" outside. Inside there were a ship's galley, and substantial wine-bins. The rooms were

used as a roystering place for the young "Bucks" of their day.
In the same building are housed other interesting nautical objects.

PEEL, "the Sunset City of the West", is in no way bound up
with its cathedral as is Castletown with its castle. Its inhabitants
through the ages, and up to the present day, have been famous
for their complete independence of thought, and freedom in
expressing their opinions. It is a place that has felt the passage
of time less than anywhere except perhaps Castletown. In the
Market Place, the ruin of the old church of St. Peter has been
nicely converted into a garden of rest. The new church built in
1884 from money collected by Bishop Rowley Hill for the
reconstruction of the old cathedral had, when completed, a
graceful spire, but this was much damaged by a storm in 1907
and taken down. The town remains very much as it was in
mediaeval times, its houses, built of the local red sandstone,
cluster along a maze of narrow streets, too narrow for two-way
traffic. The Promenade, singularly ineffective as such, is entered
at each end by reasonably broad roads starting from "nowhere
in particular", while the roads running up through the old
houses must be accepted in faith. The motorist will eventually
come out "somewhere" if he drives with care. Peel has most
interesting "kipper-curing" houses which ought to be seen by
all visitors in the season.

RAMSEY, "Queen of the North", lies under the shadow of
North Barrule. It makes a very pretty picture when seen from
the Mountain road. At its southern end lies the Queen's Pier.
It is used by anglers, but no longer (as in the past) by passengers
disembarking from the steamers. Since the chief wind in the
Island is from the south-west, Ramsey is the most sheltered town
in the Island, and its gardens and the near-by glens are always
about a fortnight ahead of the rest of the Island. In spite of its
shallow bay, Ramsey has through the ages been the landing place
of royal visitors. The habit was begun by Godred Crovan, who
landed here in 1079. Robert Bruce too landed here in 1313
before subjugating the Island for Scotland. Queen Victoria in
1847 landed here with Prince Albert, who climbed up into the
hills in order to get a good view of the town, and to whose honour
the Prince Albert Tower was set up, on the spot where he stood.
The landing was to have been made at Douglas but the weather
there was too bad. The Governor and other officials waiting
there to receive their royal visitors had no telegraphic communication with Ramsey, and by the time a horseman messenger had

reached Douglas, and the waiting party had obtained coaches, and sped post-haste to Ramsey, the royal party had re-embarked and were on their way to England. King Edward VII and Queen Alexandra had been forced to land there in 1902, and King George V and Queen Mary in 1921. The Island weather for some perverse reason always seems to misbehave when a royal visit is made. This is ascribed to the jealousy of old Manannan McLir, the Island's wizard king, who in time past always threw a blanket of fog over his domain when any stranger tried to get to the Island. One of the most astonishing examples of the old wizard's tricks occurred in 1955 when Queen Elizabeth II and Prince Philip visited the Island in August. Up to the day of arrival the weather had been daily, day-long sunshine and bright, clear nights. As *Britannia* approached an impenetrable fog settled down over the Island, which reached a maximum as the Royal Yacht moved into Douglas Bay. Her Majesty sailed away in the evening into the same wretched fog, and as the distance increased the clearest of clear nights returned to the Island and for weeks the sun returned daily. Can it be wondered that there lies the least spot of superstition in the Manx mind?

The oldest building in Ramsey is Ballure Church, a tiny church built over an ancient keeill site, but of quite unknown dedication. It was restored in 1850 and dedicated to St. Catherine.

THE PARISHES

It is customary in the Isle of Man, in any matters dealing with all the parishes, to begin with Patrick, and "follow the sun" round the Island, and that forms a very convenient method of reviewing such points as have not been deemed important enough for consideration so far.

PATRICK. This parish is large but sparsely populated. The new ecclesiastical parish of Foxdale has been separated from it. However, it makes up in beauty what it lacks in population; the whole of its coastline (and every parish except Marown has a seaboard) is a dream of loveliness from the Lag-ny-killey, where it begins, to Peel Island, where it ends. The Patrick-Port Erin road runs parallel to the coastline, and provides one of the most beautiful scenic feasts in the Island, but a walk along the crest of the cliffs from Peel Hill southwards should not be missed by anybody who loves walking. Peel Head lies in Patrick, and its seaward bluff is known as "Contrary Head". At its base are some very interesting sea-eroded caves well worth exploring, and reached by a very steep path down the cliff-face. On its summit stands a grim, wind-swept tower known as "Corrin's folly", which was built as a mausoleum for one Corrin, a staunch Free-churchman of German, who wished to demonstrate that it was possible to be buried in non-consecrated ground. He had the remains of his wife and children transferred from Patrick church-yard to his own small burial ground beside his tower, and was later buried there himself. The tower now serves as a land-mark for the fishing fleet. Further south a descent must be made to Glen Maye, the outlet of lovely Glen Rushen. Ascent of the south side and a further ridge brings one to Dalby with a grand view of the mass of Cronk-ny-irrey-lhaa descending preci-pitously into the sea, and beyond it the Carnanes, and the head-land of Bradda and then the Calf. In Patrick parish too is the Foxdale waterfall, the most considerable fall in the Island, which gives its name to the village, Foxdale = fosdaile (Nor: Fos, a waterfall). Nearer Patrick Church is Knockaloe Government Farm, an experimental farm of great interest and value in insular agriculture which has replaced the gigantic German internment camp of World War I. The boundary from German runs along the river Neb to St. John's, including in Patrick, Slieu Whallian, the Witches' Hill, sometimes known as the Hill of Witness, which frowns down upon Tynwald ceremony. Patrick Church is of slight interest, but its little churchyard contains a pathetic cemetery of graves of the prisoners of war who died in the camp, and one even more pathetic grave of a sailor washed ashore during the same war, with its sad epitaph "Some Mother's Son".

GERMAN lies immediately north of Patrick, and contains the town of Peel and the village of St. John's, both of which have been commented on. Its coast, less bold than that of Patrick, is at its southern end red sandstone but changes back again to the shale and crush conglomerate of the main mountain mass and at Gob-y-deigan (the Devil's Mouth) there are caves and quaintly-carved rocks and a perfect bathing beach. High above the shore, the line of the old Steam Railway track can still be followed along the coast. Through Glen Helen (more correctly Glen Rhenass) runs the T.T. Course before it climbs over Cronk-y-Voddy, up Creg Willy's Hill, one of the stiffer climbs in the course. Away to the east of Cronk-y-Voddy lies the secluded little com-munity of "Little London", one of the least known and most picturesque spots in the Island. The wild expanse of the Beary

Mountains north of St. John's (and ending to the east in Colden and Greeba mountains) affords some of the loveliest, loneliest wandering ground in the Island.   At the foot of Greeba, and beside the Peel-Douglas road, stands Greeba Castle, the former home of Sir Hall Caine, the famous Manx novelist. Another pleasant excursion to be made either on foot or by car, not known to nearly so many folk as it ought to be, is the Lhergy road from Ballig Bridge, near Ballacraine, to the coast road just north of St. German's Station, a road running along the side of the foot-hills, and affording a lovely view of Peel.   It passes the " Giant's Fingers " tumulus at Kew, and further on the Giant's Grave stone-circle at Lhergy-dhoo.   It crosses, too, the even more intriguing Bishop's road just above St. John's Mills.   This delightful track runs north and south, forming part of the original bridle road from Rushen Abbey to Bishopscourt more or less parallel to the main road through Glen Helen.   It emerges eventually at Michael through Glen Mooar.   On the coast road at Ballakeighan farm near the Devil's Elbow was discovered an ancient tree-boat adjudged to be of the Neolithic age, and beside the road on the land side close by is a large cairn or stone tumulus which has not yet been excavated.   Tynwald Hill stands in German and this gives rise to the local quip that " on July 5th the law is read in Manx and in English and in German ".

MICHAEL.   Is one of the few villages that has sprung up round its parish church.   The present church, rebuilt and consecrated in 1835, has no architectural interest.   It has a pleasant modern lych-gate built to house its wonderful collection of ancient crosses,. but these have since been moved into the church. They include the very beautiful Dragon cross, the massive Joalf's cross and Gaut's cross with its boastful runic inscription, " Gaut made this and all in Mann ".   Gaut was a Norse sculptor of the mid-tenth century whose interlaced designs started a " school " which lasted to the end of the Scandinavian period in the Island. Five Manx bishops are buried in the churchyard, the great Bishop Wilson, his immediate successor Mark Hildesley, George Mason, Claudius Crigan and Leonard Thornton Duesbery.   All lie within the shadow of the solitary remnant of the chancel of the ancient church which preceded the present one.   In the churchyard in 1975 was found a Viking coin hoard, which is now on display in the Manx Museum.

The village which lies at the heart of this parish is administered by the Kirk Michael Village Commissioners, which are the smallest byelaw authority in the British Isles. The Mitre Hotel is reputedly the Island's oldest inn, dating from 1786. About a mile to the south, a pleasant footpath leads up to the waterfall of Spoyt Vane, which plunges into the upper section of Glen Mooar.

BALLAUGH is a dual community. There is a very small group of houses around the ancient church near the shore. The real village is on the main Peel-Ramsey road and here the present church was built in 1832. The village green lies half way between the two villages.

The Bishop's glen has a mound on which is set a stone commemorating the sea-fight between the French ship *Belleisle* and H.M.S. *Aeolus*, each with subsidiary vessels (1760). The French ships were in charge of a young captain, Thurot, a man of gentle birth. Earlier he had been engaged in the smuggling trade between France and the Island and knew Ramsey well. He sailed up the channel and sacked Carrickfergus, where he re-victualled. The *Aeolus*, with two frigates under Captain Elliott, had been in Kinsale when the news arrived of the sack of Carrickfergus. He hastened northward to try and intercept the Frenchmen. They met just off the Ballaugh shore. Bishop Hildesley watched the battle from the "broughs". The *Belleisle* was sunk. Thurot's body was washed up on the shore at Kirk-maiden, Wigtownshire, and was buried in the little churchyard on the shore of Luce Bay. Timbers from the *Belleisle* were washed ashore near Bishopscourt and set upon the mound in the Bishop's glen, which he called "Mount Aeolus". Edward Forbes began his studies of zoology and botany on Ballaugh shore. The coast from Ballaugh to the Ayre is being gradually eroded. Only one ancient cross has been uncovered in Ballaugh, but it is a very interesting cross, carved also by Gaut, raised by Olaf Liotulf-son. It is of very great interest that Liot is the stem of the name Corlett (Mac-ur-liot) and the Corletts have held land near Old Ballaugh Church from time immemorial. The old church has a very ancient font which had been built into a window seat and has the Manx inscription "Tavun chiarn, un Credjue, un Vashtey, Un Jee as Ayr jeh ooilley" (There is one Lord, one Faith, one Baptism, one God and Father of all). The doorway arch is of Norman type with a studded oak door, and the gateposts have leant together for many many years in apparently a delightful state of inebriation. From Ballaugh Bridge, Ballaugh Glen runs into the mountain side, from which the lovely Druidale mountain road is entered.

L

JURBY also has a church dedicated to St. Patrick, standing now very near the shore. The cliffs have been eroded here more seriously than anywhere else in the Island, and several fields have disappeared since the Ordnance Survey of 1868. Most of the parish that is not curragh was formerly occupied by a military airfield, some of which is now used as an industrial estate. The sand dunes, running from the church to the parish boundary of the Lhen river, are typical and lovely. The curraghs, which are continuous with those of Ballaugh, are of absorbing interest. In the curragh aforetimes lived the old miser Mylecaraine, of the Manx ballad translated by George Borrow:

> In the turf-bogs of Jurby, from history we learn
> There lived an old miser called Mollycaraine.

There is a genuine Mylecaraine pendant cross, part of the dowry he left to his daughter. The cross was stolen over a hundred years ago from the last of the line. But a duplicate, made for the Museum, was designed from drawings that were extant. The result, however, was interesting, for in 1946 the genuine cross was presented anonymously to the Museum, where it may be seen.

ANDREAS is the chief village of the northern plain. Its church has a dedication due to the Scottish missionary inflow, which was responsible to an " Iona " influence shown in several dedications on the eastern side of the Island. The church had a high, slender detached tower forming a landmark for the northern plain, now considerably shorter. It has a magnificent display of stone crosses, including the Odin-Ichtus cross and the Sigurd cross. A field in the rector's glebe known as Foyn ny Hoalan (the field of the sacred bread) was left that the rent might in perpetuity pay the cost of the communion bread. In Andreas too is Knock-y-dooney with its ship burial, and at Ballachurry the famous Derby Fort.

BRIDE is the most northerly parish and includes the Ayre, a wide expanse of sand and heather, the nesting place of many kinds of birds. Much gravel is extracted here for use by the building trade. The Bride hills are formed from the sandy deposits left by a melting glacier. From the top there are glorious views of the Ayre, Southern Scotland from Galloway to Solway, and Northern Ireland. Two men from Bride were aboard the *Victory* at Trafalgar, John Cowle, a quartermaster, and John Lace, who lost an arm by the same bullet, it is reported, as that

which killed Nelson. There are some good crosses including an
" Adam and Eve ", another Gaut and a Thor.

LEZAYRE is a parish of outstanding interest. It is the largest
parish in the Island. The whereabouts of its ancient church is
not certain. A church was built by Bishop Wilson in 1704, but it
quickly fell into disrepair, and the present church was built in
1835, one of the many churches rebuilt through the efforts of
Bishop Ward. Its windows are locally interesting, since they were
designed and made by a Manxman, Daniel Cottier, and illustrate
the Christian virtues. The parish contains in its boundaries
Snaefell, Beinn-y-Phott, Glen Auldyn, North Barrule and Sulby
Glen, as well as a large stretch of curragh land. It contains also
the famous Skyhill (Scacafell), the scene of Godred's great victory
over the Manx, 1079, the earliest recorded event in Manx history.
Somewhere in the parish stood the small abbey of Mirescogh.
The *Chronicon* contains a pleasant story of one Dofnald, a " noble
old man ", a friend of Harald Olaffson, captured by craft from
the Abbey of Rushen, and imprisoned in Mirescogh by his
enemy Harald Godredson (1250), who was miraculously set free.
Chronicon ends the story with the comment, " This we record as
we had it from his very lips ". Milntown near Ramsey was the
home of the famous Christian family. The family was Scandinavian in origin and the name was originally McCristen, modified
later to Christin. They held Milntown for 400 years, and produced more men famous in Manx history than probably any
other family. Another family closely connected with Lezayre is
that of the Standishes. The first Standish recorded was 1577.
In 1610 there was a Standish, Clerk of Lezayre, and another John
Standish of Ellanbane, also Clerk of Lezayre. Myles Standish,
the Pilgrim Father of the *Mayflower* (1584-1685), the American
colonist and military leader in New England, was probably born
at Ellanbane. His two successive sister-wives Rose and Barbara
were Manx. The family held extensive lands in Lancashire and
the oldest document concerning these lands was signed by
Johannem Standishe de Insula de Mane. Myles claimed to be
the owner of these lands described in his will as " surruptuously
detained from me ". Robert Standish, who acquired this property
in 1502, signed the deed of purchase with two Manx officials,
Henry Halsall, steward to the first Earl of Derby, and Thomas
Hesketh, Receiver General of the Island. The " surruptuous
detention " appears to have been due to Myles' grandfather who,
not having heard of Myles since he left for New England, left the

lands to his grandson William, Myles' nephew. But the Island can claim this very strong link with New England, and that should be of great interest to American visitors. At Cronk-yn-How in an ancient keeill was found the interesting engraved stone of the Bronze Age (p. 33), and at Cronk Aust was found the beautiful Bronze Age beaker exhibited in the Museum.

MAUGHOLD also has many important relics of Island history and pre-history. Its church is of very great interest and contains much more ancient work than any other church in the Island. In the porch it has one intriguing "capital" of a Celtic arch, with a human face in front, and beasts at each side. The work is said to be of the tenth century. In the porch is a piece of arch-moulding of about the same period. These are evidently parts of a very early Celtic church which probably was the enlargement of an ancient keeill. The font is old and large, evidently meant for total immersion. The chancel is not in a straight line with the nave. The churchyard of five acres is the largest in the Island. In it are the ruins of two ancient keeills, of which there are eleven in the parish, one for each treen. The church was in ancient days fortified with a wall and a ditch. In the church are still used the collecting pans for the offertory alms. These are strange-looking objects somewhat reminiscent of small warming pans and known locally as "scoops". They are half-covered, and made of copper. Most Manx churches have similar "scoops", but those in Maughold are engraved "The gift of the Revd Henry Allen and Jane Allen to ye Pshe of K.K. Maughall 1751". The Allens were a famous Maughold family of vicars, of whom there were five in sequence between 1625 and 1754. They were descendants of the first protestant minister of Castletown, who fled to the Island from East Anglia to escape the persecution of "bloody Mary". During the examination of the church walls a gold coin was found of the date of Louis le Debonnaire son of Charlemagne. It was presumably part of a pirate hoard brought by some Scandinavian. It is in the Museum. There are thirty-three crosses well housed under shelter, some of outstanding interest. In former times the parish was granted to the Abbot of Furness. It is highly probable that there was a Celtic monastic settlement here before the Scandinavian incursions. There is a reference in *Chronicon* to the taking to Maughold Church of the pastoral staff, presumably of the Abbot of Rushen, in order to provide a sacred symbol against the wiles of one Gil-column, an ally of Somerled, Thane of Argyll about 1160. The staff has since disappeared, but about 70 acres of the land around the church is "staff" land, apparently land of which the rent provided for the safety of the staff. Today the tenure of the land rests neither on statutory right, nor is it supported by any documentary evidence.

Along the cliff edge runs a path leading to St. Maughold's well, reputed to have been used as a baptismal well by St. Maughold. The village cross, one of the most interesting "pieces" in the Island, has been moved from the village green, where it formerly stood, to the greater security of the churchyard. It is the only remaining market-cross. It has several times been "restored". The capital carries four shields, one bearing the Three Legs of Man (q.v.). The others are not heraldic. One is a cinquefoil device, another an open book, the fourth a chalice. There are two side shields at the top, one a much worn heraldic design, the other the double rose. The rood proper bears on one side the crucifix, and on the other the Virgin and Child. The top of the cross has been destroyed. In Maughold parish stands the Neolithic horned barrow, Cashtal-yn-Ard (q.v.) and there are two lovely and unspoilt glens, Glen Mona, running down to Port Cornaa, from whence starts the telegraph cable to St. Bees in Cumberland; and Glen Dhoon, a very steep ravine with several pleasant waterfalls.

In this parish too, close beside the old Maughold Road, running down from Hibernia, is the Quakers' burial ground, Rhullick-ny-Quakeryn, where lies, close to his old home of Ballafayle, the much-persecuted William Callow and other Quakers who were so heavily persecuted by Bishop Barrow. It is a peaceful little cemetery amid glorious surroundings. But it brings a lump to the throat to think it possible that in the name of Christ-the-kind-hearted an ecclesiastic could persecute such good-living, simple-minded people. Today the insular authorities have rebuilt the wall-surround and planted trees, a pleasant official act of grace.

LONAN includes the village of Laxey with its lead mines, its great wheel, and the two glens, Glen Roy and Laxey Glen. The dedication of the present church is to St. Lonan, otherwise Lonan McLaire of the Irish Church. But Old Lonan Church near the Onchan parish boundary is deemed to have been dedicated to St. Adamnan of Iona. Every one of the twelve treens in the parish has a Scandinavian name. The best known son of Lonan is Captain Henry Skillicorn (1678-1763), who developed Cheltenham Spa. His record is given at length on his memorial in

Cheltenham Parish Church: "Born at Kirk Lonan, Isle of Man, taught by Bishop Wilson. When young went to sea . . . in the employ of Jacob Elton of Bristol . . . whose relation Sarah Goldsmith he married . . . she dying . . . he in 1731 married Elizabeth Mason . . . quitting the sea after 40 years . . . they came to live upon their estate in Cheltenham . . . where he gave his mind to increase the knowledge and extend the use of Cheltenham Spa. He made the well . . . brought the waters to just estimation and extensive use. . . . He died aged 84. He could do business in seven languages . . . so temperate as never once to have become intoxicated. Religious without hypocrisy, grave without austerity, of cheerful conversation without levity, tall, erect, robust and active; he lived and died an honest man." He left a considerable sum of money to Lonan Church.

In the parish occurs the interesting double barrow known as King Orry's Grave.

ONCHAN (more accurately KIRK CONCHAN) is the name of both the parish and the village within it. Onchan village has expanded greatly in recent years; although still technically a village, and administered by its village commissioners, in population it is now second only to Douglas, which it adjoins. The present church dedication is to St. Peter, but this is comparatively recent. For the ancient keeill dedication there are three possibilities, all of them Irish saints: Conchanus, a traditional bishop of the Manx Church; Conanus, who is somewhat later (*circa* A.D. 600); but the most likely is St. Conchem, the Irish equivalent of St. Christopher. He is figured in the Celtic Church as a "dog-headed" man. Conchan Fair was celebrated on St. Christopher's Day, and further, three Runic crosses found in the churchyard all have crude carvings of the dog-headed man, so it may fairly be assumed that the original keeill was dedicated to St. Conchem. The Communion plate is a handsome set of the time of Charles I. Captain Bligh of H.M.S. *Bounty* was married in Onchan Church in 1781.

BRADDAN. This is another parish of fascinating interest. The dedication of the church is to Brendan, another Scottish saint, claimed to have met, baptized and taught Maughold on his arrival. It has two churches close together. The old church, surrounded by trees, has a quaint tower, probably added when the church was restored in 1773. There are Norman-type coigns in the walls and there is a three-decker pulpit. Its chief antiquarian glory is a superb granite finial at the east end of the roof, a twelfth-century sculptured "crucifixion". Inside the church are five ancient Scandinavian crosses.

The new church is just across the side-road, a very worthy building, airy and light and well designed. On the west side on a steeply banked field the famous Sunday morning outdoor services have attracted thousands of visitors. Under the shadow of Carraghan in the treen of Algare, East Baldwin, is the site of another Tynwald Hill. This may have been the scene of the Al-thing of the south, and an assembly was certainly held there in 1428. Below it, the plain little church of St. Luke stands on the site of an ancient keeill. In Kirk Braddan, too, at the Strang, are the Mental Hospital and the Old People's Home. At Algare in 1750 was born John Kelly, the Manx grammarian and lexicologist. The son of a cooper, he attracted the attention of Vicar Philip Moore because of his aptitude in the Manx language. He assisted in translating the New Testament into Manx, and the fee he received from the Society for Promoting Christian Knowledge allowed him to go to Cambridge (St. John's). After his ordination he built up a polyglot dictionary, Manx, Irish and Gaelic. The Manx section became the standard Manx dictionary. While translating the Old Testament into Manx he had occasion to transport his MS. from Douglas to Whitehaven. The boat in which he sailed was wrecked and young Kelly had to swim. He did so, and maintained his precious documents over his head above the water for five hours and so the text of the Old Testament from Deuteronomy to Job was saved for publication.

In Kirk Braddan Vicarage was brought up one of the Island's favourite sons, Thomas Edward Brown, the Manx poet (1830-97). His father, Robert Brown, chaplain of St. Matthew's and later vicar of Braddan, had bitterly opposed Bishop Barrow's Trust Fund being spent on founding King William's College. But he sent his son there to become a brilliant scholar. He was a contemporary of F. W. Farrar, afterwards Dean of Canterbury. Farrar went up to Trinity, Cambridge, and Brown to Christ Church, Oxford. This was probably the worst college for the rugged Manxman, for he was surrounded by a host of snobbish English fellow students and undergraduates, who sneered at this uncouth "foreigner". However he took a first in Classics and a first in History and Law, and in 1853 was made a Fellow of Oriel, a post which he resigned to become Vice-Principal of King William's College. From there he was appointed headmaster of the Crypt School at Gloucester and then joined Percival as second master at Clifton in 1864. He was a great figure in the life of Clifton, from which he retired in 1893. The affection in which he is held in the Island is the result of his innate Manx-ness. He was body and soul part of the Island. He stood for all that is best and noblest in the Manx character. He had a fund of humour, a vast friendliness, a power of understanding for his fellow men, and, what is probably as precious to the Manx mind, a rugged directness and inability to "suffer fools gladly". Any-body who wishes to understand the Manx and the Island spirit must read his poems and letters. Of him his pupil and friend W. E. Henley wrote:

> "He looked half parson and half skipper; a quaint
>   Beautiful blend, with blue eyes good to see,
> And old-world whiskers. You found him cynic, saint
>   Salt, humorist, Christian, poet; with a free
> Far-glancing luminous countenance; and a heart
>   Large as St. Francis's."

His best poems are comparable to those of Wordsworth and Blake, but in the Island the dialect poems, such as "Foc'sle Yarns" and "Betsy Lee", have pride of place.

In the field of the open-air service there stood in by-gone days a stone circle and alignments which have been so much mutilated as to be indecipherable. About two hundred yards away in the wall of the road between Kirby and Ballaughton is the "saddle-stone", which appears to have been taken from the stone circle. Various theories have been put forward to account for it. Was it a "penitent" stone on which offenders against ecclesiastical laws were made to sit? Or possibly an "ordeal" stone placed in some perilous position to try the truth of a victim? Many folk-lore stories hang around it, mostly modern; and many concern the "little people". But it undoubtedly has a "fertility" repu-tation locally, even today.

The ancient fort at Castleward has been mentioned. In the Baldwin valley, dammed at the southern end of Injebreck glen, the Douglas reservoir makes a gallant stretch of water, which, viewed from the higher end, provides a pretty picture of perfect scenery "far from the madding crowd". In the parish of Braddan too, along its southern sea border, runs the Marine Drive, a cor-niche road of very great beauty high up above the sea along cliffs of contorted shale. One detached rocky pinnacle, the "Nun's Chair", is traditionally the penitential throne of naughty nuns from the Nunnery.

MAROWN is a parish named after another Scottish saint, Ma Ronan, St. Ronan. It is the only parish without a seaboard. The present church is modern, but the old church up on the hill above Crosby, is in a sad state of disrepair. It has mouldings taken from St. Trinian's Church (q.v.). About half a mile south of the old church is St. Patrick's chair, a small group of standing stones, two of them with incised crosses. Popular superstition suggests that from this spot St. Patrick preached, and blessed the Kingdom and Church of Mann. Consequently persons who sit in the "chair" and rest their backs against these incised stones will never again feel fatigue. St. Trinian's Church, we have seen, was formerly a small monastery with a "hospital". One of the best-known families, the Quilliams, had farm-land in Marown. Along the side of Slieu Whallian runs a road known as Quilliam's road. A member of the family in the time of Bishop Barrow was found guilty of adultery in the Vicar-General's court, and pleaded that instead of the bishop's prison he might do some useful work. This took the form of making a road to the top of the hill. But when Bishop Barrow was translated to St. Asaph, Quilliam left off his work, and now it is a "road that leads to nowhere!" On the other side of the valley, on the edge of the grounds of Greeba Castle, but in Marown, St. Patrick had another "chair", this time a rocky bluff, giving a lovely view along the central valley towards Douglas.

SANTAN (spelt wrongly on the map as "Santon") has a church dedicated to the Irish St. Sanctain. In the post-Reformation days it was thought to be a corruption of St. Ann, and indeed Santan headland is called on the maps St. Anne's Head, and the church communion plate perpetuates the error. It is the smallest Manx parish and its church is very isolated. There is little of interest in the church building, but in the graveyard was found a Latin inscribed stone, the "monumentum Aviti", which now stands beside the door of the church. If its origin is Roman, it is the only such relic in the Island, but its history is quite unknown. In the churchyard stands a gigantic tombstone of undressed shale weighing nearly two tons. It covers the grave of the Cosnahan family, many members of which were clergy in the Island church, and five of them with their wives are buried under this great stone. There are three headland forts on the coast of Santan parish, and of these one, that at Cronk-ny-Merrieu, just north of Port Grenaugh, has recently been carefully excavated (p. 44).
About a mile south of Grenaugh is the Jackdaw Cave, reputed

to have taken a great part in the smuggling trade, for it is so
isolated that boats would be laden and unladen without any
observation. On the hillside above Ballalona Bridge is a fine
top-heavy monolith, and at Ballakelly the stone circle already
mentioned. There is another unexcavated fort at Moaney, one
mile west of Mount Murray.

MALEW offers another puzzle in nomenclature. The "Ma"
stands for Saint, but the "lew" is less certain. The oldest record
of church is in a bull of Pope Eugenius III (1153): "Sancti
Melii, and the Abbey at Rushen in the parish of St. Leoc."
Engraved on the old paten in the church is "Sancte Lupe ora pro
nobis" (1525). Evidently two saints have been confused, the
Irish saint Lua and the French saint Lupus. The old fair day,
July 25th, corresponds to that of the Irish St. Molua or St. Lua.
In the ancient parish are included Castletown, the village of
Ballasalla and the smaller villages of Derbyhaven and St. Mark's.
The church is of the usual Manx form but has a wide north
transept. In the nave lies buried Illiam Dhone, who was executed
at Hangohill. The parish is almost entirely "Abbey Land"
and contains some of the best agricultural land in the Island,
much of it put out of use by Ronaldsway Airport. Derbyhaven
was the port of the Derby family. Later it was the port of a
considerable number of boats of the fisher folk and there
were kipper-curing sheds, now in a ruinous condition.

St. Michael's Island, on the south side of Derbyhaven Bay,
joined by a causeway, has the small chapel of St. Michael, a
picturesque little ruin built probably in the eleventh century
on the site of a Celtic keeill; and the round fort, built about 1540,
but re-equipped by the Earl of Derby at the time of the Civil War.
At the north shore of the bay stood Ronaldsway House, given by
his father to William Christian, Illiam Dhone, but knocked down
to make a safe runway for the airport traffic. On Langness stands
a tall cylindrical tower, which was built about the year 1800 for
some uncertain purpose. It may have been a watch-tower against
the fleet of Napoleon, or more likely a beacon tower or a "huer's"
tower. On the Castletown side of Langness, near the Lighthouse,
there is a series of natural archways, already mentioned.

Here, too, is the glen of the little people, Ballaglonney. It has
become customary (though the custom is of comparatively recent
origin) to salute the little people on crossing the small road bridge.
Folk living south of the bridge, i.e. "over the bridge", are
specially favoured. The custom of lifting the hat when one

crosses the bridge is probably due to the fact that here one enters (or leaves) the former lands of Rushen Abbey, and acknowledges the sanctity of the Church.

In front of King William's College, in the centre of the sweep of Castletown Bay on a very squat hill, is a small ruin, all that remains of a summer banqueting house of the Stanley family. The hill is now known as "Hangohill" and also as "Mount Strange" (a subsidiary title of the Stanley heir). The date of the building is uncertain. It is recorded as being in use at the end of the seventeenth century (1689). The mound was not built to carry the building. It was thought it might have been a ship burial, but excavation showed it was not. Much of the mound and of the building had fallen into the sea before the present sea-wall was built. There was a farm known as Hangohill which with the neighbouring farm of Ballagilley (now covered by the airport) was "attached" by Bishop Barrow for his Educational Trust Fund. Aerial photography suggests that this farm building was about 200 yards north of the ruin. Around the mound have been found several graves. It is alleged that here was the Castletown gibbet in Stanley times. Indeed Thomas Durham's map marks the spot with a gibbet (1610). Illiam Dhone of Ronaldsway was "shotte to death" on Hangohill in January 1663. The Manx never forgave the Stanleys for this "murder", and it has been suggested that in order to wipe out this "foul blot" the hill was re-christened Mount Strange, and the banqueting house built to cover the spot where Christian died. But to be feasting over the grave of Christian within thirty years of his "martyrdom" would seem unlikely behaviour of the Stanleys.

ARBORY. The name of this parish is also derived from its church dedication to the Irish saint, Caerbrie of Coleraine. Its earliest record is in a papal bull of 1153, where it is described as "terra Sancti Carebrie", but less than a hundred years later is given the dedication of St. Columba, and its designation changes again in 1798 when it is called "Chairbrae or Colum killey". Its fair day, the only one to survive without a break apart from St. John's, is St. Columba's Day, June 20th (O.S.). The church is of the usual Manx style but the old bell turret was replaced a few years ago with a square squat tower. It contains a monument to Captain John Quilliam, who was a quartermaster aboard the *Victory* at the Battle of Trafalgar. Quilliam was born in Marown, ran away from farming and went to sea, being ultimately 'pressed" into the Navy. At the Battle of Camperdown his coolness and courage brought him under the notice of Admiral Duncan, who promoted him to lieutenant. At Copenhagen he was on the *Amazon*, engaging the forts, and having a bad time. All her officers, senior to Quilliam, were killed, and he took command. When the ship withdrew Nelson himself went aboard, and not being received on deck called below "How are you getting on?" only to be answered in good Manx accent "Augh middlin'! middlin'!" Nelson was so pleased with him that he invited him to join the ship's company of the *Victory*. At Trafalgar *Victory* had her rudder shot away, and Quilliam rigged up an emergency steering below deck, which he himself controlled in the battle. For his pluck and resource he was promoted post-captain. He came back with good prize-money, bought the estate of Ballakeighan, married one of the Stevensons of Balladoole, became a Member of the House of Keys, took a great interest in the Peel fishing, designed a new type of fishing boat, and set forward the scheme for building the protective breakwater at Derbyhaven. He lies buried in the churchyard at Arbory.

In Arbory, at the Friary Farm, is the only remaining portion, the Chapel, of the small Franciscan House, known as Bemaken Friary. This was for centuries used as a cattle shed of the farm. It has now been cleaned out and such repairs carried out as will maintain it till the time when some restoration will be possible. The site assigned by the Earl was "in the village of St. Columba" and leave was given to the Irish branch of the order to build "an oratory, bell-tower, cemetery house and necessary offices, for twelve brethren, without infringing on the rights and appurtenances of the parish church". In Arbory the estate of Balladoole held for centuries by the Stevenson family has proved to be of absorbing interest, for here on the hill behind the farm in a small area excavated by Dr. Bersu have been found traces of six civilizations.

1. A Neolithic settlement.
2. A pre-Christian Celtic burial ground of about 500 B.C.
3. A pre-historic fortified site showing a bank faced with stones enclosing a space of what was probably a palisaded "keep".
4. A Celtic Christian burial ground, the graves of cyst type.
5. A Viking ship burial of which were found a cloak pin, gilt buckles, and ornamental buckles, all of Scandinavian origin. A massive silver buckle, stirrups, spears and harness ornaments of Irish design. Sword and spear had rusted away

but the shield-grip remained. There were burnt bones of horse and ox. The date was the ninth century.

6. Close by, a Christian keeill surrounded by a small graveyard.

In Arbory, at Colby, was born the Manx lexicographer, Archibald Cregeen (1774-1841). Like the other Manx lexicographer, John Kelly, he was also the son of a cooper. He was trained as a stone mason. He was deeply interested in Manx literature and the language generally. He was appointed coroner of Rushen. Independently of Dr. Kelly, whose work he had not known about, he compiled a Manx dictionary. His list of words took him twenty years to collect, and his dictionary was published in 1838. Of Cregeen George Borrow wrote: " I reverence the very ground on which that man trod because he was one of the greatest natural Celtic scholars who ever lived."

RUSHEN is a very large parish occupying all the south-west of the Island. Its name is a puzzle, since it is not confined to the parish but is the name also of the sheading, of the abbey, and the castle. The earliest record of the name is in *Chronicon* 1134 " *in loco qu vocatur Russin* ", referring to the site of the abbey in Malew. The most usual derivation of the name is from Ros, " promontory ", of which the diminutive is " roisen ". The church is dedicated to the Holy Trinity and, as at Lezayre, is known as Kirk Christ. It is built on the typical Manx style with a plain nave without aisles or chancel, with west door and a west gallery. In Rushen are the villages of Port St. Mary and Port Erin and the much smaller Cregneish, which remains the most Manx of all Manx villages, and has still retained a number of typical Manx thatched cottages. It is perched at the top of a steep hill and from it there is quite a " dream " panorama of sea, sky, and heatherland. The headland to the south is known as Spanish Head and it was held that a ship of the Spanish Armada was wrecked there, and that survivors of the Spanish Navy settled down and intermarried with the inhabitants, thus accounting for the swarthy appearance of some of the Cregneish folk, and their alleged love of gay colours. The story is obviously fanciful, since every ship of the Armada has been accounted for, and none came near the Island; moreover there are no Spanish names in the locality, nor have any Spanish words survived.

Cregneish today houses the Folk Museum, comprising a farmstead, a weaver's shed, turner's shop and smithy, and Harry Kelly's Cottage. Harry Kelly's is a typical Manx fisherman-crofter's cottage, thatched in the traditional style. Its open peat-hearth and the chimney together form the "chiollagh" or chimney-corner. The hanging-pot, "slouree", and fire-irons are there, and other hearth implements. There is also a display of Manx cottage furniture downstairs and in the bedroom. With the help of the Carnegie Trustees the farm buildings were bought and added to the Museum in 1940. They are being restored, and will become a Manx-farm Museum showing agricultural implements of various periods and farm furniture and dairy vessels. Close beside Harry Kelly's Cottage is a small thatched outhouse fitted up as the workshop of a Manx joiner, and containing woodworking tools with treadle lathe and gear. In the Weaver's Cottage is set up a hand-loom, on which, in the summer, demonstrations of the making of Manx tweed and broadcloth are shown. The loom was removed hither from Ballafesson on the opposite hill where till his death in 1939 it was worked by Alfred Hudson (Hudgeon the fiddler), the last of a family of Manx home-weavers. The idea of this Folk Museum was based on communication from Scandinavia, where such Folk Museums are popular. Lord Bledisloe at the Museum Conference of 1939, of which he was chairman, said: "With regard to Folk Museums in general, we still lag far behind. It has been left to the Manx Museum to set up in the Isle of Man the first Museum of this kind."

Port St. Mary or Puirt le Moirrey is the most Manx of the small ports of the Island. It is superbly set about its harbour, built with local limestone; its ancient streets and irregular cottages mount up in a delightful manner as seen from the sea. In the summer, this is a popular resort. The quays are often busy but there are fewer fishing boats than in years gone by.

Port Erin has developed very strongly during the past fifty years and for a great many persons is the most popular of all the holiday towns, catering like Ramsey for a special type of holiday maker, especially family parties. At Port Erin is the Marine Biological Station attached to Liverpool University. It owed its inception to and preserves the memory of Professor W. Herdman, F.R.S., who spent much of his busy life on the Island and was always a scholarly and scientific observer of Manx affairs. The work of the station is two-fold, teaching and local research, while in addition its fish hatchery, subsidized by the Isle of Man Board of Fisheries, does a great deal to maintain the stock of local fish and crustaceans. It undertakes research work in all branches of marine science and puts back into the sea several million young plaice and crustaceans each year. In both these cases the greatest mortality occurs in the egg and early larval stages. About the year 1864 an attempt was made to make Port Erin a harbour of refuge, by building a breakwater across much of its narrow bay entrance. The "god-father" of Port Erin in those days was William Milner, the Liverpool safe-maker. When the first load of stone was lowered, he gave a great feast to the inhabitants. The breakwater was duly completed, of gigantic concrete blocks, but it was all washed away by a terrific storm in 1884. Its remains still act as a "blanket" to soften the attack of westerly gales. The tower on Bradda Head was erected to Milner's memory.

THE CALF. "All Man glorieth in its Calfe" writes a seventeenth-century visitor to the Island, and indeed this islet of the Calf, forming part of the Parish of Rushen, is a gem of beauty. It is sad that the word "calf" has not a romantic meaning, but it is just simply "a calf". In Scandinavian place-names all islets standing at the side of a larger island are in Norse known as "calf", usually spelt "kalfr".

The first written record of the name is on the Manorial Roll of 1511, where it appears as "le Calf". The best view of it is the surprise view as one arrives over the top of Cregneish, especially when seen in the blaze of a summer sunset when the Island is aglow with gorse and heather. In size and shape it is about a third of a square mile, more or less rectangular. All its shores are precipitous and the only two possible landing places are in the small rocky cove opposite Kitterland (the small grassy island nearer the main Island) and at the southernmost tip, opposite a grotesque rock, known as the Burrow. The rock is pierced right through by a sea-passage called "The Eye" and giving the rock the appearance of a gigantic horse rising from the sea, its nose still submerged. It is a very difficult matter to climb the Burrow from a boat, but on its summit is a curious cruciform hollow , surrounded by a wall, with the appearance of a "look out". The Calf was presented to the National Trust in 1937. The Trustees immediately declared it a bird sanctuary. There is a fixed fee for landing, but no visitor is allowed without a special permit during the nesting season, between early May and late July. The Calf has always been famous for its sea-birds. John Ray in a letter in 1691 describes his visit to the Calf, in the same letter in which he described the Manx shearwater. The Puffin or sea-parrot (*Fratercula arctica*) is still common. Ship passengers passing to the south get quite a different view of the Calf from that seen from the main island. On the western shore stand the two disused lighthouses, now joined by a third, which has been in operation since 1968. Three-quarters of a mile off-shore stands the lonely and graceful tower on the Chicken Rock. The only habitations on the Calf today are the farmhouse occupied by the custodian and the keepers' accommodation beside the lighthouse. Nearby are the foundations of a keeill, near which was found the " Calf Crucifixion Stone ". The highest point (420 feet) is the top of the northern cliff.

In 1621 there arrived on the Calf one Thomas Bushell, a man of considerable ability, and scholar of Balliol. After Oxford, he had joined the band of young scholars under the patronage of Francis Bacon, Lord Verulam. He specialized in metal-mining, and was adviser on all matters concerning mining to his patron. In spite of this, he lost most of his money, as so many men have done, in investments in unsound mines. For some unspecified reason, the most probable of which is said to have been disgust at the arraignment of Lord Verulam for bribery, Bushell chose to live a life of seclusion on the Calf. He lived there for three years before returning to London, where he became a great favourite with Charles I, owing largely to his scientific ingenuity. He survived the Commonwealth, and was equally appreciated by the " Merry Monarch ". His life on the Calf gave rise to many fantastic contemporary stories, but it may be a possibility that he "dwelt in a cave". One very unusual structure ascribed to him remains in a ruinous condition, a long narrow trench with two "transepts". The length of the main trench is about 55 feet, with width 6 feet, while the "transepts" are 16 feet by 10 feet, all sunk into the ground. The main trench is almost exactly north and south and the suggestion is made that possibly he had an intention of setting up a large transit telescope. In 1511 the Calf was the property of the Stevenson family of Balladoole, Arbory. It was withdrawn from them by the Great Earl (1648) on the ground that he might place a garrison there against the Parliamentary forces, but in return granted the Stevensons an annual supply of 500 sea-parrots. John Ray (1661) described the Calf as "*Inculta prorsus aut duobus tribusve tantum turguriolis nuper extructis habituta*". John Quayle, clerk of the rolls, owned the Calf in 1776 and he took over red deer and grouse, hoping to establish them there for shooting. They soon disappeared. He is reported, too, to have built a banqueting house, but, if he did, not a trace remains. Geologically the Calf is covered with glacial drift in contrast to the alluvial drift over most of the remainder of the southern part of the Island, and the deep soil contains an unusual number of transported boulders.

APPENDICES

M

SUMMARY OF MANX HISTORY

Date	Lord of Mann	Date	Bishop
		447	Germanus
		474	Romulus
		498	Machutus
	SCANDINAVIAN PERIOD		
		1025	Brandon
		1070	Rulwer
1079	Godred Crovan I	1079	Hammond (A Manxman)
1095	Lagman		
1096	Donald (Regent for Olaf)		
1099	Sigurd		
1113	Olaf I	1125	Walter de Coventry
		1135	Wimond
1153	Godred II	1150	John of Seez
1158	Somerled		
		1154	Gamaliel of Peterborough
		1158	Christian of Bangor
		1164	Michael (Manx)
1187	Reginald I		
		1204	Nicholas of Argyll
		1217	Reginald
1226	Olaf II	1225	John
		1229	Simon of Argyll
1237	Harald I		
		1248	Lawrence
1249	Reginald II	1249	(Vacant)
1249	Harald Godredson		
1250	Ivor the Usurper		
1252	Magnus		
		1253	Richard of St. Andrews
1265	Magnus died		
1266	Alexander III		Vacant
		1275	Mark of Galloway
1284	Margaret of Scotland		
1290	Edward I		
1298	Edward II		
		1305	Alan of Galloway
1313	Thomas Randolph	1321	Gilbert McLelland
		1329	Bernard de Linton
1333	William de Montacute I	1334	Thomas of Dunkeld
1344	William de Montacute II	1348	William Russell
		1374	Donkan (Manx)
1392	William le Scrope	1392	John Sproton

Date	Governor	Notes
		Traditional dates only (Jocelin Vita Patricii)
		Buried at Maughold. *Chronicon.* Godred probably " Orry " of Manx folk-lore
		1103 defeat and death of Magnus Barfod, K. of Norway
		1134 Rushen Abbey founded
		Consecrated at Trondheim Cathedral started Perished at sea Reginald II buried in Rushen Abbey
		Magnus died at Castle Rushen, buried in Rushen Abbey Isle of Man sold to Scotland for 4,000 marks
1285	William Huntercombe	
1290	Richard de Burgh	
1293	John Balliol	
1310	Antony Bek	
1311	Piers Gaveston	
1312	Henri de Bello Monte	Castle Rushen taken by Bruce 1313 Castle Rushen rebuilt Consecrated at Avignon
		Mann bought by Scrope

Date	Lord of Mann	Date	Bishop
1399	Henry Percy of Northumberland		
1405	John Stanley I		
1414	John Stanley II	1410	Richard Payl
		1429	Richard Pully
1432	Thomas Stanley I, First Baron		
		1433	John Burghersh
		1435	John Seyr
		1455	Thomas Burton
		1458	Thomas Kirkham
1460	Thomas Stanley II, First Earl	1483	Richard Oldon
		1487	Huan Blackleach
1504	Thomas Stanley III, Second Earl	1503	Huan Hesketh
1521	Edward Stanley, Third Earl	1523	John Howden
		1546	Henry Mann
1572	Henry Stanley, Fourth Earl	1568	Vacant
		1576	John Meyrick
1593	Ferdinando, Fifth Earl	1599	George Lloyd
1594	Queen Elizabeth I		
		1599	George Lloyd
1603	James I	1604	John Phillips
1607	Henry, Earl of Northumberland		
	Robert, Earl of Salisbury		
1627	James, 7th Earl of Derby (The Great Earl)	1633	William Foster
		1635	Richard Parr
		1644	Vacant
1651	Commonwealth		
1652	Lord Fairfax		
1660	The Restoration, Charles Stanley, Eighth Earl	1661	Sam Rutter
		1663	Isaac Barrow
		1671	Henry Bridgman
1672	William Stanley, Ninth Earl		

Date	Governor	Notes
		Mann given to Percy by Henry IV
1405	Michael Blundell	
1417	John Litherland	
1422	John Walton	1423 First recorded Tynwald Manx "Magna Carta"
1428	Henry Byron	
1496	Peter Dutton	
1497	Henry Radcliffe	
1508	Ralph Rushton	
1511	John Ireland	
1518	John Fazakerley	
1521	Thomas Danport	
1527	Henry Stanley	
1532	John Ffleming	
1536	George Stanley	1536 Suppression of Monasteries
1545	William Stanley	1548 English Prayer Book
1552	Henry Stanley	
1576	John Harmer	
1580	John Sherburn	
	Bishop Meyrick	
1593	William Stanley	
1594	Ranulph Stanley	
1595	Thomas Gerard	
1594	Ranulph Stanley	
1595	Thomas Gerard	
1596	Piers Legh	
1599	Cuthbert Gerard	
1600	Robert Molyneux	
		The first Manx Prayer Book
1609	John Ireland	
1623	Frederick Liege	
1626	Edward Holmewood	
1627	Charles Gerard	
1639	Ffoulkes Hunckes	
1640	John Greenhalge	
1651	Philip Musgrave	Battle of Bolton, 7th Earl executed
	Colonel R. Dukinfield	Castle Rushen surrendered
1652	Matthew Cadwall	
1656	William Christian	
1659	James Chaloner	
1660	Roger Nowell	
1664	Bishop Barrow	Bishop Barrow's Trust founded
1673	Henry Nowell	

Date	Lord of Mann	Date	Bishop
		1682	John Lake
		1684	Baptiste Levinz
		1693	Vacant
1702	James Stanley, Tenth Earl	1698	Thomas Wilson
1736	James, 2nd Duke of Atholl		
1764	Charlotte, Duchess	1755	Mark Hildesley
	John, Third Duke of Atholl conjointly		
1765	George III	1773	Richard Richmond
		1780	George Mason
		1784	Claudius Crigan
1820	George IV	1814	George Murray
1830	William IV	1827	William Ward
1837	Victoria	1838	James Bowstead
		1840	Henry Pepys
		1841	Thomas Vowler Short
		1847	Walter Shirley
			Robert John Eden
		1854	Horatio Powys
		1877	Rowley Hill
		1887	John Bardesley
		1892	Norman D. J. Straton
1900	Edward VII	1907	Thos. W. Drury
		1911	James Denton-Thompson
1912	George V	1925	Chas. Leonard Thornton-Duesbery
1936	Edward VIII	1928	William Stanton-Jones
	George VI		
1952	Elizabeth II	1943	J. Ralph S. Taylor
		1955	Benjamin Pollard
		1966	G. Eric Gordon
		1974	Vernon S. Nicholls

Date	Governor	Notes
1677	Henry Stanley	
1678	Robert Heywood	Lake, one of the Bishops in the Tower
1690	Roger Kenyon	
1693	William Sacheverell	
1696	Nicholas Stanley	
1701	James Cranstoun	
1703	Robert Maudesley	
1713	Charles Z. Stanley	
1718	Alexander Horne	
1723	John Lloyd	
1725	Thomas Horton	
1736	James Murray	
1744	Patrick Lindsey	
1751	Basil Cochrane	1756 Printed Manx Prayer Book
1761	John Wood	1775 " Manx Bible " first edition
		Act of Revestment
1777	Edward Smith	
1793	John Murray, later Fourth Duke	Castle Mona built
1808	Cornelius Smelt	Last edition " Manx Bible "
1832	John Ready	King William's College built
1845	Chas. Hope	
1860	Francis-Stainsby-Conant-Piggott	1862 Government moved from Castletown to Douglas
1863	H. B. Loch	1866 First " elected " House of Keys
1882	Spencer Walpole	1881 Women Suffrage
1893	John W. Ridgeway	
1895	Lord Henniker	1904 Car Races
1902	Lord Raglan	
1918	Sir Wm. Fry	1907 Motor Cycle Races
1925	Sir Claude Hill	
1931	Sir Montagu Butler	
1937	Vice-Admiral the Earl of Granville	
1945	Air Vice-Marshal Sir G. Bromet	
1952	Sir Ambrose D. Flux Dundas	
1959	Sir Ronald Herbert-Garvey	
1966	Sir Peter Stallard	
1974	Sir John Paul	

SOME MANX PLACE-NAMES

The following names have been used in the course of this book:

Name	Parish	Derivation	Language

A

Name	Parish	Derivation	Language
Agneash	Lonan	Eggjarnes, edge nose	Scand.
Algare	Braddan	Ealgar, the place of justice	Scand.
Andreas	Andreas	Andrew	
Arbory	Arbory	Caerbrie, an Irish saint	Celtic
Archallagan	Patrick	Ard-talachan, the little height	Celtic
Auldyn (Glen)	Lezayre	Aldyn, a proper noun	
Aust	Lezayre	Ottarstad, Ottar's farm	Scand.
Ayre	Bride	Eyrr, a pebbly beach	Scand.

B

Name	Parish	Derivation	Language
Baldrine	Lonan	Balla-drine, of the black-thorns	Celtic
Baldwin	Braddan	Boldalr, the valley	Scand.
Balla		Farm, homestead	Celtic
Ballachurry, Ballachurrey	Andreas and elsewhere	Curragh, the curragh	Celtic
Balladoole	Arbory	Dubhail, the black stream	Celtic
Ballagilley	Malew	Gil, the servant	Celtic
Ballahot	Malew	Cott, the cot	Celtic
Ballakeighan	Arbory	Keggin, proper name	Celtic
Ballalona	Malew	Glion, in the glen	Celtic
Ballamodha	Malew	Moddey, the dog	Celtic
Ballaqueeney	Rushen	Queen, proper name	Celtic
Ballaterson	Ballaugh	Terson, of the crozier	Celtic
Ballaugh	Ballaugh	Ny-lohey, by the lake	Celtic
Ballure	Maughold	Euar, the yew-tree	Celtic
Barrule	Malew and Lezayre	Warool = Wardfell, watch and ward	Scand.
Beinn-y-Phott	Braddan	Mount of the Turbary	Celtic
Bemaken, Byma-can or Bimican	Arbory	Bola-machan, Machan's tent	Celtic
Berk	German	Borgarvik, the fort by the creek	Scand.
Billown	Malew	Balla-lodin, proper name	Celtic
Bradda	Rushen	Bradhou, broad headland	Scand.
Braddan	Braddan	St. Brendan	Celtic
Braaid	Marown	Breid, the gullet	Celtic
Bride	Bride	St. Bridget	
Burrow	Rushen	Borg, a round hill	Scand.

Name	Parish	Derivation	Language

C

Name	Parish	Derivation	Language
Carnanes	Rushen	Cairnane, cairn	Celtic
Cashtal-yn-Ard	Maughold	Castle on the height	Celtic
Cass-ny hawin	Santan and elsewhere	The end of the river	Celtic
Castleward	Braddan	Cashtal-ny-waaid, the sod castle	Celtic
Chibbyr		A well	
Chibbyr Pheric	Lonan and elsewhere	Patrick's Well	Celtic
Clagh Ouyre	Lezayre	Grey height	Celtic
Colby	Arbory	Kollabyr, Kolli's farm	Scand.
Colden	Braddan	Kollrin, summit	Scand.
Conister	Conchan	Kion-y-sker, end of the reef	Scand.
Cornaa	Maughold	Quern, a water-wheel	Scand.
Cranstal	Bride	Kraun's stadt, Kraun's farm	Scand.
Cregneish	Rushen	Craukness, the ness of the crows	Scand.
Cronk Aust	Lezayre	Ottar's farm	
Cronk crogher	Michael	Hill of the gallows	Celtic
Cronk-ny-irrey-lhaa	Rushen	Hill of the dawn	Celtic
Cronk-ny-Merrieu	Santan	Hill of Death	Celtic
Cronk Urleigh	Michael	Eagle hill	Celtic
Crosby	Marown	Crossbyr, the croft of the cross-roads.	Scand.
Crossag	Malew	The little crossing	Celtic

D

Name	Parish	Derivation	Language
Dalby	Patrick	Dal-byr, the croft in the glen	Scand.
Dhoon	Maughold	Dhoon = dun, fort	Celtic
Douglas	Conchan	Dughglais, the dark stream	Celtic
Dreswick	Malew	Drangsvik, the creek in the rocks	Scand.

E

Name	Parish	Derivation	Language
Eary killey	Lezayre	The church shieling	Celtic
Ellanbane	Lezayre	The white island	Celtic

F

Name	Parish	Derivation	Language
Fleshwick	Rushen	Fles-vik, green creek	Scand.
Foxdale	Patrick	Fors or foss-dale, valley of waterfall	Scand.

G

Name	Parish	Derivation	Language
Garff	Sheading	Grafir, a ravine	Scand
Garraghan	Braddan	The rough place, Carrachan	Celtic
Garwick	Onchan	Gjar-vik, cave creek	Scand.

Name	Parish	Derivation	Language
Glencrutchery	Onchan	(Mc)Cristory's glen, proper name	Celtic
Glenfaba	Patrick, name of Sheading	The Glen of the Faba (river)	Celtic
Glen trammon	Lezayre	The glen of the elder-tree	Celtic
Gob-y-deigan	Michael	The mouth of the devil (caves)	Celtic
Gob-y-volley	Lezayre	The mouth of the old road	Celtic
Greeba	German	Gneba = Gniba, a peak	Scand.
Grenaby	Malew	Gren-byr, the green farm	Scand.
Grenwick (Grenaugh)	Santan	Gren-vik, the green creek	Scand.
Gretch veg	Lonan	Grettistor's (farm) (the lesser)	Scand.

I

Injebreck	Braddan	Inga-brekka, Inga's slope	Scand.

J

Jurby	Jurby	Jngvar-byr, Invar's home	Scand.

K

Kentraugh	Rushen	Cinn-tracht, end of the sand	Celtic
Kew	German	Kew's farm, proper name	Celtic
Kilabban	Braddan	Keeill Abban, Church of St. Abban	Celtic
Kitterland	Rushen	Kidja island, the kids' island	Scand.
Knockaloe	Patrick	Knock aloe, hill of Olaf	Scand.
Knock-y-dooney	Andreas	Hill of the man	Scand.

L

Lag-ny-killey	Patrick	Church hollow	Celtic
Langness	Malew	Long headland	Scand.
Laxey	Lonan	Laxa, salmon river	Scand.
Lezayre	Lezayre	Church in the Ayre	Celtic
Lhen	Jurby	A trench	Celtic

M

Malew	Malew	Ma Lua, St. Lua	Celtic
Marown	Marown	Ma Ronan, St. Ronan	Celtic
Maye (Glen)	Patrick	Glen muigh, the yellow glen	Celtic
Meayll or Mull	Rushen	Maol, bare	Celtic
Milntown	Lezayre	The place of the mill	Celtic
Mooar (Glen)	Michael	The great glen	Celtic
Mirescogh	Lezayre	Myrerskoge, miry wood	Scand.

N

Niarbyl	Patrick	Yn arby, the tail	Celtic

Name	Parish	Derivation	Language

O

| Orrisdale | Ballaugh | Orrastadt, Orry's farm | Scand. |

P

| Peel | German | Pile, a fortress | Scand. |
| Poylvaish | Arbory | Poll ghais, the pool of death | Celtic |

R

Ramsey	Maughold	Rams, island of garlic	Scand.
Raneurling	Michael	= Cronk urleigh (q.v.)	
Rhenass	German	Rheynneas, the divided water-fall	Celtic
Rhullick-ny-Quakeryn	Maughold	Cemetery of the Quakers	Celtic
Ronaldsway	Malew	Ronald's wath, Ronald's boat-path	Scand.
Rue (point)	Jurby	Red (point)	Celtic

S

Santon	Santan	= St. Sanctain	
Sartfell	Ballaugh	Swart-fell, dark hill	Scand.
Scarlett	Malew	Skarfakluft, cormorant's ledge	Scand.
Scholaby	Rushen	Skollabyr, Skoll's farm	Scand.
Skyhill = Scacafell	Lezayre	Skogar fell, wooded hill	Scand.
Slieu Freoghane	Michael	Mountain of whortleberries	Celtic
Slieu Ruy	Lonan	Red Mountain	Celtic
Slieu Whallian	Patrick	Mountain of Allen	Celtic
Snaefell	Lezayre	Snae-fell, snow mountain	Scand.
Soderick	Braddan	Sol-vik, sunny creek	Scand.
Sulby	Lezayre	Solabyr, Sola's farm	Scand.
Sumark (Cronk)	Lezayre	Sumark, primrose	Celtic

T

Tholt-y-Will	Lezayre	Tolta-yn-wooliæ, the hill of the cattlefold	Celtic
Trollaby	Marown	Trolls byr, the home of the troll	Scand.
Tromode	Conchan	Thrumms oddr, Thrum's home	Scand.

W

| Wyllin (Glen) | Michael | Glen myllin, the mill glen | Celtic |

INDEX

STIRLING
DISTRICT
LIBRARY